DATE DUE

This book was originally published as *The future of shopping*, LannooCampus Publishers (2017).

D/2018/45/696 – ISBN 978 94 014 4723 2 – NUR 802

Cover design: Peer De Maeyer
Interior design: Gert Degrande I De Witlofcompagnie

LannooCampus Publishers is a subsidiary of Lannoo Publishers,
the book and multimedia division of Lannoo Publishers nv.

LannooCampus Publishers
Erasme Ruelensvest 179 box 101
3001 Leuven
Belgium
www.lannoocampus.com

THE
FUTURE

JORG SNOECK & PAULINE NEERMAN

OF
SHOPPING

WHERE EVERYONE IS A RETAILER

LANNOO
CAMPUS

// CONTENTS //

Preface

In many ways, the past year has been a dream come true. One year after *The Future of Shopping* originally appeared in Dutch, we are incredibly grateful and proud to present the English edition of our critically acclaimed book.

It has been an amazing roller coaster, leading up to this updated, international version which — we are excited to announce — appears both in an English and a Chinese language edition. We are profoundly grateful that our very first book already won the prestigious award 'Managementboek van het Jaar 2018' (which translates into management book of the year 2018) in the Benelux.

According to the professional jury *The Future of Shopping* is an accessible must-read, not only for everyone active in the industry, but also for policy-makers, educators, students and beyond, as (retail) consumption touches upon every aspect of society and every one of us.

As a result, we have been on the road virtually non-stop for keynote lectures, panel discussions and university guest lectures all over Europe. And of course, in doing so, we have been finding even more retail inspiration, encountering innovative new ideas and meeting visionary thinkers and entrepreneurs. Quite a few of these progressive insights have found their way into this revised edition.

Retail is changing ever so rapidly, shifting and shaping as we speak. Yet, our ground work has proven to be stable: throughout the tumultuous changes of the last decades, we have been able to lay bare the ground rules and underlying factors of that change.

In every chapter of this book we drill down on each of the crucial elements shaping today's dynamics in the FMCG and retailing industry. From new consumer demographics (think of the continuous population growth) to new distribution channels (from mobile commerce to automatic replenishment), producers, processors and distributors must all change their approach to succeed.

Each and everyone involved in the supply chain must adapt. By offering myriad examples and case studies from across the world and across all branches, the aim of this book is to inspire and enlighten, as well as to give readers food for thought and for discussion. Our insights are meant to be shared, both inside and outside your companies, because sharing knowledge and practices is more important than ever.

We hope you will enjoy this updated and internationalized edition. Have an inspiring read and feel free to reach out — to us and to others. Only through honest sharing we can make the industry future-proof and ready to tackle the challenges that lie ahead.

Jorg and Pauline

Retail has a
permanent new face

How can brands and retailers survive in the future of shopping? Day after day, they need to prove their added value to increasingly difficult shoppers. But how can they do this, now that Alexa and your smartphone already put together your shopping list and automatically provide you with meals for the whole week?

Retail, as we have known it for centuries, is dead. Economic, demographic and technological developments have killed it. Or, rather, have made it unnecessary. Traditionally, it was the role of shopkeepers to buy products in large quantities and then sell them in smaller, more manageable quantities (de- and re-bundling), allowing these products to be brought closer to people, their customers.

// Retail, as we have known it for centuries, is dead. Economic, demographic and technological developments have killed it. Or, rather, have made it unnecessary. //

Today, the internet has eliminated the need for shops to be close to people. Digitalization has turned the world into a single large marketplace, a dream that has been around for a long time, but has now become a reality. Nowadays, no-one gives it a second thought if a package from China arrives in their letter box or if their friends bring back cheaper electronic goods from their trip to the United States. Whereas in the past retailers could see their competitors simply by looking out of the shop window, the whole world is now a potential rival.

What's more, everyone can open a shop or even become a producer, selling goods directly to customers. Today's 'shops' transcend the original meaning of the word. What is a shop nowadays? There are many different forms: physical shops, websites, apps, posters on the wall, virtual spaces, holograms and various intermixtures of all the above. Anything can be a shop. No matter how crazy your idea, someone has probably already thought of it. And for modern consumers, the crazier, the better - as long as it doesn't take things too far. A new type of consumer has been born: multi-cultural, self aware and... grey.

Falling purchasing power since the 1990s, the continuing ageing of the population and increasing migration are leading to a new kind of purchasing behaviour. The economic crisis of 2008 further diminished consumer confidence. People continue to hunt for the best bargains and the lowest prices, a search that has been made easier than ever before thanks to the ability to compare things online. This revolution in transparency has both emancipated shoppers and given them a powerful weapon.

Retailers are being forced - if they want to remain competitive - to cut back on their number of stores (i.e. close them). Otherwise, they will end up in the same boat as Toys "R" Us, Mexx, RadioShack and countless other retail traders. All the things that retail used to stand for are now up for discussion. Everything needs to be reinvented. And that is the purpose of this book: to allow retailers to get back in touch with the consumers of today and tomorrow.

This book has been written specifically for retailers, brand producers, wholesalers, distributors and anyone else closely connected with the industry, but also makes an eye-opening read for students and for the shopper in each and every one of us. After all, we are all consumers and, as this book will show, we are increasingly becoming retailers as well. The book deals with online and physical retail, for both food and non-food, mainly in Western Europe and the United States .

Because we are convinced that all retailers and producers focused on consumers need to profile themselves as a brand, we have used the term 'brand' in this book in the wider sense of its meaning. We will use the supermarket branch, where all the recent trends and evolutions come together and which was the last branch to switch to retail 4.0, as a case study. So let's now enter the new world of retail. Get ready for a fascinating journey!

New game,
new rules

There is an epidemic of bankruptcies that is striking terror into the heart of many retailers. The finger of blame is usually pointed at digitalization, but the problem goes much deeper than that. It is actually down to a combination of circumstances, which have changed the face of retail as we know it.

Retail is in a state of revolution. It is not the first revolution it has experienced and it won't be the last. But it does mean that things will never be the same again. Running parallel with the recent revolution in society, which has radically altered traditional thinking about how we live, where we live, with whom we live and for how long, we are standing on the threshold of a new economic and industrial era. This fourth industrial revolution is powered by smart technology, which for the first time is now capable of self-learning. In addition to the physical world, there is now a new digital dimension, which is starting to intertwine itself inextricably with the corporeal.

// Today, everything can be a shop or a sales point and everyone is a potential retailer. //	

Retail has changed for good, but there is more of it than ever before. Nowadays, retail is everywhere. You can find it at all times and in all places. Shopping is no longer an activity that you go somewhere to do. Except for an occasional day out or a little bit of pleasure shopping, it is now something you do intuitively, constantly and wherever you like. Today, everything can be a shop or a sales point and everyone is a potential retailer.

Welcome to the new consumer

The world is in flux. The global population continues to grow. There are more old people and they are living longer. People in some parts of the planet are plagued by problems caused by climate change, political unrest, scarcity of natural re-sources and terrorism, so that many now wish to seek a better life in the more stable and more prosperous West. The result is a new melting pot of cultures, all with different backgrounds and different frames of reference.

This requires us to look again at our own frames of reference, also as retailers and brands. New socio-demographic profiles now determine demand, purchasing behaviour and exactly how those purchases are made. Multiculturality, societal ageing, single parent families, blended families... these are all phenomena that lead to shopping patterns very different from those of 'the Joneses' retailers and brands we used to love so much. Global is becoming local, with influences from all over the world now within the reach of even the smallest village. But local is also becoming global: digital contacts and interactions bypass national boundaries as though they no longer exist, resulting in parallel import and cross-border trans-actions.

It may sound paradoxical, but the growing availability and dominance of the 'glob-al' is actually rekindling interest in the 'local'. An American study by Deloitte and others (2016) revealed that the desire for transparency is more important than demographic or regional factors. The demand for authentic local products and brands is increasing, from both the conservative and the progressive segments of society. It is not just the 'millennials' and the well-to-do whose purchasing be-haviour is changing. More and more shoppers of all types are starting to take new impulses into consideration: health and welfare, safety, social impact, experience, etc.

This move towards a more conscious consumption is already in full swing. More than ever before, shoppers now insist on being be well-informed. They search for information online, via social media and mobile applications. Brands that want to win will need to provide the information the customers want via the channels they most like to use.

As a result, earning models are set to change. People now like to buy things as directly as possible, based on the conviction that this will give them back control over what they consume. They become shareholders in a co-operative, have their dividend paid through the harvest and dine at the table with the farmer. This sharing or peer-to-peer economy transforms the consumer into a producer. In the sharing economy, which has changed from being controversial to mainstream almost overnight, apartments become hotel rooms (thanks to Airbnb), amateur cooks become restaurateurs (thanks to Homemade and the likes) and a taxi company like Uber can turn a whole industry on its head. Thanks to the power of the internet, access has become more important than ownership. This has created a whole new playing field.

The consumer is changing fundamentally and this poses a serious challenge for manufacturers and retailers. It means they need to try and understand the consumer by remaining in constant dialogue with him. Fortunately, today's sophisticated technology makes it possible to interpret behavioural data and purchasing intentions in real time, which in turn makes it possible for companies to create relevant communication and experiences at the individual level. Welcome to the age of hypercontext, predictive personalization and so much more!

From push to pull

For decades, the consumer was overloaded with consumption goods that he was constantly told he simply couldn't do without. Neither time nor money was spared to employ every available channel to sell him an amalgam of products. Every possible means was used to attract his attention and excite his interest, in the hope that this would persuade him to make a purchase. This was the classic 'purchase funnel'. But today that funnel looks very different.

Consumers are no longer willing to blindly follow the stories told to them by retailers. If you want to attract the attention of modern consumers, you first need to look at your own set-up, to make sure you are offering them what they really want. It is no longer possible to pull people on board of your train; they need to get on voluntarily - and they will tell you when they are ready to leave, from which station, which special services they require on the way and where, ultimately, they intend to get off. And don't forget your letter of recommendation from satisfied past customers; you are going to need it more than ever!

In other words, it is now the shopper who decides the fate of brands and stores. He determines whether they do well or not. And don't think you can convince him simply by banging your own drum and telling him how good you are. He will use his own network to find out if he really wants to do business with you - or not. To a large extent this will depend on whether you can offer him a unique experience and a fantastic story. The brand that can create a community of enthusiastic brand fans to sell its story will be the brand that has the best chance of success.

Retail is everywhere - and everything

During the past decade, the digital selling process has switched from the laptop to the mobile and now finally to super-smart applications inside your home. We are on the eve of the breakthrough of the 'internet of things', machine-to-machine retail and FMCG. These changes are dramatic: from buy buttons in apps on our smartphones, we are evolving towards buy buttons in our homes and fridges that fill themselves. Over the course of 2016 and 2017, we went from Siri, who told you the way to the nearest shop, to Alexa, who orders whatever you want and has it delivered to your front door. And we ain't seen nothing yet.

 // In less than a few years, we went from Siri, who tells you the way to the nearest shop, to Alexa, who orders whatever you want. //

Apart from greater ease, retail is also evolving towards more service and better experiences. Since the 'non-fun' element has now been automated out of shopping, people now have more time and energy to immerse themselves in the shop experience. Technology is the perfect ally to provide more inspiration, better service, more comfort, a more personal offer and more appropriate pricing.

A virtual shelf is never empty, while shops are great at focusing attention on best-selling products and the most eye-catching articles. The interaction between digital and physical finds its expression in a non-stop retail experience into which the shopper can dip as and when he pleases. The customer journey no longer has a beginning and an end: the shop simply follows him wherever he goes.

Quite literally. In the near future, the smart mirror in your house will record all your sizes and measurements, which you can then use anywhere to filter the online offer for what you need. Even in the shopping streets you can try products and have them kept to one side, without the need to buy or pay for them immediately. You do this with your mobile app, but only after you have first shown your partner later that evening the 3D film you made in the fitting room. Your television will then show you a range of matching products, also filtered to reflect your personal preferences. Add what you like to your shopping basket and simply pick it up the next morning.

Shops are moving closer to the customer, even literally, with mobile shops, pop-ups at places where demand is predicted to be high, or virtual shopping spaces and kiosks. To make this possible, data is the key. Data is the future of retail. Channels will give way to a single integrated experience, targeted at the individual purchaser.

The same is true for service: seamless live shopping means that people will continue to be helped in the same well-informed manner, but now that can happen just as easily at home or at work as in the shop. Depending on the time and place, this service will be provided by chatbots, human staff, brand fans, hologram presentations or robots. Robots know where to find everything and can lead shoppers to what they need or even fetch it for them. Being ready for the customer, around the clock, is a prerequisite for the future: retail must become a new kind of 24/7 business.

What the hell happened?

From top to bottom, from producers to trader, and from trader to consumer. For more than a century, that was the logical order of things. The producers provided the products, the trader added on his margin and the consumer paid the end price. That's what we all learned, isn't it?

But today, that no longer holds good. The whole value chain is on the point of disintegration: shops are no longer the only sales channels and the typical top-down approach, with companies at the top of the ladder and customers are the bottom, has now been superseded. We are living in a period of change.

What kind of change? The consumer now approaches purchasing from the opposite end. He is in command and to a large extent dictates the value chain. In this world of rapid change, all the links in the consumer-retail-industry chain need to work together if they want to remain up to date instead of out of date.

 // The world is in flux. Its population continues to grow, but the gap between rich and poor is getting bigger all the time. //

The world is in flux. Its population continues to grow, but the gap between rich and poor is getting bigger all the time. The West is getting older, while some fast-growing regions are confronted with a scarcity of resources, the consequences of climate change and political and social instability (nowadays described under the collective name of 'terrorism'). This results in new patterns of migration, resulting in a very different looking and more diverse streetscape in Western Europe, concentrated above all in rapidly expanding urban centres.

At the same time, technology has led to a shift in the balance of economic power, placing at our disposal endless rows off shopping shelves from Albania to Zimbabwe. Faced with this cornucopia, shoppers are searching for ways to make their lives easier and technology ensures that this ease take new forms. The consequences are making themselves felt, especially in the shopping streets. We can probably all name a number of shopping chains that have closed down entirely in recent years.

In the United States the term 'Retail Apocalypse' has even been coined to refer to the large number of store closures and bankruptcies. In 2017 nearly 7,000 stores closed, twice as much as the year before and a record-breaking number for the industry —exceeding even crisis year 2008. Western Europe follows the American trend: whereas in 2011, 78 chain stores in the Netherlands had a total of 6,687 branches, by 2017, their number had fallen to 3,239 branches, a drop of 52%, according to a survey by Ebeltoft en Q&A (2017). In UK high streets 5,855 stores closed in 2017, meaning a staggering average of 16 store closures a day (see **FIGURE 1**).

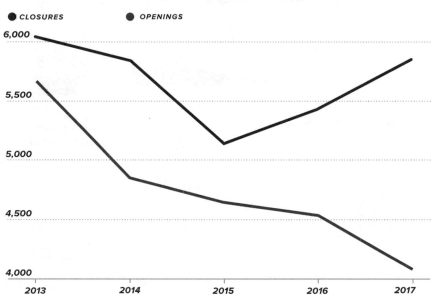

5,855 outlets closed on UK high streets in 2017, at a rate of 16 stores a day

● CLOSURES   ● OPENINGS

6,000

5,500

5,000

4,500

4,000

2013   2014   2015   2016   2017

FIGURE 1 • 5,855 outlets closed on UK high streets in 2017

Source: The Local Data Company for PwC

Retail is moving into a new phase: a phase of total (omnichannel) and personal retail (me-tail). We call this current phase Retail 4.0 (see **FIGURE 2**). Indeed, it is the fourth major (r)evolution in the retail sector, the best examples of which are still in the process of formation.

Source: Fun/Fundoo & McKinsey

FIGURE 2 · The four phases of retail

Retail 2.0: the glory years of mass consumption

When people in retail talk about 'the good old days', they generally mean the years between 1950 and 1970 in the West, the high-water mark of the consumption society and the golden age of the high street shop. After the Second World War, everyone wanted to move forward. The years of shortages and deprivation were behind them, and people wanted to show it. Ever since the large department store first made its appearance at the end of the 19th century, the shopping street had become a feature of every town and city, both great and small. After 1945, the influence of American culture gave a new impulse to this phenomenon, with new supermarkets, shops, stores and even hamburger joints sprouting out of the ground like mushrooms.

Family budgets increased substantially, in large part because women also began to get jobs. The middle class blossomed. When things are going well, more children are born, and these children wanted to have things better - much better - than their parents had experienced during the war years. As a result, they studied longer and joined the labour market later. This new category of young twenty-somethings had greater purchasing power than the previous generations and was easy to reach, thanks to the mediums of radio and, increasingly, television.

In fact, the television made it possible to reach all segments of the population, without the 'noise' of other channels interfering with the message. And this message - in the form of advertisements for new and surprising products - was lapped up by a curious and enthusiastic public. The economy was booming: more purchasing power, more people who wanted the same assortment, more rotation. In short, more of everything. The golden age of retail had dawned.

Thanks to mass production and the advent of the welfare state, new groups of people were gaining access to consumption. The key to success was the ability to boost supply - because the demand was already there, at an all-time record level. This was the birth of mass markets, mass consumption and Mad Men mass marketing. It was also the time when retail changed from local to national: even the small independent retailers of the past began to think increasingly in terms of chains. And as the mobility infrastructure improved, so the size of their chains grew, both in terms of the number and the size of their stores.

To generate scale and traffic, the offer was made bigger, better and broader, in the hope of creating a handy 'one-stop shop' for consumers. Because if you can buy everything at a single retailer, why should you ever need to go anywhere else? Grocer's stores first became supermarkets and then hypermarkets, while 'big box' formulas like IKEA also saw the first light of day.

Disappearing borders reshape the world

Society, of course, continued to evolve. In the face of recurring oil crises, the Cold War and the Gulf Wars, the first signs of saturation began to appear in the 1980s. Some industries began to realize that things could be made more cheaply elsewhere and moved en masse away from Europe. Employment became harder to find in the developed West and wages stagnated.

'Industry without borders' opened the eyes of many people outside (Western) Europe and led to new flows of migration and protest. The world moved in the direction of becoming a more connected whole, with the fall of the Berlin Wall in 1989 as a truly symbolic moment. At the same time, consumer needs slowly began to display different profiles: people were no longer satisfied with the same uniform range of products.

The balance between supply and demand shifted: due to the ever increasing supply and the rise of efficient distribution systems, shoppers were granted an almost unlimited offer and unlimited access. Especially when the logistics infrastructure improved in the eighties and it became even easier to import exotic products. Not only was everything available the heart desired, there was more than one could long for. The production-driven economy turned into a marketing-driven economy: production capacity was no longer the bottleneck, demand was.

The year 1995 saw the first emergence of the company that has today become the largest online retailer in the world and the bogeyman of every physical store: Amazon. It was the start of an era when we could no longer ignore names like Facebook, Twitter, Apple or Samsung. Around the turn of the century, internet made a huge leap forward in terms of availability and effectiveness with the arrival of broadband. The Google search engine had just been launched and Apple opened its first physical stores.

 // The consumer, armed with the internet, now took control of the strings of shopping power. //

The consumer, armed with the internet, now took control of the strings of shopping power. He now determined the offer he wanted and actively went in search of the best place to buy it. There was no longer such a thing as a 'loyal' customer. And it was very clear that 'one size most definitely does NOT fit all'.

Retail 3.0: the pre- and post-Amazon era

Amazon is the symbol par excellence for the third phase of retail (retail 3.0) and for the start of a new fourth phase (retail 4.0). The birth of e-commerce, for which Amazon helped to lay the foundations, shook retail as it then existed to its core. So much so that we can reasonably speak of a pre-Amazon and a post-Amazon era. Many companies failed to survive the bursting of the dotcom bubble - but Amazon did, with flying colours.

> // Amazon is the symbol par excellence for the third phase of retail (retail 3.0) and for the start of a new fourth phase (retail 4.0). //

It was able to move beyond pure e-commerce, so that it was ready to launch the next - and current - developmental phase: retail as me-tail, which is characterized by platforms, hyper-competition and polarization. Today, Amazon is one of the 'Big Three' technology companies, along with Google-holding Alphabet and Apple.

Amazon turned retail on its head by making an agreement with Ingram, a book wholesaler. Amazon founder Jeff Bezos asked for and was granted access to Ingram's full range of titles and offered these for sale in his online shop. All he needed to do was arrange collection, packaging and dispatch to the customer. Which, to begin with, he did from his own garage. With these minimal costs, it was possible to keep his prices low - or at least lower than in the physical bookstores in his neighbourhood.

And so Amazon was born. Not exactly rocket science, is it? This is something that Jeff Bezos also understood. He knew that his model was easy for others to copy. So how could he make the difference? By staying the biggest and the fastest - and by growing as quickly as possible and innovating as much as possible. This is also typical of the visionary nature of Amazon: there is no place for number 2s in today's markets. Bezos continued to expand and invest, even during the first six years when Amazon made no profit.

But it was not just in the field of digital revolution that Amazon set the tone. The online giant brought its own 'private labels' to market to undermine the power of the brand producers. It started an all-comprehensive marketplace, without the need to hold a supply, but with an almost limitless offer, which it was prepared to use - and sometimes even sacrifice - in aggressive price wars. It is reaching for consumers' homes and hearts with new, unseen services and hardware. It aims to make shopping as automatic and boundless as possible, be it in stores or online. In almost every respect, Amazon stands as a symbol for retail in the new world.

Beyond Retail 3.0 to 'New Retail'

Amazon adding physical stores to its portfolio proves that the former e-commerce pioneer is no longer thinking in terms of different channels but is aiming to achieve full channel integration. For Amazon, a shop is simply an extra touchpoint with the consumer, just like a site or an app. It is all about the customer journey: the path the consumer follows and all the places along the way where it is possible to come into contact with him. If university students in cities like Seattle or Portland want to enjoy an offline moment to sniff around in traditional bookstores, Amazon wants to meet them there. If people are in a hurry to grab a snack or office lunch, Amazon wants to meet them there.

Much the same is true of Amazon's take-over of the Whole Foods supermarket chain. It brought Amazon closer to the massive food sector and allows them to learn the tricks of the physical retail trade. They want to be the everything-and-everywhere retailer of the 21st century: a new and omnipresent Walmart for the digital age. 'If we want to become a 200-billion-dollar company, we need to learn how to sell food and clothes,' predicted Jeff Bezos as long ago as 2007. Proving he is a very quick learner, Amazon's highly technological and fully automated convenience shops Amazon Go are popping up throughout the United States. Only days after Apple shattered the 1,000 billion dollar stock quotation ceiling, in September 2018, Amazon was valued at 1,000 billion dollars as well, merely 165 days after it was listed at 600 billion dollars. How? By focusing heavily on both food and clothes.

With Prime Wardrobe, Amazon signals more clearly than ever before that fashion retail is its next big target. Prime shoppers can order up to 15 items of clothing at the same time, keep them for seven days, and return them free of charge if they do not want them. A series of delivery and collection lockers in apartment buildings in combination with the use of the Whole Foods store network for the same purpose means that Amazon's logistics outstrip their rivals. At the same time, Amazon is also selling exclusive capsule collections in collaboration with up-and-coming designers, like streetwear brand Nicopanda.

On the other side of the world, Alibaba is taking all the same steps. The web retailer has grown from an online marketplace for local Chinese traders (Taobao) into a complete eco-system for consumers worldwide; from an online warehouse with international A-brands and retailers (Tmall.com), through own brand labels, a mobile payment system and video services, to state-of-the-art physical retail.

Like Amazon, Alibaba is now moving in to high-tech supermarkets (Hema) and developing a voice assistant - Tmall Genie - as the contact 'person' to bring together all these services in people's homes. In fact, the Hema omnichannel supermarkets have even put Alibaba a step ahead of Amazon. While Amazon is moving into food retail one small step (or Amazon Go opening) at a time, Alibaba is already in full expansion in China. According to Alibaba CEO Daniel Zhang, these stores 'are not supermarkets and not food markets, but a completely new model' (Bloomberg 2017).

In Hema stores, Chinese shoppers can choose fresh sea produce, have it prepared the way they like and delivered to their homes within half an hour, thanks to online in-store picking. If they need more information, they simply scan the barcodes with their smartphone and when they are ready to check out they can pay using AliPay. As if that were not enough, the Hema app also gives personalized product suggestions. The innovative supermarket chain is expanding quickly, at an average rate of one new store every six days.

Next to the company headquarters in Hangzhou, Alibaba Group even opened its own five-storey mall. The MAO Mall not only hosts the Hema flagship store, but also features unmanned registers, delivery services and the first physical shop for the company's online marketplace Taobao. Alibaba also owns a major stake in Chinese hypermart operator Sun Art Retail Group and is helping Western retailers or brands, such as Intersport, open stores in China's high streets. According to founder Jack Ma, nearly 10,000 unmanned stores will open within China in the next few years.

His aim is to set the standard for 'new retail', the harmonious integration of online and offline that Alibaba sees as the future. Rightly so, because shoppers in the future will want to find what they want, where they want it and when they want it, all the time and everywhere. And by the way, it has to be quick and easy as well.

Beyond capitalism?

When the new millennium opened with worldwide fear and uncertainty about the so-called 'millennium bug', few people realized that this would be the prelude to a new era of general fear and uncertainty. The internet bubble, which from 1997 to 2001 hung above the heads of many internet start-ups like a latter-day Sword of Damocles, finally burst with predictably dire consequences. The limitless enthusiasm with which many investors had embraced this story and the promises of the internet entrepreneurs were shown to be horribly misguided. Neither the mentality not the technology were ready to make the expected commercial breakthrough and managers, carried away by the spirit of the moment, put growth before everything - including sound management. Only the strongest survived when the bubble finally burst.

This was followed in 2008 by the bank crisis, another symbolically important moment. What had previously been whispered in the background for years finally became clear to the masses: namely, that capitalism is not flawless. Unbridled consumerism and the neo-liberal discourse of endless growth and prosperity were suddenly revealed to have been responsible for many people losing everything: their house, their job and their credit-based welfare.

The firmly rooted 'traditional' idea of people as consumers first took shape in the in the 19th century when a middle class emerged, bringing with it for the first time the real prospect of improving your material and social position in life. This social position was no longer determined by aristocratic title, but by the riches you could earn with the sweat of your own brow. The enticing prospect of upward social mobility was accompanied by the rise of marketing: it was now seen to be possible to encourage people to do things or buy things that enhanced their quality of life and status. Prosperity was now within everyone's reach - or so people were led to believe - if only you worked hard enough.

Only in recent years this core idea has come under increasing criticism. Globalization and the universal availability of information have allowed us to see more clearly than ever before the inequalities and the problems that surround us. It is no longer possible to close our eyes to the things that are wrong with the world.

In other words, capitalism is now under fire, not least because the gulf between rich and poor is getting wider again in the West, leaving the middle class feeling increasingly threatened. Will everything turn out well if there is enough growth? If we work enough and buy enough? Marketeer and lecturer Herman Toch (2013) has described this growing questioning of capitalism as 'a total system crash' for the world as we know it. According to him, we are standing at a crossroads that will lead us to a new world where the consumer will once again become a person.

Our desire for prosperity is being replaced by a desire for well-being. Our first reaction when faced with the growing insecurity and stress-inducing speed of modern life is to seek greater certainty, honesty and transparency. This is leading to new kinds of economy: we now have the sharing economy, the exchange economy and the social economy, but also the local economy and the experience economy.

The customer as person
It is not only classic retail that has died. The classic customer is dead as well. In a world where marketeers and retail experts beg for companies to put the customer in the central position, this might seem like a contradictory statement, but it is important to make a distinction between customer, consumer and person nonetheless.

// It is not only classic retail, but also the classic customer who has died. //

A customer only exists from the perspective of the seller, the retailer or the brand. The people who buy things from him are 'his' customers. The possessive pronoun says it all: it is a proprietorial relationship. Once the retailer has persuaded the customer to buy, he believes that this customer belongs to him - and to no one else. Sadly for this way of thinking, that kind of customer no longer exists. The era when retailers and brands could 'appropriate' customers is history. Today's shoppers are no longer loyal the way they once were. With the exception of a limited number of 'love brands' (Nutella, Apple, BMW, etc.), purchasing preferences are now highly varied. Modern customers are emancipated and demanding. You cannot capture them and keep them anymore.

This is the mistake that traditional retailers have made and they have paid the price accordingly. Many have disappeared; the rest are suffering badly. Even an institution like Macy's had a sticky patch when it failed to realize that 'their' customers were no longer prepared to automatically offer their unconditional support. Likewise, the German department chain Kaufhof belatedly recognized the need to find new ways to lure back all its lost customers.

In a second phase, we have the person as consumer: someone who fulfils his needs by purchasing products. In contrast to the customer, it is the consumer himself who is in control and decides what, where and when he will buy something. Marketeers have been working for decades to reach this consumer, so they can persuade him to satisfy his needs with a particular brand or store. They have done this by, amongst other things, analyzing the consumer, placing him in segments and targeting him accordingly. It wasn't really all that difficult, because there were always so many new things to try. Within the span of a single lifetime, people saw the advent of the car, the washing machine, the television the computer and the smartphone. For a long time, retailers and brands were convinced that a flourishing and ever-expanding middle class would continue to be willing to buy more and more, and would never tire of going in search of new products and services to consume.

However, those same brands and retailers are now discovering that there is no such thing as limitless growth. In the production field, innovation is slowing down; it is only really in the technology and consumer electronics sectors that creativity is still on fire. One of the knock-on effects of this development is that instead of addressing consumers, marketeers now have to speak to the person behind the consumer - or so says Toch (2013). A person is more multi-dimensional than a consumer, with changing and sometimes incoherent priorities and fickle purchasing behaviour. In other words, someone who is autonomous but still connected. With a consumer, it's all about having. With a person, it's all about being.

To activate people to make a purchase, brands need to go further than simply convince them of the value of their product; nowadays, the product needs to give added value to people's lives. Even a sales expert like Doug Stephens says (2017):

'Nobody really needs your product'. In other words, products and services need to fulfil higher needs by playing on people's reason, emotion and intuition. Brands that want to be successful with people - as opposed to consumers - need to connect and humanize. People are value-driven. When faced with the huge mass of product and service providers, they will choose the ones that most closely match their own values and help them to live their lives the way they want. It is only when it satisfies this criterion that a brand will be able to have a differentiating usefulness for the purchasing person.

People are value-driven

We are currently experiencing a transition from a consumer-oriented retail industry with fast moving consumer goods (FMCG) to a more person-oriented industry, in which relationships and value-driven content are central. People are no longer the target public of brands; in today's open and transparent world, companies have become the target public for people everywhere.

// Modern customers are emancipated and demanding. You cannot capture them and keep them anymore. //

More and more brands are starting to profile themselves as a 'person', with a set of values, dreams and visions. Civic mindset brands, as futurist and trend-watcher Stefaan Vandist (2017) calls them, realize that they have an important social role to play. Like people, they are a part of society and therefore need to make a contribution. They can see the problems and challenges facing our world and decide of their own accord to do something about them.

Patagonia is a classic example of a value-driven or purpose-driven brand. As an outdoor brand, it cherishes nature and demonstrates this commitment by donating 1% of its turnover to environmental organizations. It also actively seeks to combat overconsumption by encouraging people to buy less and by awarding them points when they bring back their used or damaged clothing to the store, so that it can be repaired and sold on their own second-hand website.

In contrast, brands that fail to address the person behind the consumer soon find themselves punished where it hurts most: in falling sales. Classic, even iconic retailers such as Sears and Marks & Spencer learned the hard way that people are no longer looking for consumption warehouses with a hotchpotch of different types of products. People see these companies as lacking a clear identity, with a vague and ill-defined offer. No values, no story, no humanity.

Retail 4.0: at the heart of the fourth industrial revolution

Together, we all send 10,000 Snapchat photos every second and half a billion tweets per day. Tens of thousands of apps are competing for our attention. Is it any wonder, then, that our concentration levels have dropped since the advent of the mobile phone? Our span of attention is currently limited to about eight seconds, which (according to a famous marketing myth) is shorter than that of a goldfish. Although this claim can probably be dismissed as 'fake news',[1] it does nonetheless highlight a crucial feature of our modern world: everything needs to be done at lightning speed.

Even change is taking place much faster than in the past. Electricity had to wait 46 years for its real breakthrough. It was just 35 years for the telephone. The CD player managed to do so in 12 years, but the smartphone took only two! And this is just the tip of the iceberg, as Peter Hinssen explains in his book in *The Day After Tomorrow*. Gordon Moore, the founder of the IT company Intel, predicted that (computer) technology has the ability to increase its power and performance at successively greater speeds, whilst at the same time cutting the associated costs. This evolution - now generally known as Moore's Law - does not take place linearly, but in an exponential curve.

Although it is now evident that computer power is not increasing at the rate that Moore hoped, we nonetheless find ourselves in the middle of a new industrial revolution, in which change is taking place at a pace never previously seen in human history. This fourth industrial revolution - following the manufacturing revolution of the 18th century, the steam revolution of the 19th century and the internet revolution of the 20th century - is, like its predecessors, a technological revolution. Even so, as Klaus Schwab, Chairman of the World Economic Forum and author of *The Fourth Industrial Revolution*, has put it: 'In scale, scope and complexity, what I call the fourth industrial revolution is different from anything mankind has ever experienced before.'

Wherein lies the difference? A number of key technological breakthroughs have coincided in recent years: artificial intelligence (AI), robotics, the Internet of Things (IoT), self-driving cars, 3D printing, nanotechnology, biotechnology, material sciences, energy storage and quantum technology. This has had ramifications in every business sector. New business models have emerged, existing models have been disrupted and all the elements of the value chain have been redrawn. Production, consumption, transport and delivery methods have all been given a makeover.

But the impact of the fourth industrial revolution extends much further. Now that billions of people are connected to each other via their mobile devices, there now exists a hitherto unseen processing and storage capacity, allied to an unlimited access to knowledge. 'This not only changes what we do, but also who we are,' says Klaus Schwab. The changes we see taking place around us cannot be dismissed as temporary or transitory.

The business world influences the fourth industrial revolution in four different ways:

- consumer expectations are changing as a result of the availability of information;
- new products are being created on the basis of data;
- innovation is taking place through collaboration;
- new operational models are being developed.

In the future, these four elements will be found increasingly in retail and FMCG. If technological developments kick-start a sector into movement, the ball will start to roll faster and faster, until collision becomes unavoidable. The resulting impact releases new and disruptive forces - more specifically in retail, a horde of young companies with challenging business models - which will push change in the sector into an even higher gear.

// It's not the technology that is so disruptive; it's the speed. //

The changing speed of change

'It's not the technology that is so disruptive; it's the speed. Speed is the disruption of this era,' says retail consultant Frank Quix of Q&A Consultancy. To stay competitive, companies need above all to be fast and flexible. Nowadays, it is not so difficult to make a product that solves a problem, but this is inevitably followed by a whole range of variants and copies. And while it might not seem fair, it is not the best product that wins but the product that can attract the most customers quickly. That's how it was in the past (think of VHS and BetaMaxx) but today the process is many times faster.

// It is not the best product that wins, but the product that can attract the most customers quickly. //

Although Toyota has been working for years on the technology for an electric car, Tesla has beaten them. Why? Because Toyota was reluctant to cannibalize its own products and consequently decided to first launch a hybrid. This gave Tesla the chance to step in and claim the electric market. It is also significant that Tesla is willing to share its technology and knowledge with others to make traditional cars more sustainable, whereas Toyota has always refused to take this step. This suggests an old way of thinking, in which knowledge and innovation need to be fiercely protected. But change now happens so rapidly that innovation is only possible through collaboration and the general increase of common knowledge.

In the previous two decades, volatility in the retail sector - as recorded in the Deloitte Retail Volatility Index - has increased significantly. The largest retailers in the United States - with the exception of Amazon - have all seen their share of the market fluctuate, which means that the stock listed companies have had to sail through troubled waters as share prices see-saw erratically up and down.

Deloitte Retail Volatility Index

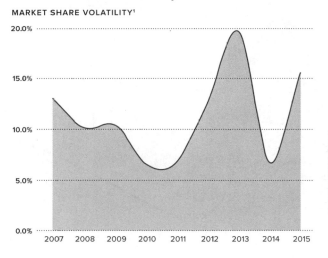

MARKET SHARE VOLATILITY[1]

BASED ON THE
TOP 153 US RETAILERS

1 Market share volatility is
measured as the weighted
standard deviation; retailers
contributing most to annual
volatity.

FIGURE 3 • Deloitte Retail Volatility Index

Source: Deloitte

In the retail sector, more change will take place in the next ten years than in the past century. Technology has reached the point where many disruptive innovations are now ready to become mainstream and have a real and lasting impact in the market. Within five to ten years, virtual home shopping will be commonplace and all different kinds of smart devices will be introduced that give retailers a different role in the chain.

According to the Gartner Hype Cycle, once an innovation reaches the peak of its cycle (the hype), a phase of disillusion usually sets in. It is only after this phase that the technology reaches full maturity and is embraced on a mass scale. This is when the technology becomes self-evident. For example, the current hype surrounding contactless payment is more or less over, so now it is gradually starting to be introduced in many places.

FIGURE 4 • Hype Cycle 2018 by Gartner

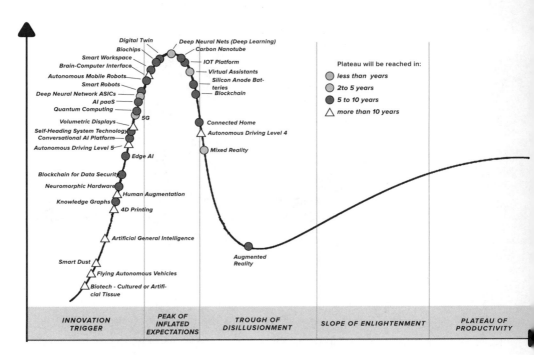

The hypes around the Internet of Things and big data reached their peak a few years ago; now we are starting to realize that they are not the panacea everyone once thought. This is positive, because if we follow Gartner's logic this means that in the near future the Internet of Things and big data will be embraced by friend and foe alike. Data-driven retailers can already gear their own stock purchases to the predicted purchasing behaviour of the customers. In the same way, virtual reality and robotics are now ready to make their 'comeback' following their premature launch in the 1990s. The time is now ripe, thanks to the omnipresence of powerful internet connections, allied with current levels of computer processing power and the drastically reduced price of the hardware.

Technological innovations are following each other at an ever greater speed and are influencing the behaviour of the consumer during the customer journey. In the years ahead, only the companies who can tap into the 'now' moment, by making the most personalized offer in the right place at the right time and on the right device, will survive. For the others, the future looks bleak.

The platform revolution

Pushing internally developed goods and services onto the market is becoming outdated. Many companies that have grown spectacularly in recent years - think of Airbnb, Uber or Alibaba and eBay - have a clear external focus: the value is created by the users, which is then shared on both sides of the value chain.

Revenues at marketplace platforms will double from 18.7 billion US dollars in 2017 to 40.1 billion dollars by 2022, with a special thanks to the growing sharing economy (Coresight Research 2018). Over half (57.2%) of the total 2022 revenue is expected to come from the Americas, but all over the world marketplaces are becoming forces to be reckoned with.

Three types of marketplaces are becoming especially successful: vertical marketplaces that specialize in specific categories, local marketplaces (such as Flipkart in India and Taobao in China) and service providing platforms that support sharing economy initiatives (think of TaskRabbit).

Hence, the typical linear value chain, in which the end user (as the name implies) only appears right at the very end of the chain, is passé. Logically, this chain was associated with a push model: the finished products - or well-defined services in the service industry - were pushed onto the market, with the intention of selling them to as many consumers as possible. It was not the consumer who asked for what he wanted; instead, companies offered what they had. In other words, it was a supply-driven market, but this no longer makes sense.

Networks are turning the economy upside down

What typifies marketplace companies is the way they create a platform on which the network then searches for value. The impact of the network economy is still often underestimated, but it is destined to change almost every sector - and change them for good. In fact, it will do more than change them: it will turn them on their head: not an evolution, but a platform revolution (Parker e.a., 2016).

A platform is a place where value exchanges between external producers and users are facilitated by offering an open and participative infrastructure. This can sometimes mean marketplaces, like Amazon, Alibaba, Etsy and eBay, but it can just as easily mean social platforms (Facebook, dating sites, Pinterest, etc.) or platforms like Tripadvisor, Buzzfeed and Uber. These are all companies that exist to bring people, other companies and brands into contact with each other. And nowadays there are lots of them. An awful lot.

They turn the entire value system upside down because their growth is generated by network effects. Not by internal factors, such as economies of scale, growth in the number of sales points or the diversification of the product assortment, but by using one side of the system as a lever to allow the other side to grow: the phenomenon of two-sided network effects. For example: if more people offer things for sale on second-hand sites like eBay, more people will be able to find what they want to buy, and so will use the sites. More buyers will then attract even more sellers, creating a snowball effect that results in exponential growth. Upsizing has never been easier!

That being said, the earning models of the platform companies can differ considerably. Whereas Amazon charges traders a commission on each sale, Alibaba charges traders nothing on its Taobao marketplace. Their income comes from advertising and from traders who pay to have greater visibility. Increasingly, platforms — Ahold Delhaize's online daughter Bol.com among them — offer both: in addition to paying commission, traders can also pay for sponsored search results, display advertising, brand pages or weblogs.

According to Leung and Lesco (2014), a platform company needs to fulfil three roles to function - and keep on functioning - successfully:

- match buyers and sellers;
- build up confidence by curating and by quality control;
- facilitate interactions.

Match supply and demand

It is self-evident that matching supply to demand is of crucial importance. However, when both these elements come from outside the company, you can easily end up in a chicken-and-egg situation: why, for example, should people offer the things they want to sell in a new online marketplace if they don't know in advance that there are lots of potential buyers? The reverse is also true: how can you attract visitors to your platform if you don't have many sellers?

So where should you focus your initial investment if you want to start a platform? Successful examples like Spotify, Pinterest and Tripadvisor use social media to achieve fast brand recognition and to collect data about their users. Via the often seen 'log in with Facebook' option, a network company immediately knows not only who its users are, but also gains access to their network to recruit new users.

In addition, a platform company must ensure that the potential buyer can easily find the kind of offer he is looking for (Molenaar, 2017). Certainly with the larger and more successful platforms, it is sometimes difficult as a visitor to see the wood for the trees. A random search on sites like Etsy, eBay or AliExpress illustrates why good selection filters, high-quality search functions and smart algorithms are essential.

Monitor quality to win confidence

Building up confidence is one of the most difficult aspects when developing a network initiative. Airbnb and Uber are the most obvious and well-known examples of platform companies where abuses are regularly reported in the media. In view of their status as disruptors and challengers, it is only logical that the opponents of the platforms - usually competitors working with traditional models who are being hit hard by their new rivals - should do all they can to give maximum publicity to every incident where things go wrong. And this is only right and proper, because the risk of things going wrong is real.

In a model in which the users hold all the strings, a downward spiral can quickly lead to disaster. In view of the huge scale inherent in any successful platform, the manual checking of quality is simply not feasible. The only option is to develop an excellent system of feedback and reviews, supported by filtering algorithms. In other words, a self-controlling system.

// Building up confidence is one of the most difficult aspects when developing a network initiative. //

Where competition is fierce, it is of great importance for suppliers/sellers to maintain their good reputation. They do this by making use of reviews and customer ratings, which together create a personal scoreboard for each supplier/seller. According to Clark's biography of Jack Ma (2016), the traders on Alibaba's Taobao network keep a close watch on their online reputation and are even willing to show their products to potential customers visually via webcam. It is also common for them to add 'extras' to each package after sale - and all to preserve their good name. Why? Because a good name is gold: 'Your reputation precedes you, Mr. Bond'.

If disputes nonetheless arise between buyer and seller, a number of *xiaoers* act as arbitrators. These are often young people who work long hours to ensure that everything on the platform runs smoothly, but it also allows them to earn a good living. Alibaba consciously pays its *xiaoers* a good salary to guarantee their loyalty and independence. They are regarded as key figures in the business model. They have the power to close down a 'shop' on the platform or to reward good traders with marketing campaigns. Corrupt or negligent *xiaoers* can expect little mercy from their employers. This also explains why Amazon wages a fierce war against false reviews, because reviews are the control mechanism that determines whether or not confidence in the platform stands or falls.

In order to build up confidence, sustainable relations with the community are indispensable. A network model based on peer-to-peer contact in which thousands of people can be 'active' at the same time without any of them actually being 'employed', is not without risk. The independent operatives who drive for Uber, knit for Etsy or cook for Meal Sharing do that for a fraction of the cost for permanent employees, but on the reverse side of the coin do not enjoy the protection and security conferred by a formal contract of employment. If the platform fails to offer a sustainable and flexible framework for this growing group of flex-workers, the community will soon collapse.

Facilitating up to the sale and beyond

The third and final role of platform managers is facilitation: they need to develop a safe and secure system for completing transactions. In the case of a service platform, this often means little more than a good payment module, as the seller and buyer arrange delivery between themselves. However, if they sell products, platforms often need to deal with the logistical part of the transaction as well. Both Amazon and Alibaba are pulling logistics in-house, giving them control over the crucial 'last mile'. This allows the companies to remain in contact with the end user, to whom they provide useful added value in terms of good service, which all enhances their reputation.

That being said, perhaps the most important facilitator - and therefore source of confidence - is the payment mechanism. Being able to pay and receive money easily and safely is a *conditio sine qua non* for both buyers and sellers. This is why PayPal was taken over by eBay. And what PayPal is to eBay, AliPay is to Alibaba. Clark (2016) even thinks that AliPay is Alibaba's most important trump card. It has grown to become the largest online payment system in China and deals with more than three-quarters of a billion dollars' worth of online transactions in a year. Amazon could not afford to be left behind and has introduced Pay Places, which allows users to make mobile payments at physical locations.

H&M

H&M launches its own multi-brand platform

'There's a seismic shift in the world of retail and we're here to change it', says the announcement of Afound, a marketplace selling discounted fashion and lifestyle products by H&M Group.

Interestingly, the digital marketplace and physical stores of Afound not only sell the vertical retail group's own brands, but also 'a wide range of well-known, popular brands for both women and men'. H&M is consciously trying to partner up with other brands, as a part of the 'seismic shift' in retail it is preparing for.

Although carefully curated, over 60 brands are participating in the new concept, using the platform as an outlet channel, and H&M keeps looking for more. The Swedish fashion giant invests in digitalisation and platforms because that is where its younger target audience increasingly is to be found: in 2017, the year before the launch of Afound, H&M Group faced turnover setbacks, store closures and significant quantities of unsold stock. The turnover growth it did book, was mostly thanks to increasing online sales. By investing in new distribution models, among which the multi-brand platform, H&M wants to reconnect with consumers, even if it requires a very atypical move for the pioneer in integrated, vertical fashion retail.

Verticalization from Apple to Zara

The internet brings people into contact with each other, all across the world. For whatever reason, including to do business with each other. Whereas in the past the retailer was the sole and necessary intermediary between supply and demand, between producer and consumer, in our new globalized and digitalized world the producer and the consumer can find each other directly, cutting out the middle man. This is a return to economic basics: a single integrated chain from production to end user. Whether you are talking about a webshop or a self-run flagship store, verticalization is the new norm: retailers are becoming brands and brands are becoming retailers.

As a result of direct sales via the internet, the necessity to invest in strategically located shops and large stocks, with their huge fixed costs, has fallen away. Large shops with large stocks no longer have an added value, hence they can no longer be charged as an added value to the customer in the price. Using technological and online interfaces (internet terminals, tablets, etc.) everything the shop has to offer can be virtually present on the shop floor.

Until recently, the entire distribution model was built around this concept of large stores and large stocks. Retailers even calculated their margin based on these "essential" costs: turnover per square metre. The entire earning model (the retailer earns on the margin) was based on this system. However, this type of classic retail has now come to an end. There are new players in the game who have the full chain in their control, from production to final sale. Brands have become their own retailers and some retailers have turned themselves into brands. Well-known examples include Apple, H&M, Nike, IKEA and even Louis Vuitton: they are all among today's most trendsetting and successful retail companies.

Their huge advantage is that they are not dependent on other brand producers to obtain favourable conditions, nor are they reliant on external retailers to display their products in their stores. Or at least not completely - because even in integrated vertical chains it is still possible to find a number of variants.

The first and purest form is the completely vertical chain, where companies only offer their own products via their own channels. This is the concept behind Zara and IKEA. A second, more hybrid model involves a mix of the kind used by Apple. The company's own flagship stores and online sales are supplemented by the use of partners, multi-brand retailers and mono-brand retailers, who are also permitted to offer the product lines. Apple still determines the pricing and the marketing, so that price competition between the different channels becomes impossible, while also projecting the same brand image to the consumer wherever he shops.
It is also noticeable how many food and FMCG brands are taking steps to approach consumers more directly via flagship stores, webshops, pop-up shops and anything else they can think of, although the bulk of their actual turnover is still realized through external retailers.

Nowadays, consumers also demand the best price, which means that the margin-consuming intermediaries are gradually being squeezed out of the chain, one by one. Physical retailers, and certainly the supermarket chains, have become like drug addicts - or so says Corstjens (2015). They do everything they can to win the price wars with their rivals, but at the expense of cutting away at their own margins, which they desperately need to pay their high fixed costs. As a result, they effectively end up cutting their own throats.

// Physical retailers, and certainly the supermarket chains, have become like drug addicts. //

In response to these developments, some retailers have tried to become producers, by launching new brands and private labels of their own. Of course, retailers have had their private label products for some time, but today they are no longer the white products we used to see on supermarket shelves. Now they are image builders. Even hardcore retailers like Amazon and Zalando are starting to focus more on private label products. They see these house brands not only as a way to differentiate themselves from the crowd, but also as a method to re-establish a shorter and more vertical value chain, which will give them greater control over their offer, allow them to push up their margins and relieve them from some of the pressure exerted by brand producers and price-comparing shoppers.

A few giants make the world a smaller place

Is there still a future for retailers who only sell the products of others (horizontal retail)? Yes, there is - but that future will be very different from the past. Nowadays, what people expect most of all from retail is ease and convenience - and this can take many forms.

If convenience means speed, there will still be a need for the one-stop shop. When speed is of the essence, you want to find the things you need as efficiently as possible. This why Amazon and Zalando are so keen to become total sellers, stocking anything and everything, like the 'people's warehouses' of the past, such as Sears, Marks & Spencer and Galeria Kaufhof, all of which have now lost their positions and are frantically searching for a new model. Why? If every product supplier is a brand and if every retailer is also a brand, then every supplier is also a competitor.

You can already see this competition operating internally in the multi-brand retailers, where the A-brands are locked in battle with the house brands, with further rivalry being brought in from outside via the shopper's smartphone or via the rival listings under your search results in Google.

Fighting every day to secure your product's position on the shop shelf: it is hardly an attractive prospect, and certainly not in the long term. Yet this is exactly what happens in many supermarkets and at horizontal retailers like Amazon and AliExpress. Or as retail designer Rodney Fitch once said: 'Only one of them can be the cheapest; all the others will have to think of something else'. This applies equally to the fastest and the most complete. The new one-stop shop needs to be all these things.

To keep on fighting this war, you need to be big. Very big. There are only a few players who can manage it. At national level, there are a small number of local leaders, like Bol.com in the Benelux, but even their situation is precarious. For years, Otto was the market leader in Germany, but it is now trailing some distance behind Amazon: it has to be satisfied with second place and 3.8% of the market share, compared with 13% for Amazon.

The list of largest global retailers has changed fundamentally over the last decades. Only four of today's top ten retailers were already on the list in 2001 (Deloitte 2018). New stars have risen, and these stars are shining ever so brightly. The revenue of the world's 50 fastest-growing retailers grows four times (20.9%) faster than the total revenue growth of the entire top 250 group. These ten top players also keep growing their share of all retail sales: nearly a staggering third of all revenue of the top 250 retailers goes to them.

Source: Deloitte, Global Powers of Retailing 2018:
Transformative change, reinvigorated commerce (2018)

FIGURE 5 • Top 10 of the world's largest retailers (by revenue)

Deloitte, Global Powers of Retailing 2018:

FY2001	FY2016
1. Wal-Mart	1. Wal-Mart
2. Carrefour	2. Costco
3. Ahold	3. Kroger
4. Home Depot	4. Schwarz Group
5. Kroger	5. Walgreens Boots Alliance
6. Metro	6. Amazon
7. Target	7. Home Depot
8. Albertson's	8. Aldi Group
9. Kmart	9. Carrefour
10. Sears	10. CVS Health

Given the high concentration of power, competition among this top list is fierce. As the 'winner takes it all' in the future of shopping, the world's leading retailers feel pressured into ever-growing consolidation and globalisation. Deloitte's Top 10 retailers focus on strong foreign operations - Aldi, Schwarz Group and Carrefour already make over half of their retail revenue abroad - hyper-efficient operations and industry leading inventory control. As a result, their return on assets is almost twice as high as the ROA of all Top 250 retailers taken together.

Hence, the gap is widening between the top and bottom players of the retail pyramid. How to compete in the current hyper-competitive environment, where margins are so tight and prices under such pressure? While brand producers are learning to approach customers directly - by opening a webshop, engaging in social commerce via social media or investing in flagship stores - retailers are trying to secure their own network, so that they can remain in the front line in shoppers' minds. Their tactics include house brands, but they also go online with their own platforms and form international alliances, as will be discussed later on in this book.

Retailers and brands will feel increasingly obliged to work together if they want to compete against companies that are not interested in making profits as such, but are more concerned about generating non-stop growth. You can either swim with the current or against the current. You either make use of the services offered by the big players or go your own way. But trying to take on the big players and beat them at their own game is - to put it bluntly - pointless in this 'winner-takes-all' market.

'Future of the Consumer': demographic shifts - or earthquakes

The population of Western Europe is starting to look very different. Certainly older: Westerners have never lived for so long. In combination with a falling birth rate since 1965, this means that Europe is increasingly greyer rather than greener. The countries outside Europe where more children are being born are in many cases subjected to the consequences of war, poverty and climate change. This in turn leads to increased migration - usually to the richer West, which leads to a more diverse population in our streetscape. What's more, this population is increasingly concentrated in urban areas, where the composition of households is also undergoing radical change, with more singles of all ages, as well as single parent families, co-housers and larger f(r)amilies.

In the meantime, the process of far-reaching globalization continues unabated. A significant middle class is being formed in the lands with developing markets, so that the world is gradually becoming a single large market, assisted by exponential technological development. Because information is now available at all times and in all places, people can immediately find what they want, no matter where they are. They might want contact with like-minded people; or they might simply want products they can't find at home. If so, they can check the claims of companies everywhere, but at the same time they can learn what things are really like on the other side of the world.

In this way, concern for and commitment to solve the problems of the planet grows. This is reflected in consumer behaviour. Whether people are motivated by fear or idealism, the demand for local, organic and authentic products is on the rise. Companies need to make clear what they stand for and how they intend to contribute to a better world. In fact, many companies are being bypassed, with people turning to local agricultural markets and online platforms, or else co-owning or sharing their possessions with others.

Whereas for decades 'average' was regarded as being good enough, today being 'choosy' has become the norm. Coming from a past with much less choice and where everything was new and deemed necessary, certainly with the privations of the war years still in the back of people's minds, the days of 'keeping up with the Joneses' are now over: the new generations exalt the individual above the mass while middle class in developed Western countries is slowly but surely shrinking: Mr. Average does not live here anymore.

The new normal

We often speak about different generations and give them names, such as generations Y and Z (also known as the millennials). We even still talk about the baby-boomers of the 1960s. But these are nothing more than easy pigeon holes in which to categorise people, primarily for marketing purposes. Every market research survey makes full use of these categorizations to decide who is in which target group and how they can best be reached.

Age, however, no longer says it all (if it ever did). We are all living longer and remaining healthier for longer. And even if we are not healthy, improving health care succeeds in keeping us alive in comfort much better than ever before. Nowadays, age does not necessarily mean that you feel old - not like the typical grandmas and granddads of yesteryear. What counts now is the individual's mindset: a fifty-year-old can sometimes have the mindset of a thirty-year-old, but with twenty years more life experience.

People, of all ages and in all markets, have never been so free to establish their own identity. This means that their patterns of consumption are no longer determined by traditional demographic segments, like age, gender, location, income, family status, etc. There is a new wind abroad, which disregards the pigeon-hole thinking of the past. The traditional idea of 'settling down' and starting a 'nuclear family' - job, house, marriage, children - has lost the universal appeal it once had. Nowadays, it is even possible to experience more than one phase of life at the same time!

Close the Loop

H&M captured the new spirit of the times graphically in its advert for the recycling of clothes: everyone is free to choose who he or she is, young or old, man or woman. The trendsetting world brand also used the most diverse models in its campaign, from people with a transgender background to sprightly seniors.

Especially the number of single-dwelling, older women will continue to grow considerably. Nevertheless, women in the single target group in our society do better than the men: they study longer, grow a career and marry later in life. When their marriage fails, women today are also a lot more empowered because often they have reached financial independence. We are heading towards a *Sheconomy*, observes trend watcher Kjeldsen from the Copenhagen Institute for Future Studies.

// Patterns of consumption and lifestyles not only vary within the same household, but also within the same individual. //

It doesn't stop with family composition either: patterns of consumption and lifestyle not only vary within the same household, but also within the same individual. One week a person might eat vegetarian, whereas the next week he/she might choose to eat halal with his/her partner. In most of the world, people have never had such freedom to define their own person. This means that society needs to adapt to new and flexible forms, so that hyper-specialization becomes essential. We are evolving towards a world of niches.

An example: if superstar Beyoncé chooses the wheelchair user Jillian Mercado as the role model for her merchandizing collection, this indicates a clear change of accent from idealized physical beauty to mindset and individuality. But this was by no means a first for fashion blogster Mercado, who was born with a debilitating muscular disease: in 2014 she was also one of the faces for the campaign of the Diesel fashion brand, in which she figured with other young influencers from her generation.

The clash of generations

Today, the clash of generations is largely about the problems associated with growing up in a rapidly changing succession of different worlds. This means that it is not easy to understand and (especially) communicate with each other. Even though there is no longer a linear connection between age clusters and consumption patterns, the categories are still useful, particularly if we are talking about the lifestyles of different generations. And even though we still need to bear in mind that there are often as many differences within generations as between them, everyone grows up within a certain 'era', with its own social, economic and political context that shapes people.

For example, the 'millennials' generation is characterized precisely in terms of its confrontation with previous generations and the way in which their lifestyle puts the social system under pressure. The welfare state is based on the premise that the young, working generation will provide the financial support (pensions, health care, etc.) for the old generation. This was logical in the 1950s, when the majority of the population was 'young', so that there was a sufficiently broad basis to carry both the economy and the social security system.

However, the population pyramid is starting to turn, with a broader top of older people and a narrower base of younger ones. How long will it take before the pyramid cracks under its own weight and brings the whole system crashing down?

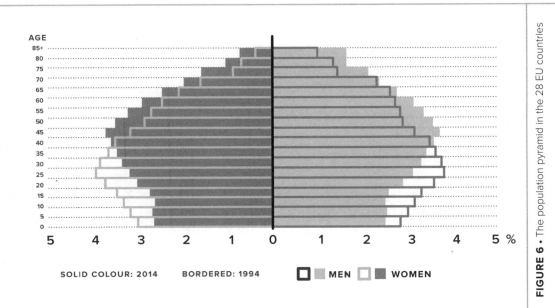

AGE

5   4   3   2   1   0   1   2   3   4   5 %

SOLID COLOUR: 2014   BORDERED: 1994   ☐ ▨ MEN   ☐ ▨ WOMEN

FIGURE 6 • The population pyramid in the 28 EU countries

Source: Eurostat

Average life expectancy in Western Europe rose by 25% between 1950 and 2010, while during the same period people joined the labour market six years later and retired much earlier: at the age of 65 years in 1950 to an average of 59 years in 2010. This trend has shown no signs of being reversed in the past decade: the effective retirement age almost everywhere in Europe continues to be much lower than the official retirement age, which is still 65 years. In other words, many people are still stopping work much earlier than the system foresees.

After their retirement, these early stoppers enjoy life and their regained freedom, as long as their health permits. And evolutions in health care, medicine and general life style ensure that 'as long as health permits' is getting longer as well. Some people now spend more years in retirement than they ever spent in work. But somehow this needs to be financed, beyond people's own savings.

Source: OECD

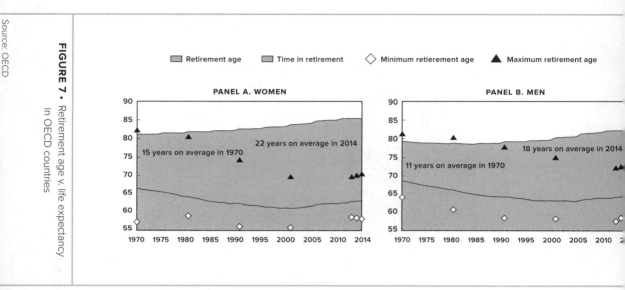

FIGURE 7 · Retirement age v. life expectancy in OECD countries

However, the younger generations now have generally lower wages and pay high-er taxes for the social security of the older generations. In 2050 Eurostat expects that the amount of elderly people (65+) will increase to 48 percent in relation to the working age population. This means that every working couple becomes re-sponsible, financially and theoretically, for a non-working elder. In 2015, the de-pendency ratio of older people was only 26 percent. The pressure on the working population is therefore twice as high. This gap creates tensions: how do we make it financially sustainable?

Because life expectancy continues rise (and is expected to keep on rising), in West-ern Europe we will soon have five active generations for the very first time. The children of tomorrow will not only know their grandparents and great-grandpar-ents, but also, in some cases, their great-great-grandparents. A child of five with parents of thirty has grandparents of fifty-five and great-grandparents in their seventies. This means that the great-great-grandparents would 'only' need to live to around ninety-five to meet their great-great-grandchildren. Nowadays, that is not such an unlikely prospect as it once was.

And if the grandparents continue to take early retirement at the age of fif-ty-five, this means that one working generation will need to support three old-er, non-working ones. Is there a solution? The World Health Organization (WHO) argues that, from a purely physical perspective, people are comfortably able (on average) to work well into their seventies. In other words, we need to get more people - more generations - back into labour market. The challenge for the future is to find ways to allow three generations, each with their own different skills, to work together to support the very oldest and the very youngest non-working generations.

The silver consumer

The chance that someone in their fifties is only halfway through life has never been greater. Statistics show that average life expectancy in Europe increases by two years with each new decade. We are living longer, and falling birth rates mean that there are proportionally more older people than ever before.

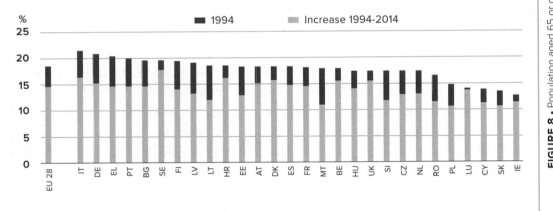

Population aged 65 or over on January (% of the total population)

■ 1994   ▦ Increase 1994-2014

FIGURE 8 • Population aged 65 or over (% of the toal population)

Source: Eurostat

In European countries, 38.5% of the population is already older than 50 years of age, according to Eurostat (2015). By 2030, that figure will have risen to 44.1% and by 2050 even 45.9% will be fifty-plussers. In France in 2014 there were more people older than sixty than younger than twenty. It is the same story in the Netherlands as well: the over-65s now form 18% of the population and in 2019 it is expected that for the first time in Dutch history the 18-49 cohort will be smaller than the 50+ cohort. As a result, the majority of tomorrow's shoppers will be grey rather than green.

Ageing research carried out by Q&A suggests that the spending patterns of older people are different: they spend more on services and less on products, both in terms of amounts and frequency. It is not just that there are more seniors and that they are living for longer; they are also fitter and more dynamic than they have ever been. Young pensioners often feel young at heart (61% say they feel at least nine years younger than they actually are, according to a Boston Consulting Group survey), regularly travel and keep active by looking after their grandchildren and maintaining a busy social life. The once common idea among the young that 'old people are past it' no longer holds water.

In part, it is media consumption that helps to keep older people young at heart: Europeans aged between 50 and 75 years spend more time on the internet and watching television than other age categories (Neuvy 2016). This means that older consumers are well informed, up-to-date and eminently reachable for marketeers. When it comes to buying online, there is no essential difference between the behavior of seniors and non-seniors either. Although seniors do like to go shopping a bit better: almost half of them just likes to visit stores and therefore does not buy online. A vast majority says that they want to see and feel products first.

Desigual

Seventy-year-old model for Desigual

The Spanish fashion brand Desigual, which consciously tries to focus on diversity in its campaigns, decided to launch a new denim line for young people with a model who was anything but young: Alicia Borrás, a sprightly seventy-year-old and former Miss Spain. With her dancing and her motto of 'Life is great!', this elegant lady certainly catches the eye. 'I do it because I love fashion and because I think it's time for a change,' Borrás told the Spanish newspaper *El País* in 2016. 'Older people have knowledge and experience, and that's a big plus!'

Grandparents with cash

The silver generation makes an active contribution to both society and the economy. Even after their retirement, they want to keep busy: in France, millions of pensioners do so-called 'invisible work' in societies or as volunteers. An increasing number are also still active in the labour market: 600,000 French pensioners supplement their income with paid employment. They are making their presence felt in the relational market as well: the number of seniors who remarry is also on the rise.

According to the sociologist Guérin (2015), no less than 48% of all consumer expenditure in France is made by the fifty-plussers. Further research by Q&A shows that the emphasis of this expenditure is on services and food: they take more frequent and more expensive than average holidays, eat out more and buy more expensive foods for daily consumption. But they spend less on non-food, because they have less need of new things. If they do need to make savings, this is where they do it.

// Entrepreneurs of the future will no doubt set their sights on the fifty-plusser as a demographic target group. //

Entrepreneurs of the future will no doubt set their sights on the fifty-plusser as a demographic target group. And certainly on the babyboomers - or grandparents with cash, as they are often known - who were born between 1946 and 1964. They are regarded as the most successful generation of the 20th century; in part because they are the last generation who will be able to retire before the age of 60 (although about half the babyboomers are still working), in part because they were able to benefit from the years when interest rates were sky-high, allowing them to build up a capital nest-egg that survived the various banking crises of recent times.

'Too old to be called young, but too young to be old': that is how the babyboomers feel, according to Filip Lemaître of The Silver Ones consultancy bureau. 'Fifty-so-methings and sixty-somethings often feel like privileged thirty-somethings. The kids have left home, the grandkids are within shouting distance, their mortgage is paid off and they still have cash in the bank at the end of the month.' Life expectancy statistics suggest that the babyboomers can still expect between another 12 and 20 years of life - and they intend to make good use of them.

Even so, all that glitters is not gold - especially for the people who rely on their state pension to make ends meet. Two in 10 pensioners in the UK are living in poverty: whereas in 2012, 13% of British pensioners were living below the poverty line, by 2017 this number had risen to a level of 16% (JRF 2017). Their savings no longer earn the interest they once did and the likelihood that they will need to sell some of their possessions to get by is on the increase. The babyboomers will probably also be the last generation to inherit from their parents - if there is anything left to inherit. Many boomers are already making significant financial contributions to the care of these parents, eating into their resources. There probably won't be all that much left over to pass on to their own children, the millennials. Economists predict that many babyboomers will get into financial difficulties because they have put too little aside for the medical care they will need in later life. Even selling their own homes might not be enough to dig them out of this financial hole, predicts Lemaître.

As if this were not enough, many people now feel that the babyboomers have the 'total system crash' on their conscience. Many of the problems facing the world today - such as climate change, the ageing of the population, the breakdown of capitalism - were ignored during the 'golden years' of the late 20th century, so that these same problems are now being handed down to the next generation. However, the babyboomers will no longer be around to solve them. They were content to make hay while the sun shone, but now they are gradually withdrawing from the labour market, leaving it to others to clear up the mess. We are about to enter a huge transitional phase, the results of which are far from clear.

Accessible consumption

Retailers can no longer ignore seniors. Instead, they are better advised to respond to the specific needs of this large group of consumers. For example, the Danish supermarket chain Netto is already highly active in this area. They have a dedicated seniors' policy and develop measures to attract and keep both older customers and older employees. Initiatives of this kind can increase both consumer satisfaction and profitability: older customers like to be served by older staff and visit more often when this is the case.

With this in mind, Netto has created three senior supermarkets, where at least half the staff is older than fifty years of age. After an initial lead-in period, Netto claims that these supermarkets are now performing just as strong as the best branches in their chain. Staff costs are relatively higher, but this is compensated by significantly lower levels of sickness and absence. Customer satisfaction levels are also well above average.

People generally want to live at home and function independently for as long as possible. But a long life inevitably means that sooner or later we are all confronted by medical problems of one kind or another. To help meet these circumstances, many seniors are enthusiastically turning to home delivery services, not only for their daily groceries but also for their meals. Both these trends are likely to grow in the future, as resources are cut for the social services that currently help many older people with their cooking and shopping.

French supermarket group Intermarché launched Bien Chez Moi, a store and service center for seniors. The store of about 200 square meters is to be found in a mall in Normandy and is completed with a service formula for 'active seniors'. Bien Chez Moi wants to combine innovative products and activities like adapted food products, diet advice, cooking lessons, sporting sessions, administrative assistance and assisted shopping for an older clientele. As the name gives away (Bien Chez Moi translates to Happy At Home) the aim is to help seniors live at home longer.

In the Netherlands, the Spar supermarket network already introduced a service package geared to meet the needs of the elderly. In addition to a meal service, they also offer a wide range of other services, such as a dry cleaner's, a photo service, a package service, self-care and even medicines. It is a kind of one-stop shop for less mobile customers. As a result, many older people now regard Spar as almost being a friend of the family, especially as it is often the local shop keeper himself or one of his staff who delivers the products to their home.

It is predicted that in Western markets sales of incontinence materials - nappies, etc. - for the elderly will soon exceed sales for babies. In fact, this was already the case in Japan as early as 2012.

The silver economy is a billions economy, with huge potential for entrepreneurs and retailers who are able to approach its possibilities constructively, particularly in the areas of food, services and (para)pharmacy. What's more, with better care and greater openness for the individual (and his/her diversity), attention will also grow for those who are confronted with mobility problems for reasons other than old age. Perhaps this is where the future lays for many retailers? According to Frank Quix of Q&A the ageing population is set to put a bomb under traditional non-food retail: the elderly spend much less on non-food and are also becoming an increasingly large part of the population. So why not switch the focus to providing them with the services they need?

The 'work hard, play hard' generation

The professionally active age group between the young starters and the *fin de car-rière* babyboomers is a highly desirable target group for marketeers, retailers and brand producers. When we think of people in their forties or early fifties, we think of active men and women. They have started a family and built a career. It is an age group that is open to consumption in all its many new forms. They are ready to make premium and luxury purchases, while they still have budgetary room to do so.

Today's late thirty-, forty- and fifty-year-olds belong to Generation X (born between 1961 and 1981), the so-called 'lost generation'. It is a large generation in terms of numbers and its consumption behaviour is not dissimilar to the babyboomers, but it has a more pessimistic, perhaps even cynical outlook. Generation X-ers started their careers as the Cold War was ending, turning the political landscape on its head and resulting in a massive shift of employment to low wage lands. They were also the generation of increasing divorce and frequent changes of home, as people tried to climb the housing ladder.

The current cohort of working forty- and fifty-somethings know that they will never be able to build up a reserve of capital the way their parents did, and that consequently their children will have to make do with less. At the same time, they feel obliged to care for their long-living parents, while also struggling to maintain a good work-life balance. This age group stands with one foot in the analogue world and the other foot in cyberspace. They have learnt to adjust to the new technology of recent years, although they did not grow up with it. Unlike their children, they are not digital natives. As a result, marketeers can easily lose sight of Generation X, even though they form the largest part of the active professional population.

// Generation X is truly omnichannel: they like to make use of online video services, but also still like to watch television. //

So the question is how you can best reach them: online, offline or both? When confronted with new technology, the Generation X-ers usually manage to find their way, although their responses differ: some are early adopters, some (but only a very few) are digital illiterates. Generation X is truly omnichannel: they like to make use of online video services, but they also still like to watch television. They read an online newspaper during the week, but a real paper one at weekends. They combine online shopping with regular trips to the high street stores.

It is worth noting that marketeers also claim that professionally active people in their forties and fifties display a certain degree of brand loyalty. In general, they are in the phase of their life where they work hard and play hard, with a preference for convenience and the certainty offered by known brands. They were brought up in the era of A-brands and consequently still see certain brands as a form of status symbol. They associate premium brands with comfort and peace of mind, which fits in well with their 'work hard-play hard' philosophy, in which materialism plays an important role.

The youth of today: welcome to the 'smart shopper'

People who have worked hard deserve a comfortable retirement. This principle dates back to the 19th century. To 1889, to be precise, when Otto von Bismarck passed a law to introduce the first state pension fund for German citizens over the age of 70. The problems started when average life expectancy continued to rise, while longer studying children entered the labour market at a later age and the pensionable age fell to levels sometimes as low as 59 years.

Today's seniors live ten years longer than their parents and therefore need significant savings to see them safely through their old age, which means that they have much less to pass on to their children than in the past. This has produced a whole new generation of young people with no accumulated capital, which in turn has resulted in a mind shift in the purchasing behaviour of this large but capital-deficient cohort. Consequently, chains like Primark, Lidl, Action and KiK now have the wind in their sails (and sales).

The young have become what they themselves call 'smart consumers'. How does this manifest itself? For example, by buying house brands in supermarkets. Whereas in the past everyone wanted to upgrade, many younger people now find it more sensible to downgrade. Expensive top-of-the-range products still sell pretty well, but the middle segment is being squeezed by the growth of low-end products that are often equally good in terms of quality.

This new reality has also encouraged young people to rediscover the value of making things for themselves. They combine craftsmanship with the latest technology to develop new products and new opportunities. Blogs, YouTube and specialized communities allow like-minded people from all over the world to come into contact with each other. For them, creativity and collaboration are the answer, and they excel at both. It might seem as though they never look up from their computer screens, but the young people of today are actually in the process of making a radical new economy.

It is natural that teenagers should be ambitious and today's generation is no differ-ent. What's more, in recent years many of them have rediscovered their interest in entrepreneurship. During a 2016 survey by Accent Jobs, no fewer than 50% said that they one day hoped to have their own company. Retailers and brands should be on their guard - because these teenagers could turn out to be serious compet-itors in the years ahead! If they do go into business, you can be certain this will automatically mean omnichannel. And you can be equally certain they will be able to reach their target group faster and more intuitively than all the marketing plans of recent decades put together.

'Millennials' and 'digital intuitives'

Within the broad category of 'young people', sociologists and demographers make a distinction between Generation Y and Generation Z. Both types have been the subject of much discussion, since they are the first real online generations, with the potential for establishing a new political and social world order. Young people who experienced the start of the new millennium grew up with fear: fear of the millennium bug, fear of a world economic crash and fear of a guerrilla war be-tween the West and Muslim fundamentalism. They also grew up with omnipres-ent internet, pocket-sized technology and easy connection with other parts of the world (both physically and virtually).

Generation Y (born 1975-1995) is a famous generation with many different names: the millennials, the lost generation and even Generation Everything. They were the first generation to have cell phones as teenagers but had to wait until adulthood to get their hands on a smartphone. In other words, they almost grew up in the digital world - but not quite. As a result, they had to adjust to digital developments, both at home and at work.

Generation Z (born 1995-2010) is the first generation that truly grew up in both a digital and a physical world. They are no longer digital natives; they have become digital intuitives. As children, they did not need to learn digital technology; they were born with it. They recognize no boundary between the digital and analogue worlds and navigate effortlessly between them. In their eyes, Facebook and Twit-ter are already outdated; they prefer Snapchat, Instagram and YouTube. Photos and videos are their preferred means of communication. If you want to reach Generation Z, a picture says more than a thousand words. This is hardly surprising: the staggering speed of the digital world is also their speed.

Young people still need something to hold on to. But they no longer seek this from 'higher up' - from their elders or the establishment - but at their own level, from people and communities who they feel are on the same wavelength as themselves. They form horizontal relationships with peers and equals, no matter where they might be in the world.

This constant experience of others via the internet makes them afraid they might somehow get left behind. There is even a term for it: FOMO or 'fear of missing out'. They are equally wary of the 'comfort zone'. They don't want the comfort of the familiar; they want the thrill of the moment. Generations Y and Z prefer the short term, things they can photograph and share via social media. In short, they put experiences and services before goods. This finds its expression in high migration, which sees a nomadic - but comfortable - lifestyle as the ideal: the unattached freelancer who roams the world and has a succession of loose but often lucrative 'jobs' as a photographer, blogger or Instagram influencer.

The best way to attract the fleeting attention of Generation Z and also Generation Y is with pop-up stores and shop-in-shops, where shoppers can continually move from one experience world to another. This satisfies their need for speed and their desire for non-stop stimulation.

The self as a religion

Making connections is second nature to young people. They search for and find kindred spirits all over the world. This allows them to broaden their horizons to such an extent that their own family, which is geographically closest to them, no longer necessarily plays the most important role in their lives. Friends become a part of the family and vice versa. This leads to the creation of what Filip Lemaître and Amélie Rombauts call 'framilies': an amalgamation of family and friends.

Friendship is highly valued by Generation Y and the older members of Generation Z. They spend a lot of time and money on maintaining these friendships. Social consumption is one of the biggest expenditure posts for Gen Y-ers: a visit to the wellness centre, a shopping trip with friends, a meal in a star-rated restaurant. These are the things that make life worth living for Generation Y.

These little indulgences - treats for yourself - are seen as a well-deserved reward by the current generations, whereas for the babyboomers and even many Generation X-ers they are more of a sin (albeit a harmless one). Nowadays, self-care and (briefly) putting yourself in first place is no longer regarded as egotistical. On the contrary, it is a sign of a healthy and balanced life. In this search for the self and self-realization, Generation Y is more open to spirituality than Generation X: mindfulness, yoga, philosophy, etc. are all things that can allow individuals to go through life more consciously. Moreover, this awareness extends beyond mere mental health: Gen Y-ers also devote plenty of attention to their physical health as well.

Even so, they are not always consistent in their approach: new fast-food chains, Takeaway.com and Deliveroo all do big business with Generation Y. In their busy lives, ease and convenience still often come in the first place. If there is one thing Generation Y doesn't have, it is time. Outsourcing is their answer. Cleaning their shoes, ironing, cooking, doing the groceries, buying clothes, transport: if there is a service for it, they will use it. And if there is no service, someone should create one - and fast!

It needs to be remembered, however, that today's starters have been hard hit by the 2008 financial crisis and have fewer savings in the bank to fall back on, thanks to their longer-living and spendthrift grandparents. As a result, many young families have to struggle to make ends meet. They live in smaller houses or apartments, need to pay back huge bank loans, and frequently both have to work (assuming there is a partner) if they want to pay their bills at the end of the month.

They need to be economical, even thrifty, but they often turn this need into a way of life, something of which they are proud: buying second-hand, sharing cars, exchanging in local (online) networks, recycling, upcycling, shopping at discount stores, waiting for the sales... These are no longer things of which they are ashamed; on the contrary, they willingly offer tips to help family and friends. School kids and students have turned the wearing of free clothes into a kind of sport: sponsored clothing from brands or advertising t-shirts from companies, preferably with flashy logos. For these teenagers, even Zara is premium.

This desire to consume less is a product of saturation. There is too much of everything. Most middle-class Westerners already have all they need. And once these basic needs are satisfied, people tend to focus more on self-fulfilment through seeking experiences rather than buying new things (although searching for bargains will always remain a favourite pastime). Of course, there are many places in the world where segments of the population still do not enjoy the same level of material prosperity as in the West, so that consumption and the purchase of goods is viewed in a different light.

// Most middle-class Westerners already have all they need. //

Gender under fire

Gender, the difference between 'm' and 'f', is no longer a constant determined by birth, but can just easily be something in which Gen Y and certainly Gen Z reach their own conclusions. What it means to be a man or a woman is no longer irreversibly fixed in tablets of stone and brands or retailers who try to impose a traditional stereotype are likely to find themselves in trouble. Children who complain in toy shops that they can only find pink things amongst the girls' toys or boys who want to dress up for Halloween as a Disney princess are all the rage on social media. Their impact is huge and they are usually supported by their parents, the millennials, who were the first to regularly challenge time-honoured gender patterns.

The next generation, Generation Z, looks set to take things even a stage further, by questioning binary m/f thinking in its entirety. In its place will come a whole range of gender identities, such as agender, transgender and androgynous. More than half the teenagers in the US know someone who does not identify as either male or female and prefers to be addressed in gender-neutral terms. This gender sensitivity has an obvious knock-on effect on purchasing behaviour. Only 44% of American teenagers purchase clothes that are exclusively intended for their own sex. The same survey showed that the picture is not all that different among the older millennials generation, where just 55% purchase clothes from specifically male or female collections.

In major cities, a whole new movement has developed that embraces female armpit hair as a feminist symbol. Market research in America has revealed that the percentage of women between the ages of 16 and 24 years who shave their armpits has fallen from 95% in 2013 to 77% today. More and more women are also letting their natural hair grow on their legs. Even though their Venus razors for ladies took Procter & Gamble five years of intense R&D, it is within the bounds of possibility that the pink razors will disappear altogether from the market within the foreseeable future. The number of women who post photographs of their armpit hair or unshaven legs with equal pride on social media is increasing by the day... #bodyhairdontcare

Technology will keep us 130 years young

Children who are born today have a good chance of living to the age of 104. At least, that is what the gerontologist Professor Andrea Maier predicts (2017). While 120 years is currently regarded as the maximum possible age for the human body, Professor Maier believes that by 2050 this maximum age will have increased to 130 years. The key? Technology.

In the West, average life expectancy is already increasing by two years each decade. In developing countries, the rate of increase is even bigger, simply because they have more ground to make up.

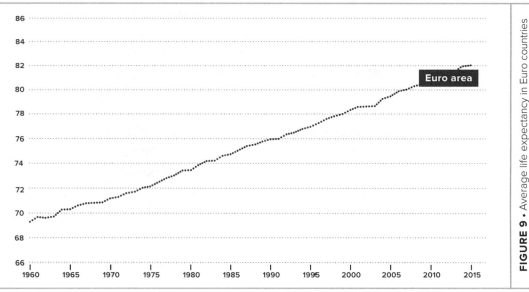

FIGURE 9 • Average life expectancy in Euro countries

Source: Eurostat

According to some doctors, Moore's Law (see 'Retail 4.0: the fourth industrial revolution') can also be applied to the medical world: technological development is taking place at such a pace that they believe it is nonsense to assume that the stable increase in life expectancy in recent years will continue to be stable in the future. As in the world of IT and technology, they expect an exponential increase.

The digitalization of the body

Today, medicine is only concerned with the solving of problems. But if we work more preventatively, by monitoring our body and maintaining it better, it will be possible to actively combat age-related illnesses and chronic diseases. Nowadays, a smart watch can measure our heart rate and blood pressure 24 hours a day and can accurately count how many steps we take. Fitness trackers connected to our running shoes can map out our physical condition in detail, while diet apps make it possible to register our calorie and fat intake.

Thanks to technology and data, it has never been easier to keep yourself well-informed about your health, and in the future things can only get better. It will probably become feasible to implant smart sensors as chips into the human body, feeding information to a whole series of connected devices that will watch over our entire physical and mental condition. Professor Maier talks about our 'digital body'.

Science fiction? Not at all. The sleep of babies is already minutely analyzed by smart monitors built into smart baby socks, which measure a baby's heart rate and oxygen levels through its feet and send all the relevant data directly to the parents' smartphone. In other words, future generations will quite literally be protected by technology from the cradle to the grave. Its presence will become second nature to them.

In fact, technology nowadays even plays a role in the procreative process - or in its prevention. Have you ever heard of i.Con? It is a smart condom that monitors the intensity of your love life, checks for the presence of sexually transmitted diseases and tells you how many calories you have used during intercourse! [3] The more competitively-minded can share their performance details with their friends and even compare them with other i.Com users, just like the popular fitness tracker FitBit.

Gimmicks aside, doctors are convinced that technology can be a useful aid to help people get old more healthily. This is something that is already happening. Calendar age and biological age are getting further and further apart. The fourth industrial revolution will not only reshape our environment, but also our bodies. The new consumer might only be as old as he feels, but his body needs to keep pace as well. This takes us more and more into the realm of genetics. Will it become normal in the near future not only to treat the symptoms of disease but also to prevent them from occurring by manipulating our DNA?

From patient to health consumer

It seems certain that to pay for the cost of living longer society will have to devote more attention to prevention. In the future, we will nearly all get old, but we will not all get old with an equal state of health. For this reason, it will therefore be important to stimulate people to work at their health proactively. People reach their biological peak around their thirtieth birthday. From then on, the body degrades quickly unless a serious effort is made to keep it in top condition. Enter the 'self-quantification movement', whose devotees like to collect and monitor as much data about their physical condition as possible. With the help of connected devices, this is now perfectly feasible. You can even add a competitive element, which some people find fun. Think, for example, of the success of apps with brain-teasers and brain-training or the way people are keen to share the details about the distance, route and time of their latest training run. Gamification is a trend that is set to become commercially interesting.

In this way, the new consumer, self-aware and demanding, will take more and more control over his own health care. We will evolve from patients into health consumers. As a result, health will no longer be the exclusive domain of medicine. Diet, sport, technology and care products will be important allies. Although this idea sometimes provokes negative reactions, it is nonetheless destined to create a market with a huge potential, also for retailers and producers. The search for healthy products and products that increase health can only grow as time passes. As soon as the legislation for online pharmacists and other (para)pharmaceutical outlets has been relaxed, there will be huge opportunities for the taking.

The end of the linear lifecycle

If we live to be a hundred and are still fit when we get there, we will need to drastically rethink our way of living. The current phases of our life are organized in the expectation that we will only live until we are seventy-something. We get 25 years to grow up and mature, 40 years to make a working contribution and 10-15 years to rest our tired bones before our candle is finally snuffed out.

// A longer life gives us a unique freedom to deal more flexibly with the different phases of life. //

But if you live to be a hundred and retire at 65, you still have more than a third of your life ahead of you before you die. These are years in which society no longer imposes any obligations on you, so that you can actually do whatever you want. A longer life gives us a unique freedom to deal more flexibly with the different phases of life.

For example, when you hit forty you can leave behind your first life, the one in which you were a marketeer and lived with your partner and two children in a detached house in the suburbs, where you bought A-brands, outlet clothing and went skiing once a year. Your mid-life crisis has revived your youthful dream of being a medic for Doctors Without Borders. After your new studies, you set off for overseas service, keeping just a small flat for your holidays and to see the children. From now on, you only buy fair-trade products, preferably organic or ecological. As a widower of 72, you find happiness with a new partner and start working together as volunteers in an animal welfare centre...

For students of marketing, this kind of long life can seem like a nightmare: for a single person, they are no longer dealing with one persona but three different personae! There is no fixed way to reach this person: there are simply too many fluctuations in the course of his/her life. In addition to these variations within a single life, the situation is further complicated by the variations between different lives. As a marketeer you know (or think you know) that health and independence are important for older consumers. And up to a point this is true. But only up to a point. Depending on their respective life pathways, two people from the same generation can easily evolve into two totally different consumers, with different needs and different customer journeys. As a result, they both need a different marketing and communication approach. Age can no longer be used as a criterion to force people into pigeon holes.

We are evolving towards one-to-one marketing and communication, although this does not necessarily mean that segmentation is obsolete. In the future, products and services will continue to be developed on the basis of general consumer segments within society, although these products and services will then need to be personalized for individual consumers.

The shopper of the future is multi-coloured

People often tend to think of people with a migration background in terms of ethnic minorities. But what if they are no longer minorities? On the contrary, in some of the world's largest cities people with 'foreign' origins now form a majority. 'In nearly all the major cities in Germany more than half of the six-year-olds already have a migration background,' says Schneider, a migration researcher at the University of Osnabrück.[4]

Europe already has a number of majority minority cities - cities where the majority of people belong to one or other minority - and this represents a 'demographic revolution that has a bigger and deeper impact than anything we have experienced since the Second World War,' according to Schneider. It also exerts a strong influence on the consumption market.

In 2014, at least one EU resident in six had an immigrant background. To show the impact of migration, the UN calculated how the population would evolve without people entering and leaving a country. In the future, according to the United Nations, the European population will shrink anyway - the current migration is not sufficient to compensate for the number of deaths exceeding the number of births - but without migration effects the population in Europe would have shrunk already.

At least four-fifths of the population growth in the 28 EU countries between 2000 and 2014 came from migration, only one fifth from natural population growth. Al-

71

though there are major differences between countries - due to the refugee crisis in 2015 and 2016, Germany and the UK experienced a strong migration peak, while many Eastern European EU Member States saw their population shrink between 2000 and 2015 - the general trend is an aging native population and limited or stagnant growth through immigration.

European residents with a migration background turn out to be younger and more urban. Among migrants of the second generation, young people (15 to 24 years) are proportionally over-represented: in 2014, the median age of non-European migrant children was eight years lower than among the non-migrant population. Likewise, three-fifths of all migrants from outside the EU live in cities (Eurostat 2017). Less than a fifth lives in rural areas, about 13 % fewer than the native population. Consequently, the differences in population and buying behavior between large cities and more rural areas are increasing rapidly.

Halal consumption is a market worth billions

Within the non-indigenous population, the Muslim community forms the largest group. Muslims accounted for 4.9% of the European population in 2016: an estimated 25.8 million people in 30 countries, compared to 19.5 million people in 2010 (Pew Research 2017). This growth trend will continue in the coming years, even if all migration were to be stopped.

Even if all borders close, the Muslim population in Europe continues to grow proportionally to 7.4% in 2050, as the Muslim population is significantly younger and fertility rates are higher than among non-Muslims. 27% of Muslims in Europe are currently younger than 15, almost double the percentage of non-Muslims. In this scenario, France would count the largest number of Muslims (12.7%). In the case of average future migration, the Muslim population is the largest in Sweden by 2050, accounting for 20.5% of the population.

This includes an acquisitive middle class with considerable purchasing power. Today, 'the migrant class is not a separate social class, but largely a part of the middle class' (Lamrabat 2016).

The purchasing and consumption behaviour of this fast-growing Muslim community is determined to a major extent by religion and culture. The annual Ramadan can give a serious boost to turnover, as shops try to meet the special needs of their customers during this month of fasting. Ramadan ends with a celebratory feast, presents and large family gatherings. In Islamic countries, clothing sales can increase by 30% during Ramadan.

In Europe, we are bombarded with Christmas paraphernalia from mid-October onwards. So why does Ramadan scarcely make an appearance in our retail landscape? If multi-cultural consumers cannot find what they want in regular supermarkets, they will go elsewhere. As a result, the supermarket chain Tanger Markt, which stocks a wide range of ethnic products imported directly from Morocco, Turkey, Surinam and Asia, has been an instant success in both Belgium and the Netherlands. The company has branches in most larger Dutch and Belgian cities and also has plans to move into Germany.

Halal has huge economic potential, for Western brands and markets as well. The total Muslim consumption of food and drink in 2015 was worth 1,452 billion euros or 17% of worldwide expenditure, according to Thomson Reuters (2017). By 2021, this figure is expected to rise to 1,625 billion euros. The consumption of halal-certified food alone amounted to 355 billion dollars in 2015. There is also similar potential in clothing. More and more of the larger chains now have collections for fashion conscious Muslim women. Dolce & Gabana, Mango, Uniqlo and H&M all have their own lines in hijabs (head scarves) and abayas (full-length robes). What's more, these garments do not need to be designed with an exclusively Muslim public in mind: modest items of clothing, like long dresses, tops with long sleeves and shawls, are popular with shoppers of all backgrounds.

The first truly global consumers

Huge migration flows will continue in the coming decades, especially from poorer to richer countries. This will have major consequences for the world economic system. In fact, the World Bank and the International Monetary Fund (2016) predict that we are standing on the brink of a new world order, in which migration will play an important role. Whereas migration growth hovered around 1% for many years, since 2000 there has been a clear acceleration - an acceleration that seems likely to persist for quite some time.

Consumers of 'foreign' origin are the first truly global consumers. When we say that 'the world has become a village', for no one is this more true than for people with a migration background. Muslims in Europe, for example, are an international community with close internal networks, so that they regularly come into contact with products and brands from different countries. Because Muslims are constantly searching for the halal products and clothes their religion prescribes, consumption goods are a key topic of conversation within this community.

// Consumers of 'foreign' origin are the first global consumers. //

Among other consumers with a migration background the same is true: they like to remain in close contact with their land of origin. Packages with local products 'from home' regularly fly back and forth. Similarly, Marks & Spencer and Albert Heijn set up special shops on the Chinese platform Tmall for a while, so that expats did not need to miss out on their favourite gingerbread while working in the Far East. Clearly, there are commercial possibilities for organizing something comparable in the opposite direction as well. The multi-cultural population also has many hard-working two-earner families, who do not always have the time or the inclination to trawl through ethnic shops and markets to find what they want.

In addition, there is also the phenomenon of parallel import. Products that are popular in non-indigenous communities and cannot be found in Germany but are available, say, in France, inevitably find their way into ethnic supermarkets and corner shops. This represents a serious loss of turnover for the traditional retailers. Lamrabat recommends that brands should think more internationally, with the new mobile consumer specifically in mind. The reality in our shopping streets is becoming increasingly diverse - and smart retailers need to respond to it.

Polarization of the extremities

The world is going through a transitional period. We are in the process of saying 'farewell' to the old economy and part of the reality of its new, global, high-tech replacement is that jobs are inevitably going to be lost. In other words, the transition will not be without its victims. The gulf between rich and poor continues to grow and the middle class continues to shrink. But these are not simply consequences of the most recent banking crisis: they are trends that have been evident since globalization first set in during the late 1980s.

The lack of future prospects for increasingly impoverished population groups leads to desperation, which finds expression in political and social unrest. The Brexit, the collapse of democracy in Turkey, the electoral victory of Donald Trump, the growth in popularity of far-right nationalist ideologies, the rise of a new radical left... These are all signs that uncertainty about the future is finding a release in polarization, radicalization, increasing nationalism, protectionism, populism and protest, by both the left and right.

The frightened vision of the future shared by these people stands in sharp contrast to the situation of those who stand to benefit from economic change. They form a largely urban class, working in creative, highly-specialized and intellectual professions that cannot easily be automated, which offers them a relative degree of financial and economic security. This group is often mockingly referred to as bobo's: bourgeois bohemians, who mostly adhere to progressive, left of centre values. This is reflected in their 'social' approach to consumption, where transparency and sustainability are among their main concerns. Even so, a growing precariat accuses them of doing little more than preaching from an ivory tower. Lack of mutual understanding continues to grow and polarization becomes ever stronger.

Be that as it may, the fourth industrial revolution is unstoppable. There are undoubtedly turbulent years ahead but this unrest, the political analysts and sociologists agree, is just the growing pains of a new and ultimately better economy, not the final shape of a new world order. Change is always accompanied by fear. Progress always has its opponents.

Flexibilization of labour
The fourth industrial revolution is making a deep impact on both the labour market and consumption. Not only is it easier than ever before to link supply and demand via the internet, it is also more feasible than ever before to outsource certain tasks and thereby link work to work-seekers. Increasing automation means that more and more human functions are being taken over by machines and technol-

ogy. It is estimated that by 2020 some 5.1 million office jobs will be lost to auto-mation. Robotics and artificial intelligent pose a bigger threat to job security than migration flows and competition from low-wage countries, according to the World Economic Forum (2016).

Nevertheless, people will continue to be indispensible for the performance of some tasks. But rather than having fixed jobs, people will have a series of loose assign-ments, which, with the aid of digital platforms, they will complete quickly and eas-ily on an independent, self-employed basis. Self-employment is nothing new in Western Europe, but until now it has been largely confined to the professions (law-yers, doctors, etc.), craftsmen, entrepreneurs, etc., who usually have a well-defined main function or a single subsidiary function. However, in the new 'gig economy' we are evolving towards a situation where work will consist of a multiplicity of different tasks, implemented on a short-term basis. Research by McKinsey (2016) showed that 162 million people in Europe and the US - 20 to 30% of the working population - are already self-employed to some extent.

This perfectly matches the mindset of Generation Z, who are gradually finding their way onto the labour market. For today's teenagers, freedom and flexibility are more important than a safe, full-time job. Why? Perhaps because they saw how hard their parents had to work in jobs of that kind, only to find after the fi-nancial crisis of 2008 that they were not quite so safe after all. As a result, many young people now have a preference for a 'mix & match' of temporary or part-time jobs and assignments.

Since the financial crisis, micro-jobs have been springing up everywhere. Of par-ticular note are the 'new' jobs now open to everyone in the consumer-to-consumer business models. Today, there is a broad range of new tasks suitable for low-skilled people, such as driving for Uber, delivering for Deliveroo or hosting via Airbnb. While job opportunities for the poorly educated are shrinking in the traditional economies of the West, the gig economy is opening up new windows of opportuni-ty - and new sources of income.

These incomes have a large impact on purchasing behaviour. Wages are no longer paid promptly at the end of each month. Flexible work - whether by youngsters starting out on their careers or by active seniors supplementing their pension -

means fluctuating income. This has a direct effect on what and when people buy, do and eat. In other words, on their consumption.

The rise of the precariat

In social terms, there is, unfortunately, a darker side to the flexibilization of labour. Even in the gig economy there is no such thing as equal opportunities for everyone. Even though personal contact in these new jobs is fleeting, the new platforms are not free from discrimination on the basis of gender, origin, physical characteristics and religion. Self-regulation is one of the foundations of these platforms, but when setting the algorithms to match people or products the discrimination factor is generally taken into consideration.

// The changing economy will create a new social class characterized by social and financial insecurity, but on a much larger scale. //

The changing economy will create a new social class characterized by social and financial insecurity, but on a much larger scale. This class will mainly consist of people who have lost their low-skilled manual jobs as a result of automation, outsourcing to low-wage lands or replacement by temporary contract labour. Deprived of any other options, these low-skilled employees must either fall back on the temporary work of the gig economy or face unemployment.

There is perhaps one other alternative. In the new economy, e-commerce will be a major new employer. Thousands of people - generally low-skilled - work each day in the distribution centres of Amazon and Zalando or with their logistical providers. Once again, however, these tend to be temporary contracts or sometimes even day contracts. Unions and the media try to highlight the questionable working conditions in these centres and accusations of social exploitation - high pressure, low wages - are commonplace.

But this is also often true for people who work in the gig economy, whether they are a driver for Uber or a delivery cyclist for a pizza joint. Sociologists refer to this new social class as the precariat, because of their precarious, uncertain position in the labour market and, consequently, in society. They are the new proletariat, but in a service and sharing economy, rather than an industrial one.

Town and country, rich and poor: a world of difference

Differences between urban centres and rural regions will increase substantially in the years ahead. The growing diversity and disparity between town and country, rich and poor regions, and regions with an ageing and migratory population represent an important challenge to retailers and brands, since consumer purchasing behaviour in all these localities is very different in each case.

The 2025 vision of the leading Dutch supermarket chain Albert Heijn explicitly takes into account the likelihood that the difference between a supermarket in a big city and a supermarket in a more rural area will continue to grow. In its large urban stores, the company plans to focus more on automation and speed, with till-free convenience shops, while in rural setting the emphasis will be more on social aspects, such as a friendly word at the check-out.

This vision is based on the assumption that in the countryside there will be fewer people with more time on their hands. Statisticians share this assumption, believing that the impact of population ageing will be most strongly felt away from the large urban agglomerations. Rural population growth will stagnate or even decline, resulting in an older average age.

The cause is to be found in increasing urbanization, which has been taking place for some time. In contrast to the countryside, birth rates in the world's major cities are rising rapidly. This results in very different patterns of purchasing behaviour. Smaller portions are bought by more single-person households in local supermarkets, while large families of non-indigenous origin drive up the demand for ethnic products, with people in all urban categories making less use of the car, thereby increasing the importance of home delivery services and proximity stores.

Of course, population growth does not necessarily mean more purchasing power and prosperity. In comparison with towns, suburbs or rural areas, cities in western EU states bolster relatively high shares of people living at risk of poverty, high shares of people living in low work intensity households or high unemployment rates (Eurostat 2016). Nonetheless, on average these cities have higher standards of living, showing rising income inequality. Likewise, geographical and social segregation by income is increasing in U.S. cities. At the same time, areas with an ageing population also risk impoverishment: incomes are relatively low, while costs (care of the elderly) are relatively high.

The result is that some urban centres, which are able to attract young, dual-earner families, become more prosperous, while ageing towns and cities get poorer. This polarization makes the adjustment of retail stores and their offer to reflect local circumstances more important than ever before.

The hot breath of the growth economies

Each year, some 83 million people are added to the population of our blue planet. This continuing population growth is accompanied in many developing economies by a comparable increase in the standard of living. The centre of gravity for this trend is in South-East Asia. If we want to see the future of retail, this is where we need to look.

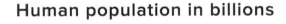

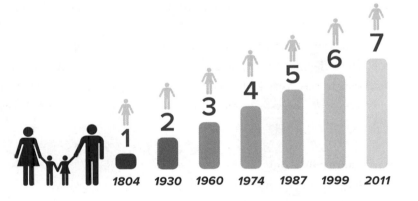

FIGURE 10 • Human population in billions

Source: United Nations Population Division

Emerging markets with their emerging generations place a strong focus on innovation, since they see no value in hanging on to anything from their poorer past. As a result, they are giving shape to a new reality, a reality to which the 'traditional' world will need to adjust. In China, for example, a large part of online retail turnover is not realized by retailers, but by consumers themselves via consumer-to-consumer sales or through *daigou* (shuttle sales). These are consumers who use their free time to fly to cities all around the world, where they pick up luxury products at good prices, which they then resell on Alibaba platforms or via social media channels like WeChat or Weibu. In this way, consumers can become retail competitors.

Growth nations like India, China and Korea are industrializing at a rapid rate, supporting their evolution towards a service economy. They are catching up to the West, because their gross national product is increasing much more quickly. In Western Europe, for example, the markets are already saturated, so that there is little potential for further growth: the population is ageing, the middle class is stagnating and the cities are increasingly home to low-income households.

In comparison, current predictions suggest that in China, the world's most populous nation, some 76% of urban residents will be in the middle class by 2022. This is equivalent to a phenomenal 550 million people! Yet as recently as 2000, only 4% of Chinese citizens were reckoned as middle class. This is comparable with the rise of the middle class in Europe and the US in the mid 20th century. Now as then, it is accompanied by a spectacular growth in consumption. McKinsey calculates that Chinese consumption expenditure will increase by 55% between 2015 and 2020.

In other words, there is plenty of demand; all you need to do is find the right way to meet it. This offers interesting opportunities for Western producers, since the Chinese associate the West with high quality. Luxury houses like Louis Vuitton and Hermès have developed a strong following among the ranks of the burgeoning Chinese middle and upper classes.

A new world (retail) order

China's GDP growth accounts for one-third of total global growth. Therefore, it should not come as a surprise that the West is losing its self-proclaimed grip on the retail industry. The role of the Western markets on the world retail stage is shrinking: in 2016, European revenue made up for 33.8% of accumulated revenue in the list of top 250 largest retailers (Deloitte 2018), a significant drop from 39.4% only ten years earlier.[22] American revenue is stagnating as well, while the Asia Pacific region accounted for 15.4% of all retail revenue, as opposed to only 10.4% in 2010.

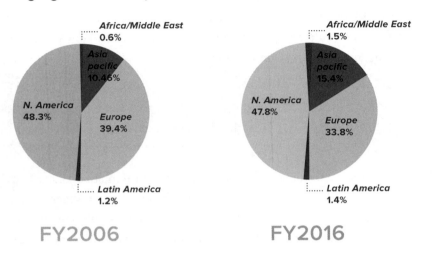

Changing share of Top 250 retail revenue, FY2006 to 2016

FY2006

Africa/Middle East
0.6%

Asia pacific
10.46%

N. America
48.3%

Europe
39.4%

Latin America
1.2%

FY2016

Africa/Middle East
1.5%

Asia pacific
15.4%

N. America
47.8%

Europe
33.8%

Latin America
1.4%

FIGURE 11 • Changing share of Top 250 retail revenue FY2006 to FY2016

Source: Deloitte, Global Powers of Retailing (2018)

Of late, however, China's working-age population is no longer expanding and the speed of growth is slowing down. Because of this, China starting is to focus on more high-quality growth (IMF 2018), as well as expanding its horizons abroad. Chinese companies are not only crossing borders, their ambition is to take the world by storm.

China has become Africa's biggest economic partner, with over 10,000 Chinese-owned companies estimated to be operating in Africa (McKinsey 2018). In countries like Ethiopia and Senegal, Chinese companies find the cheap labor they are starting to run short on at home. 'In China, no one wants to make shoes anymore,' says Chinese entrepreneur in Ethiopia Zhang Huarong (CNN 2018). The African population is estimated to reach 2.5 billion by 2050, of which Ethiopia provides the second-largest number of residents. Of the 100 million inhabitants 70% are under the age of 30, giving it tremendous growth potential.

At the same time, Chinese entrepreneurs hope to conquer Europe and Northern America through retail. All the shoes Zhang Huarong produces in Ethiopia, are destined for the US market already. Still when JD.com chief Richard Liu proclaims he will no longer just sell products from Europe to

China, but also wants to sell products in Europe, he means (retail) business. The online marketplace platform aims to distribute both Chinese and local products in Western markets, installing a vast logistics network on the European continent. Rival Alibaba is trying to beat him to it, investing heavily in its global distribution network and closing deals on the instalment of local hubs with the French and Belgian government, among others.

// The continuing growth of world population is expected to force up food prices, but it also poses climatological challenges. //

Along the way, they are forming partnerships with Western multinationals, hoping there is a slice of the huge Chinese pie in it for them. As such, Walmart and Google both have shares in JD.com. Also, Richard Liu promotes his company as a way to fight off the Amazon threat: 'A dominant player is a danger', he says, so the more competitive the retail landscape, 'the better for consumers and producers'.

Not without irony, the pressure on European retailers does however seem to be increasing substantially as a result of Chinese platforms company coming their way. The initiatives of players such as JD.com and Alibaba represent a major challenge for German e-commerce players Otto and Zalando, for example, as these two largest Chinese retail groups are growing by more than 50% per year. According to a study by management consultant Oliver Wyman, by 2025 they could reach a turnover of about 550 billion euros - more than the top ten German retailers added together.

Clearly, the rise of the new giants from the East is not to be underestimated. Analysts even put Alibaba ahead of Amazon (Jenkins 2018). When it comes to moving beyond ecommerce, into innovation (R&D), physical retail and payment technology, Alibaba seems to be the front-runner at the moment. The race is on.

There is, of course, another side to the rapid growth and development of emerging markets, illustrated curiously enough by the dramatic shortage of milk powder for babies in the Netherlands in the spring of 2013. A Chinese run on milk powder resulted in empty shelves in Dutch supermarkets, with local supplies being bought up by *daigou* or clandestine wholesalers. According to experts, this was just a foretaste of what we can come to expect: 'the world is evolving at lightning speed from an era of surplus to an era of scarcity', observed Vredeseilanden (a Dutch NGO) as early as 2014.

The world growth in meat consumption is driven by the Chinese market: when meat consumption hit the bar of 30 million tonnes in 2010, this was mostly because of the Chinese consuming over 8 million tonnes of meat – increasing at a staggering growth rate. Other parts of Asia accounted for over 4 million tonnes of meat, reaching the same consumption levels as in Latin America. However, this growth puts significant pressure on agriculture and causes scientifically proven harmful effects on the environment.

In a similar vein, there is also an on-going battle for the world's natural resources and agricultural produce. Rabobank (2011) has already predicted huge price rises and serious shortages, particularly in agricultural commodities. To safeguard their supply, the emerging economies are once again turning their eyes to the West. China already has plans for a modern-day variant of the Silk Route, an intercontinental trade highway between Europe and the Orient designed to facilitate the purchase and transport of these scarce raw materials.

Albert Heijn CEO Wouter Kolk shares this fear of shortages: 'The Chinese are already knocking on the door of our tangerine supplier in Spain. They want to buy his whole harvest. If that happens, where will I buy my tangerines? This kind of thing means that I need to secure my resources for the future - and I need to do it now.'

The continuing growth in world population is expected to force up food prices, but it also poses climatological challenges. If living standards rise, this is usually accompanied (or has been until now) by an increase in the demand for meat. This in turn requires the use of more agricultural land as pasture. Agricultural productivity urgently needs to be boosted in the developing countries, but at the same time pressures on the climate make necessary the use of more sustainable and ecological methods of production. It is a Catch-22.

According to the UN, there will be 9.8 billion people on earth by 2050. China and India will remain the most populous countries, but the current No. 3 - the USA - looks set to be overtaken by Nigeria. In other words, Africa is also an important potential growth market, increasingly so as standards of hygiene and health care improve. The need for sustainable solutions, which ease the strain on the environment and help to combat the problem of future resource scarcity, is both urgent and concrete.

Transparency and sustainability: the new prerequisites

'Retail is the biggest democracy in the world: every day the customer can decide whether or not he is going to choose you again tomorrow. You need to live up to your reputation every single day', according to Frans Colruyt, executive at supermarket company Colruyt Group. As the market leader in Belgium, he should know.

As a matter of fact, modern shoppers increasingly expect more information about what they buy and consume: where do the products come from, how sustainable is the production process, are the brands truly authentic? The price, quality and availability of products continue to be important, but buyers now also demand fuller transparency: they want to know what they eat, what they wear and what they buy.

People are more concerned than ever before about our world and their part in it, resulting in a growing demand for honest, sustainable, environmentally friendly, organic and local products, both food and non-food. As the Colruyt example shows, transparent communication about these things is equally vital. If you fail to do this, people will view you with suspicion until proven to the contrary.

Transparency: a must in the age of social media

Internet and social media are everywhere. This has given power back to the consumer. As a result, transparency is now a *sine qua non*. Retailers who deal with this new reality lightly will find themselves heavily punished. Do you remember the treatment handed out to McDonald's a few years ago when it was discovered that abattoir waste - the notorious 'pink slime' - was used as an ingredient in their meat? All hell was let loose on them. In the past, all retailers needed to do was lay low until the storm passed, but in the age of social media that has a wholly counterproductive effect.

Only when McDonald's laid all its cards openly on the table with its *Our Food Your Questions* campaign, launched a series of informative 'behind-the-scenes' videos, invited customers to visit its kitchens and opened a telephone hotline to answer consumer questions, the storm finally blew over. Lost consumer confidence takes a lot of time and effort to restore. Trust arrives on foot but leaves on horseback...

Nowadays, the public has more tools than ever before to keep itself well informed. People are no longer dependent on the retailers for information. Apps that compare prices and chart price evolutions; apps that provide information about the origin and composition of products; customers who give their unvarnished opinions via Twitter, Facebook or on review sites: these are all part of the modern retail game. As is the speed with which bad news travels around the world.

The origin app tells all

Consulting your smartphone in the supermarket to check the origin and date of catch of the fish you want to put in your bouillabaisse tonight. Or investigating which farm your eggs come from and how the chickens there are treated. Or making sure that the dress you are trying on in the fitting room has not been made by underpaid child labour in appalling conditions. All these things are possible in just a few seconds with the most recent technology.

Supplier of tinned fish John West tells the story behind each tin of tuna or salmon with its 'can tracker'. Or using the fTRACE app, a customer at German chain Metro can know that the fillet of salmon he is buying on the 25th of July was still swimming off the coast of Norway when it was caught on July 17, before being skinned, gutted, sliced and packed in a factory somewhere in Germany four days later. You can even follow the whole trajectory on a map. According to Metro, the app is especially popular with chefs in hotels and amateur chefs.

Other, consumer-led apps like Rank a Brand monitor how transparently national and international brands communicate about matters relating to sustainability, use of child labour and employment rights. 'This way, you can immediately see while you are shopping which brands are most sustainable,' claims the organization, which describes itself as 'an international community of responsible consumers who want to buy honest and sustainable products and services'. The growing number of apps of this kind serves to show that this type of information is of increasing importance to the ordinary man or woman in the street.

Reviews: a two-sided coin

With ever-increasing frequency, consumers are basing their purchasing behaviour on opinions and preferences posted on the internet by total strangers. The rise of e-commerce and the widespread availability of social media have resulted in an avalanche of online reviews. It is often open to question how well founded these reviews really are. In many of them, objectivity and know-how are hard to find. But that doesn't seem to matter: they continue to grow in popularity and importance. Research by Open Companies shows that 92% of shoppers regularly check online reviews before making a purchase; 37% use such reviews weekly; 68% say the reviews are trustworthy, with only the word of friend having a higher credibility rating (84%).

Even so, it is wise to be cautious of reviews on comparison sites, webshops and corporate sites. Websites like TripAdvisor, Yelp and even Amazon are often the target of false reviews. Sometimes these are damning condemnations written by competitors; sometimes they are glowing paeans of praise written by the company itself. It happens more often than you might think. Not so long ago, Yelp felt obliged to develop software that could identify and remove these false reviews. This revealed that 16% of all its reviews were being 'economical with the truth'. Even the authoritative TripAdvisor was once forced to admit with blushing cheeks that it systems were not as watertight as they had hoped, when an Italian newspaper succeeded in launching a local restaurant to top spot in the 'most favoured' chart.

Of course, it is next to impossible for consumers to distinguish between genuine opinions and lies. Research by the State University of Groningen (2016) concluded that even good and honest reviews lead to a higher percentage of returns.6 Not because the purchase was defective, but because the review failed to reflect the reader's high level of expectation. And the more positive the reviews, the greater the problem! This led the research team to suggest: 'Don't ask consumers to only leave reviews when they think the product is good, but also when they think it is awful...'

Whether companies like it or not, reviews are here to stay and have an important marketing function. Products that have one star more than a competing product can easily sell 10% more. The retailer has to accept, however, that this is information that he can never effectively control. All he can do - and must do - is to try and manage the online conversations about his products proactively.

> // The rise of e-commerce and the widespread availability of social media has resulted in an avalanche of online reviews. //

Economic must rhyme with ecological

The world in which we live is under pressure from all sides: climate change, shortages of raw materials, population growth, changing patterns of consumption... People understand that there is a need for a social, ecological and economically sustainable model and that this model will only be realized when producers, retailers and consumers work together, so that economic and ecological interests can finally go hand in hand.

The large multi-nationals often set a good example in this respect. In 2013, Unilever gave a commitment to halve its ecological footprint by 2020 without limiting its ambitions for growth. On the contrary. This Anglo-Dutch concern hopes to double its turnover during the same period. Kellogg's, Sony and Coca-Cola are part of a group of 114 companies that have developed their climate objectives on a scientific basis using strict criteria set by the United Nations. Together, these companies emit a total of 476 million tons of CO_2 each year, equivalent to 125 coal-fired power stations.

In their efforts on behalf of the climate, these companies consciously focus on a reduced and more efficient use of energy, a smarter transport policy, the adjustment of their industrial processes and improved waste management. At the same time, they also encourage - or even oblige - their suppliers to follow the same path, as well as anticipating the changing dietary and behavioural patterns of their customers and consumers.

From purchasing to packaging

In supermarkets and many other companies, the focus is first and foremost on sensible and sustainable purchasing, since this has the biggest impact on the entire sales chain. The buying of fish is the best proof that sustainable purchasing works. More and more supermarkets are only selling fish with a quality label, such as MSC and ASC, since research has shown that 54% of all consumers are willing to pay more for products that are certified sustainable. The sale of fish, shellfish and crustaceans with a sustainable quality label rose by 60% in two years time in the UK (Marine Stewardship Council, 2018).

In a similar vein, a number of supermarket chains in Europe also want to show their customers the real cost of fruit and vegetables. This initiative comes from Nature & More - a subsidiary of the bio-distributor Eosta - and starts from the premise that products are often sold at too low a price, a price that still allows the supermarket to make a profit but nonetheless has a negative effect.[7] The idea is to try and bring about a change of mentality, persuading the customer that organically grown fruit and vegetables are not expensive, but rather that traditionally grown fruit and veg is too cheap.

Not just the food retail industry banks on the environmental cause when purchasing, other sectors do not escape the trend of responsible and sustainable consumption either. DIY chains often opt for wood certified by the Forest Stewardship Council, while 64 international fashion companies - representing 142 different brands - committed themselves to taking concrete steps towards a circular strategy by 2020 at the Copenhagen Fashion Summit in May 2017. The first signatories included Adidas, ASOS, Bestseller, Eileen Fisher, H&M, Hugo Boss, Inditex, Kering, Reformation, Target and VF Corp.

Nowadays, no new supermarket can open its doors without solar panels on the roof, but packaging is becoming more sustainable everywhere as well. Although the plastic carrier bags in the supermarkets are a thing of the past, the British frozen foods chain Iceland is the first 'mainstream' supermarket to be scrapping all plastic packaging from its own brands. By 2023 all 1400 private brand products will be packaged in a more sustainable manner, such as cardboard or paper. Another exponent of this trend are the wastefree or packaging-free shops where the consumer brings his own containers.

In the UK, a group of former directors of retail chains such as Tesco, Marks & Spencer, Asda and Debenhams even made a joint call to stop using plastic throw-away packaging, while British Prime Minister Theresa May calls plastic waste one of the biggest plagues of our time. The United Kingdom sets about to ban all avoidable plastic waste by 2042.

Shoppers are happy to go along with all these trends, sometimes unconsciously, but increasingly from conviction. This is something that retailers can use to their advantage. Research by Lisa Magnier at the University of Delft[8] shows that environmentally aware customers are prepared to pay more for products in sustainable packaging, because they regard these products as healthier and fresher than comparable products in non-sustainable packaging.

Economic must also rhyme with ethical

Consumers' increasing ecological awareness is matched by an ethical reflex, which is having - and will continue to have - a growing impact on the consumption patterns of current and future generations.

This confronts producers with three major challenges:
- dealing with the problem of waste and surplus food;
- ensuring better conditions of work for employees in all lands (think of the growing success of fair trade products and the impact of the Clean Clothes Campaigns);
- developing even healthier products, in which health is seen as a shared responsibility of the producer, retailer and consumer.

Food wastage versus hunger in the world

Worldwide, roughly a third of all food produced is wasted. Realizing that this situation can no longer be allowed to continue, in recent years initiatives have been launched in all phases of the food chain to reduce this waste, from the farmer's field to the plate on your dining room table. When food waste is mentioned, the finger of suspicion is quickly pointed at the supermarkets. In reality, however, supermarkets are only responsible for about 2.5% of this waste. The consumer is responsible for between 25 and 42%.[9]

// Worldwide, roughly a third of all food produced is wasted. //

Even so, the distribution sector has developed numerous measures to cut its limited share of waste. This begins by seeking to reduce any surpluses by employing hyper-efficient supply and delivery systems, based on computer models that calculate the likely amount of sales of each product at each sales point. If surpluses do arise, products approaching their sale-by date are offered to customers at severely discounted prices. Supermarkets also donate about 25% of all consumable surpluses to charitable organizations. Surpluses no longer fit for human consumption - about 60% of the total - are used to generate energy (biomethanization), processed into animal feed or used as fertilizer. Only a minimal remainder is destroyed in incinerators.

Of course, this only applies to food that actually makes it to the supermarket. A large amount of food is lost before it even gets that far. Leeks are not long enough, apples are not round enough... Until recently, this rejected fruit and veg never made it into the shops. However, the British Tesco and Ahold Delhaize chains found the courage to put these 'imperfect' products into their stores - and with success. In the summer of 2015, for example, Delhaize offered a selection of these vegetables at sixteen of its supermarkets over a 14-week period: it sold more than 60,000 crates and saved 15 tons of produce from the rubbish skip.

Retailers can also reap indirect benefits from the battle against waste. Food waste restaurants are, literally, popping up all over the world: pioneer was Instock, an Amsterdam restaurant that 'puts waste food on its menu'. An idea of four ex-employees of retail chain Albert Heijn, the non-profit restaurant collects unsold products from their former employer each morning in their electric 'food rescue' cart for use in their diner. One of their initiatives: beer made from unsold potatoes! Since, ReTaste in Sweden opened a pop-up restaurant using only food waste from supermarkets and even U.S.A. luxury restaurant Blue Hill at Stone Barns (one of the world's 50 best restaurants) organizes wastED pop-up events, creating entire menus using ingredients that would otherwise go to waste.

Nowadays, almost every country has one or more 'food sharing' websites, which connect consumers, retailers, farmers and restaurants to make best use of surplus food. Sites like AmpleHarvest.org build a bridge between food banks and amateur gardeners who want to donate any surplus from their fruit and vegetable harvest. In some of the larger cities there are even so-called 'reservation sites', which seek to drum up last-minute customers for restaurants that have been hit by large-scale cancellations for which they have already bought the food.

Fair and honest, please!

It began a decade ago with bananas and coffee but has since taken firm root across the food sector: fair trade. 'After the 2008 crisis, it was only price that mattered. But now retailers are once again searching for differentiation, and that is something where fair trade can play a role. We always talk with people at director level. That shows just how important it has become. We convince them with figures, because it's not just all a question of emotion. The primary fair trade buyers are young families with children, which is a very interesting target group for retailers,' says Lily Deforce, former head of Fairtrade Belgium (Van Rompaey, 2016).

Fair trade now attracts some major players. One of the objectives of chocolate giant Ferrero is to only buy certificated cacao (UTZ, Rainforest Alliance and Fairtrade) by 2020; in 2014 the figure was just 40%. Snack producer Mondelez has started a holistic programme, Cocoa Life, to help raise the net income of cacao farmers, in part by generating improved harvests. And the retailers are doing their bit as well. Carrefour obliges its suppliers to subscribe to a charter containing 35 criteria relating to sustainability and social rights. The Colruyt Group, in collaboration with Vredeseiland, a Belgian NGO, has established a fair trade banana chain in Senegal, a country that previously has never exported bananas.

In the clothing sector, the focus is set very clearly on improving the often degrading working conditions in the Third World, particularly in South-East Asia. Since the factory disaster in Bangladesh that killed 1,200 people, some 80 large companies (accounting for 120 brands and more than 20,000 shops in over 80 countries) have signed up to be members of the Fair Wear Foundation. This includes absolute market leaders like H&M and Inditex, as well as smaller local players. The Fair Wear Foundation aims to secure improved working conditions, free trade unions and a liveable wage for hundreds of thousands of textile workers in the main production countries.

In addition to fair prices and better working practices, there is also the problem of land grabbing. Oxfam had the courage to bring this problem out into the open when it called on major internationals like PepsiCo, Coca-Cola and Associated British Foods to put an end to their 'complicity in land theft'. According to Oxfam, far too much sugar beet and soya is still being grown on land from which the rightful occupants - local farmers - have been chased away.

An app like Palm Risk tries to make companies, retailers and consumers more aware of the impact of palm oil production on forestry resources in the countries of origin. According to the initiative takers, the World Resources Institute, many producers actually unknowingly contribute to deforestation. In 2010, the members of the Consumer Goods Forum - which represents 400 companies worldwide - promised that it would reduce deforestation to zero by 2020. Time is ticking.

// Local sourcing is more than just a buzzword; it is a reality that offers a solution to 'globalization gone wild'. //

From global to local

Local sourcing is more than just a buzzword; it is a reality that offers a solution to 'globalization gone wild', with its related side effects of stifling uniformity, food scandals and mass production in low-wage countries, to name but a few. These are all phenomena that consumers do not associate with local production, where safety and quality are the main concerns. This explains why so many people have more confidence in 'small and local' than in 'big and supranational'.

The purchasing of local produce encourages a number of positives: protecting the riches of the region, supporting the local economy, shortening the supply chain, responding to consumer demand for authentic regional goods, etc. The big distributers have understood this for years and their marketeers miss no opportunity to promote the trend, whether it be via a photo of the grower on packaged apples, or a video message in which the producer addresses the customer in the shop directly, or even organized visits to local farms. Of course, in cases of this kind the local producer has to be able to guarantee a constant supply, both in terms of quantity and quality.[10]

The increased attention for local production has also breathed new life into the half-forgotten farmer's markets of the past. Thanks to the internet, they have been given a new look and a new identity. A typical example is The Food Assembly (originally La Ruche qui dit Oui!), which profiles itself as a virtual agricultural market, where farmers and neighbours can meet each other, after members have first placed their orders on the online platform. The Food Assembly is part of a European network that was first started in France and is now active in France, Belgium, Germany, Italy, Spain and the United Kingdom.

Some virtual agro-markets take the 'consumer-seeks-farmer' concept another stage further. For example, the American start-up Farmersmarket organizes an online food market where consumers can order their fresh produce from the affiliated growers in their region. The company collects all the different orders each week from the different suppliers, packages them for the individual customers, and delivers them to their home or place of work. The German Bonativo company from the Rocket Internet stable is trying to do the same thing, up until now in Berlin, London and Amsterdam.

'Future of technology': all things internet

Online, offline, mobile, in the flagship store, at the multi-brand boutique... None of it makes a difference. The consumer no longer thinks in terms of channels; all he thinks about is the desired end result. He makes no distinction between the different means that can lead him to that result. For this reason, it is pointless to talk about 'omnichannel commerce'. From now on, all retail is by definition omnichannel. Full stop. As such, each brand must become a series of touchpoints with the customer. Technological developments have made this an unavoidable 'must'. Also full stop. Nowadays, there is only a single channel: the customer channel.

The big advantage of all those touchpoints is that whoever is able to connect them together successfully will win a mine of valuable information. Data is the new gold. Large supermarket chains already know what they need to buy for you as one of their consumers before you even know it yourself! We are moving from retail to me-tail: a highly personalized form of service provision that proactively and interactively responds to the needs of the individual consumer. This bears repeating: retail had become a service - and it needs to be a personal one. So don't you forget it!

This is all possible because Google, your smart glasses and your Amazon grocery list know everything there is to know about you. And if they do occasionally get things wrong, artificial intelligence will allow them to learn from their mistakes, so that they can get it right next time. Words are unnecessary, even when you are out shopping, because in the future retailers will be able to read your thoughts.

E-commerce vs. omnichannel: the battle has already been won

The world's largest e-commerce market is China. In 2016, goods to a value of 750 billion American dollars were purchased online in China, which is more than the combined online consumption of the US and the UK. In the next five years, China expects an annual online growth of 20%, which means that it will also overtake the West in this crucial department as well. Alibaba founder Jack Ma warns with good reason that digitalization will continue to cause some people pain - quite a lot of pain - for quite some time. He predicts 30 years of anguish and social conflict before the new digitalized economy finally replaces the old one.

In China, this transition was relatively pain-free: before the arrival of e-commerce, there was no real retail sector in the country to replace. Such retail as there was, was small and local. Lack of infrastructure and resources made it impossible to build up a national network. It was not until the arrival of the internet that retailers finally had the opportunity to reach the furthest corners of the country. That is exactly what Alibaba does with Taobao: offer a platform where retailers can come into contact with consumers everywhere. Originally, Jack Ma wanted to make the Chinese internet into a kind of telephone book, a register to help people to meet and find each other. In other words, Taobao is a medium and a channel, not a shop.

This is a very different situation from in the West, where shops are firmly established in the culture and where national and international chains have been used to dominating the market as the giants of the economy for decades. In this context, the arrival of e-commerce was seen as a new way to 'play' at shopping: all that was different was the use of a virtual shop window instead of a glass shop window. At first, online retailers like Amazon, Zalando and ASOS held stock themselves, set the prices and determined the offer. But that didn't last for long.

Western retailers had to find out the hard way that there is not much profit to be made in the online sale of products. Like in physical retail, the margins are wafer-thin, with the difference that the internet is even more of a 'winner-takes-all' market, where continual heavy investment is necessary to stay at the forefront of the customer's mind. The cost of stock, logistics and returns are also prohibitive.

Faced with this situation, there are only two real options that offer a chance of making money:

- market vendors become market holders;
- from clicks to bricks.

Market vendors become market holders

The first strategy for retailers is to transform themselves into genuine tech-companies, so that in addition to retail they can also develop a wide range of ancillary activities and services that (in contrast to retail) do have good margins and which can also be used by other companies and retailers.

// Today, Amazon Marketplace accounts for over half the total sales by Amazon. //

Nowadays, Amazon makes its profit almost exclusively from its services to third parties (Amazon Services), such as its cloud services and, in particular, its Marketplace, where retailers and brands can sell their products via the Amazon platform. Amazon gets a commission on every sale made in the Marketplace, providing the company with a lucrative fixed source of income. But the secondary benefits of this way of working are also significant: no stock, no delivery costs, no returns. Today, Amazon Marketplace accounts for over half the total sales of Amazon and this wing is growing twice as fast as the company's own direct consumer sales. Third party sales account for the second-largest revenue segment of the online retail platform, after retail product sales and ahead of Amazon Web Service revenues.

It is hardly surprising that other e-tailers are enthusiastically attempting to copy this model by developing services and marketplaces for third parties. Zalando wants to profile itself as a European pioneer in the platform economy, an ambition that it shouted from the rooftops with its 'Vizions by Zalando: Europe's first conference about The Platform as Business Model'. Since 2015, Zalando has adopted a platform strategy, Zalando City, which seeks to connect all the players in the fashion industry, explains Monica Franz, Zalando's communications manager. The idea behind the conference, Zalando claims, was to make the platform economy more widely known in Europe by 'showing what platforms will mean for the future and what platforms can do for companies'.

Zalando actively keeps searching for 'start-ups and smaller players' who want to be part of their story, also in the field of technology. To make things easier for retailers - and to give themselves a 360° view - they have also launched their Integrated Commerce project: physical stores in Berlin can have their products delivered to customers anywhere in Europe within a day via Zalando. Of course, this means that Zalando in return needs a full overview of the assortments and the real time stocks of all the participating stores.

From clicks to bricks

This brings us to the second strategy for increasing profitability as an online retailer: making the bridge to offline. More and more former 'pure players' are now opening physical shops. Coolblue was the first company in the Benelux to openly admit that it saw advantages in a mix between online and offline. The electronics retailer went omnichannel with flagship stores that function as service centres, sales points and trust points.

Founder Pieter Zwart has never made a secret of the fact that where the company opens physical stores, online sales also significantly increase. Why? The stores give the retailer more visibility and create confidence. Zwart jokingly calls it the 'stone-through-the-window' principle: the consumer knows that if things go wrong there is somewhere he can go to complain or - in a worst case scenario — to throw a stone through the window!

Although trust was probably more important in the early days of internet sales, the addition of a physical touchpoint certainly gives consumers a feeling of reassurance. ModCloth - an American female fashion brand - started online, but is now increasingly opening so-called FitShops. Given the hassle of fitting and sizing, the addition of physical contact points gives a significant boost to credibility. At the same time, they serve as info-points to answer low-threshold questions or as a 'click & collect' point. Even if only a fraction of the packages are picked up from the physical stores, the web retailers still save on costs. In addition, they also give the consumer the opportunity to try out their new purchase.

Even so, physical stores like these are first and foremost a company's signboard, a form of advertising. When Zalando announced that it wanted to open flagship stores in major cities, it saw them above all as a marketing tool to increase their visibility, while simultaneously bringing the company quite literally closer to the consumer. This is really an imitation of the strategy of the large fashion brands. Just an expensive form of advertising, those flashy high-street stores? You bet - but worth the investment all the same. In contrast to online, physical presence is more long-lasting. Stores are also the ideal place to experience a product. In your own store, you can create a unique atmosphere and a unique story that stimulates all the consumer's senses. This is something you can't do online - but you can certainly use online to complement your physical set-up. It is the close collaboration between the digital world and physical touchpoints that completes the circle to provide a total experience, in which technology, sensory perception and human contact all meet each other.

In an omnichannel environment, this kind of physical touchpoint has no need of a wide range of products; a small but carefully chosen selection is sufficient. What might the shopper be looking for that he wants to take with him immediately? What would he like to see, feel, test? What can you show him that will make a good or even inspirational impression? You can show him all the rest on a tablet or screen. In this way, you make the link between online and offline as integrated and as efficient as possible.

// To create a seamless shopping experience and customer journey, a total experience is essential. //

Omnichannel means omnipresent
Omnichannel means more than simply combining online and offline. To create a seamless shopping experience and customer journey, a total experience is essential. This is something else where the West can learn a lot from the Chinese market. In China, news sites, games, videos and e-commerce are all integrated into the larger web platforms. On these platforms, it is unbelievably easy to chat in an app or via a network, watch videos, or shop and pay for what you want. The videos are shoppable and click-to-buy is the norm rather than the exception. It is no coincidence that these are things heavily focused on mobile users: in the near future, three-quarters of all online purchases in China will be mobile. This is significant: today's Chinese are the first generation of internet users who are willing to immediately embrace mobile commerce wholeheartedly.

The same trend occurs in other regions in Asia and Africa. Where there are no established patterns from the past, omnichannel and mobile technology are preferred. This means that the new generation in the West, which also grew up without real offline roots, have no problem to adjust either. And new spaces and dimensions will be added for them to explore still, thanks to virtual and augmented reality. In short, a new mixed reality in retail and FMCG will become a fact.

An all-inclusive eco-system

Whoever can create a platform that allows people to fulfil all their needs will have a license to print money. At the moment, Tencent and Alibaba are fighting a bitter war in China to get their hands on that license. Both platforms have developed into all-in-one apps where people can find multimedia, chat, or buy and sell. Chinese consumers seldom visit the websites of the producers and brands. They see what is available, gather the information they need and then immediately buy online, either via the Taobao marketplace (Alibaba) or the WeChat social network (Tencent).

A young Chinese in Shanghai can do almost everything with WeChat: order a taxi, buy metro tickets, have his evening meal delivered, transfer money to a friend... But the trend is also catching on in the West: 55% of American consumers now go directly to Amazon, if they are planning to buy something. This makes Amazon the No.1 search engine for products.

To counteract this, Google has launched Google Shopping. Facebook is doing the same with its frantic efforts to allow people to shop online without the need to leave the Facebook site. This is bad news for the brands and retailers, who are putting a lot of time and resources into their own virtual shopping environment: only 15% of those same Americans go first to a retailer or brand site when they want a product. Moreover, through their use of AdWords retailers and brands are even financing the competition created by Google and its Google Shopping platform.

Everybody wants to achieve what Tencent and Alibaba have succeeded in doing: creating an eco-system that is so large that it almost literally follows every step the consumer takes. Consumers move effortlessly through the different elements of the network (shopping, entertainment, payments) and while they are doing it all their data is captured and converted into a personal ID - a log-in they can use on all the different sites and apps of Alibaba. Like a Google account, but taking retail as its starting point!

Alibaba has massive data records about its more than 500 million monthly users, on the basis of which it has defined more than 8,000 consumer characteristics. This means that sellers on the Alibaba platform can segment and target their potential customers with extreme precision. This treasure trove of information allows Alibaba to go much further in terms of individual personalization than its Western retailing rivals.

To escape from the stranglehold grip of Alibaba's data, brands and store chains in China have come up with a surprising solution: they open their own physical shops! This is proving a fine way to boost their name visibility and allows them to follow a parallel path alongside an internet that is dominated by just a few large players. In some ways this is remarkable, because the most successful Chinese brands and retailers did not exist before the advent of internet and consequently have never had physical stores before. For them, it is the change from clicks to bricks that is revolutionary! Certainly in the larger cities, impressive flagship stores are proving an ideal way to approach the curious and acquisitive Chinese middle class. *L'histoire se répète*, in the land where the history of retail was first written.

A third space with virtual and augmented reality

Virtual reality has become part of the arsenal of retailers who are willing to invest in a unique and valuable customer experience. For nothing is as immersive and experiential as VR. Virtual reality creates a third space, a new layer in between the physical world and the digital world, because contrary to TV or video, virtual and augmented reality require the active engagement of users.

The hype-app Pokémon Go was a prime example of augmented reality. Via a GPS signal and the camera on your smartphone, it was possible to go in search of Pokémon creatures in your surroundings, which would then appear on your screen. Not only was it a fun game, there was something in it for smart retailers as well. With a minimal investment of just a few euros, you could have Pokémons appear in your shop, guaranteeing extra customer 'traffic'.

For many, Pokémon Go was their first encounter with this new, third space and it immediately revealed its potential for marketing and sales: the technology created a third shopping space that was neither a physical shop nor an online store, but an extra dimension to shop in.

Whether it is fashion or snacks, virtual reality immerses

VR technology makes it possible to detach yourself completely from the environment in which you are situated. The glasses — today easily created by using a smartphone at home or a headset at a venue — conceal that environment from view and register every head movement you make.

If you want to check out a couple of villas in the south of France without the need to drive over a thousand kilometres, this technology is the thing for you. It really does seem real when one space after another passes in front of your field of vision, without you moving an inch!

The fashion world has already embraced this solution. At the flagship store of Tommy Hilfiger you can follow their latest fashion show from the front row thanks to VR technology. It can truly feel like a unique and magical experience when by simply putting on a pair of VR glasses a retailer can show you exactly the kind of world he wants to create around you and his brand.

However, choose wisely when you try to engage consumers through virtual reality. Still today, the use of virtual reality technology has its difficulties: VR headsets are not yet readily available to consumers, even though headsets for gaming consoles are increasingly finding their way into people's homes. Nonetheless, the technology remains limited, because as soon as the use of something is clumsy or time-consuming, people lose interest. The same reason - 'too much bother' - also explains why Google Glass failed to break through commercially.

goPuff | GoPuff virtual candy land

Virtual reality is indeed a great way to activate consumers, albeit for a limited audience. GoPuff, a US based online convenience store, taps into its perfect audience: the service delivers typical convenience products such as ice cream, alcoholic beverages and snacks right at urban Gen Z and millennial consumers' doorsteps. To make ordering more fun and engaging, GoPuff trialed adding a layer of gamification through VR experience to their mobile app.

When using your smartphone as VR glasses, you could shop for ice cream in a virtual candy land. Just move your head to swipe through snacks, compare prices and order them, but in the meantime, do not forget to catch falling ice cream scoops or play a game of beer pong with just a tilt of your head. Even chocolate brand Hershey teamed up with the online convenience store to reach playful, tech-savvy youngsters with the munchies through GoPuff's VR app.

Augmenting reality for vivid experiences

In the search for ultimate consumer satisfaction, technological applications are being developed that make shopping more pleasant, easier and more fun for the customer by cleverly combining reality and fiction. A less intrusive and more accessible way to do so is augmented reality (AR).

Whereas virtual reality creates an entirely fictitious world, augmented reality adds an extra layer - a virtual dimension - over reality. The real world is still present but is enhanced through technology. What's more, the consumer plays an interactive role in this process. Concretely, AR involves you pointing your smartphone or tablet at something, which results in a message on your screen. This often happens by means of QR codes.

One of the first truly successful applications, as early as in 2011, Tesco Homeplus developed an ingenious idea that allowed them to conjure up virtual stores seemingly out of thin air at locations that in normal circumstances would be impossible: like a few spare metres of space in the corridors of an underground train station in South Korea.

The company concluded that its target group - busy commuters - had little time to shop in comfort because they lost so much time travelling to and fro on the underground. To approach these people Tesco decided to use AR to erect virtual stores that looked like illuminated advertising hoardings, which listed all the supermarket's best-selling products. While waiting for the next train, the consumer could quickly fill a virtual shopping basket by scanning the appropriate QR codes, before choosing a time for his purchases to be delivered to his home later that same evening. In a world where time is getting scarcer and scarcer, this concept clearly hit the mark. Tesco had worked out a strategy based on its knowledge of its consumers and their needs, and not purely on the basis of turnover and marketing objectives.

Covent Garden AR Christmas

Even bringing the Christmas spirit to live can be done with augmented reality. At London's Covent Garden, some 140 stores and restaurants participated in a virtual holiday scavenger hunt. During the holidays, shoppers could embark on a digital hunt to find Santa's reindeer hidden all over the shopping district. When found, not only did the virtual reindeer start prancing around, shoppers could also win prizes. Aiming a smartphone at Covent Garden's giant Christmas tree unlocked exclusive rewards as well.

Physical incentives to pop out your smartphone and start scanning were present everywhere: other AR activations were to be found in the participating stores, such as fashion tips from editors of Cosmopolitan, Esquire and ELLE. Scanning tags on select items in-store activated their tips, but also revealed gift guides and special offers.

The same creators are also developing AR indoor visual positioning, using computer vision technology. This technology transforms any indoor space into an AR experience, by pinpointing a user's precise location via computer vision and serving up augmented reality content based on that location.

Often used for indoor wayfinding, the application can guide users through stores or malls by providing directions and information — which could be anything from arrows to images or video clips popping up — directly through their camera. As it is location based, it can also be used to display restaurant menus, reviews or special offers as soon as people reach a certain location.

Big data leads to Me-tail

Data is the crucial foundation of Retail 4.0. Technology companies can make good money with their knowledge, recognition and personalized approaches to consumers, both online and in the physical world. Collecting, analyzing and selling data has even become the basic pillar of the earning model of the big internet players - and like everything else, it is increasingly taking an omnichannel form.

Computer transactions open the door to four important - and lucrative - applications, according to Hal Varain, the head economist at Google (Zuboff, 2015):
- Data mining and analysis;
- New forms of contract, thanks to better monitoring;
- Personalization and customization;
- Continual experimentation.

If we compare these four applications with what the major retailers do online, it immediately becomes obvious that data is also 'big' in retail. We are evolving towards a personalized internet and personal retail (Me-tail).

// We are evolving towards a personalized internet and personal retail (Me-tail). //	

You are what you click
'Surveillance is the earning model of the internet,' write Martijn & Tokmetzis (2016). Google, Facebook and Amazon, but also Zalando and other platforms, avidly collect the personal data of their users. The better they know their customers, the more accurately they can target their advertising. This is done both directly and indirectly.

In direct terms, it makes it possible to improve the customer experience by making the most relevant possible offer to each individual user. The home pages of large web shops are immediately personalized with offers that reflect your shopping behaviour. One-to-one personalization in this manner is not always possible, but micro-segmentation on the basis of a 360° customer profile is a viable alternative.

The data that can be used for this 360° profile includes:[II]

- Demographic details
- Customer card data
- Purchased articles
- Purchase periods or moments
- Google Analytics data
- Social media data
- Click behaviour from e-mails
- Google Adwords data or click behaviour
- Mobile behaviour in apps
- Chatbot information
- Information from customer service contacts
- Data from connected devices

With omnichannel the possibilities are even greater. Physical retailers not only analyze the purchasing data of customers via their loyalty cards, but can also follow shoppers on the shop floor via wifi or beacons, so that they know which shops the customer visits, supplementing this information from contacts with staff in their own store. This is all useful data that can be exploited to increase sales.

Even after the sale has been made, big data can be used to adjust aftercare services and their conditions. In particular, this is an area with commercial potential for service providers. When Google's Varian talks about 'new forms of contract, thanks to better monitoring', this is what he means. If insurers see from their data that one of their customers now has a more (un)healthy lifestyle than when the life insurance contract was first concluded, the premium can automatically be adjusted up or down. Similarly, food subscription boxes can be adjusted if it is clear that someone has an allergy or is on a diet. In the future, this kind of flexibility can be built into smart contracts.

Mathematician Wim Vanroose connects smart contracts here to blockchain (see later on in this chapter) and smart machines: 'With smart contracts, your smart dishwasher will be able to negotiate via the internet on an online marketplace for the energy it needs to wash your dishes. Once agreed, the machine can conclude a contract with the supplier, which will be registered in a blockchain.' You can take this idea quite far. Based on its records of its own energy use, the machine can later contact other electricity suppliers to negotiate new contracts for each fresh wash!

The sale of data is an earning model in its own right, in which retailers and brands can also participate indirectly. Data vendors have made a profession out of selling detailed personal information to advertisers and marketeers. In fact, the trading of personal data to advertisers is the sole *raison d'être* for an increasing number of websites, apps and connected devices.

We all know that Facebook constantly monitors all our online activity, even if we are not logged on to their social media platform. And we know that they sell this information to advertisers, so that the right adverts can be shown to the right people on their site. Google also allows its advertisers to make standard use of your search and activity histories, so that you can be shown personalized advertisements, a procedure known in the jargon as 'behavioural targeting'.

Cookies ensure that you are immediately recognized by web retailers and platforms, so that the available advertising space on the page you are viewing will be filled in *à la tête du client*, with you specifically in mind. Behind the scenes, live bidding takes place, with the company offering the most money winning the right to place its advert and link it to your virtual identity. The person sitting at the computer next to you in the same room will get to see a different advert at the same moment, reflecting his or her personal profile. In this way, it sometimes happens that the same advert follows surfers around from site to site.

Delivered to your home before you even order

As early as 2012, Amazon took out a patent on anticipatory shipping, the dispatch of products before a customer has even ordered them. Using data analysis Amazon wants to anticipate consumer needs or, to put it another way, know what the consumer wants before the consumer knows it himself. This is made possible by predictive analysis. By analyzing the behaviour of shoppers, data analysts can estimate what (or if) a customer is going to buy before he arrives at the (virtual or physical) check-out. By already transferring the products the customer is deemed likely to buy from distribution centres to local hubs closer to the prospective customer's home, Amazon hopes to deliver its package within an hour or less of the customer hitting the 'confirm order' button.

Of course, Amazon is currently only taking its first careful steps in this field. As soon as the system is working fully, Amazon plans to make deliveries to consumers' homes before the sale has been concluded. Have they sent the wrong stuff? No problem. According to marketing professor Scott Galloway, Amazon will send a second box with the delivery, into which you can put anything you don't want to keep. Returns, says Galloway, are an integral part of the sales process. As an alternative, Amazon is also considering allowing the customer to keep the wrong deliveries as a kind of bonus. They are so convinced about the accuracy of their data analyses that even if the customer doesn't make an order he will still find something in the delivery that pleases him, so that he will want to keep it. Besides, this is cheaper than setting the entire return procedure in motion.

It certainly sounds efficient, but will the customer be as pleased as Amazon is hoping? Some customers might find it frightening to feel that their thoughts are being read by a machine. Discount retailer Target found itself at the centre of a PR storm when it began to send teenage girls gift coupons for baby products. Target was testing a system to assess which women were most likely pregnant, based on an analysis of customer purchasing histories against a list of 25 indicative products that might suggest the forthcoming arrival of a newborn. Is someone buying lots of extra skin lotion and vitamin supplements? Then there must be a baby on the way! Mustn't there? The furious father of one teenage girl stormed into a Target store to complain about this slur on his daughter's reputation and demanded an apology. Weeks later it was the father who needed to apologize, since the girl was indeed pregnant. Target knew more about his own daughter than he did! Perhaps this was just a lucky hit, but it is a good indicator of the direction Me-tail is taking. Having said that, there is still a long way to go. According to the Gartner Hype cycle, 'big data' is only just starting to emerge from the hype phase. It is against this background that stories like the Target affair need to be seen.

In the coming decades, the next phase will first see the datafication of business processes to improve purchasing, logistics and general forecasting. It will only be at a later stage that use of data will offer opportunities to extend forecasting to individuals, with personalized product offers and lifecycle marketing. Or as Koos

Nuijten, lecturer in Computer Sciences at the University of Leiden, puts it: 'Data-fication will first lead to more efficient processes and only later to new and improved business models. All the rest is still in the hype stage.'

That being said, the predictive power of data is already being used to the fullest by many companies internally. For example, the Dutch Albert Heijn supermarket chain uses consumer data to resupply its stores automatically. AH's integrated replenishment process continuously monitors the purchasing behaviour of shoppers, predicts what people are going to buy tomorrow, and makes sure it is all on the shelves in good time.

Highly personal influencing

The step from 'knowing what the customer wants better than himself' to 'letting the customer buy what you want' is logical in marketing terms, but less self-evident than you might think. If the customer does not already know that he is going to buy something, how can you make clear to him that you have the right product and that he should buy it from you?

// Personalized marketing is the next step to convince the customer in the omnichannel world. //

Personalized marketing is the next step to convince the customer in the omni-channel world. To finally persuade the consumer, companies have many different 'tricks of the trade' they employ. Well-known sales techniques include use of an authority ('recommended by Dr. X, MD') and the creation of scarcity ('last chance to buy'). The problem is that these techniques work much better in the physical world than online.

Only five out of every hundred webshop visitors are convinced to buy by these techniques, in comparison with one in four in a physical store. According to research by Maurits Kaptein (2015), there are a number of reasons to explain this, but the most important (up to then) was the impossibility for webshops to find the right sales technique for each individual customer. This does, indeed, differ from person to person. Whereas customer A might be convinced by the argument of a famous TV dietitian who says quinoa is better than rice, customer B might only buy quinoa because a lot of his friends are already using it.

Kaptein tested this theory using a clothing webshop where visitors were immediately screened with the help of a data analysis of their browser history: did they buy the books recommended to them on Amazon, did they always opt for the last available rooms on Booking.com, etc.? The webshop offer was automatically adjusted to reflect each visitor's personal profile. This resulted in an increased sales ratio of 20% or more.

The cosmetics brand Rituals also tested out various sales techniques in its webshop and measured how surfers reacted. On the basis of these reactions, they modified their recommended purchases and then re-analyzed the surfers' subsequent behaviour. This kind of A/B test is currently the most popular way to use big data in digital marketing, because it is easier to test online how people react to different settings than in a physical environment. This is also what Valian means when he talks about 'continuous experimentation' as a possible beneficial application of digital data.

Advocates of personalized marketing see the advantages of a made-to-measure shopping environment, where consumers waste no time on things that don't interest them and are automatically offered a relevant experience. Opponents are concerned by the privacy implications, but also warn that the technique risks isolating people in a cocoon. Their vision will narrow, because they will only get to see what they already know and like.

The antidote is what trend-watchers call serendipity: the feeling of being surprised and fascinated by something new and unexpected. And whereas in the past it was the physical stores that shone in terms of the personalized approach, in the future their new strength must be this element of surprise.

Dynamic pricing: always the best price

Plane tickets become more expensive the more you search for a flight. People who fly regularly will have experienced this often. The air carriers were one of the first sectors to make use of an advanced form of dynamic pricing known as yield management, based on the principle of price elasticity: the optimal number of products are offered to the right number of customers at the best price.

In the first instance, this is a question of supply and demand-related factors, similar to the way hotel rooms are more expensive in peak season and Uber rides cost more during the rush hour. Adjusting prices to reflect the competition is the norm in many discount formulas in retail: it is the concept on which the Belgian Colruyt chain of supermarkets has built its entire earning model. Notably, the lighting fast alteration of prices if the same product is cheaper elsewhere. Prices also vary in these supermarkets from region to region, depending on the level of local competition.

Thanks to big data, dynamic pricing can now also be operated at the personal level: personal pricing. Prices online can certainly vary, depending on the consumer group to which you belong, where you live, what device you are using, your past purchasing behaviour, etc. The Easy-Jet airline has posted an announcement on its website that it makes no use of the search history of consumers to determine its prices. Which immediately implies that its sectoral competitors do precisely that!

In the near future, we can also expect dynamic pricing in physical stores, says Annick Lemaylleux, VP Global Retail Market at Atos: 'In most supermarkets and hypermarkets in France you can already see dynamic price tags. For the time being, this makes it possible to quickly adjust to the prices of rivals. But before too long the tags will be used to facilitate personalized pricing. The tags will communicate with your personal device and set an individual price based on your profile.' Research has confirmed that within the next five years fixed prices will indeed (most probably) become a thing of the past in supermarkets.[12]

Dynamic pricing can also be used for more noble purposes. In order to reduce the ever-growing mountain of waste, the Wasteless platform for food retailers combines the use of radio frequency (RFID), electronic price tags and dynamic price calculation. The prices are automatically lowered when products approach their sell-by date. The closer the date, the lower the price.

Companies that wish to contribute to society and see it as their task to help find solutions for societal problems - the so-called civic mindset brands - are also increasingly applying social price differentiation. For example, the Everytable lunch restaurant chain in Los Angeles adjusts it prices to reflect location: a salad in the poorer southern part of the city costs half the price of the same salad in the prosperous city centre. By using social price segmentation, the lunch bars wish to recognize and combat growing inequality.

'Pay what you want' or co-pricing is another possibility, which allows the consumer to decide the price he is willing to pay for a product. This is difficult as a permanent option, but it can be useful in the short term to test a product or to increase the visibility or PR around a brand.

The Big Six see, hear and know everything

Whoever has the most data also has the most power. And more and more of this power is being grabbed by a limited number of players. It is no coincidence that the largest data gatherers are also the most important and most trendsetting companies of our age. What NYU professor Scott Galloway calls the Big Four, can today be extended to the Big Six: not only Amazon, the Google-holding Alphabet, Facebook, Apple, but also Alibaba and Tencent. Google already knows, for example, what we all buy online, as revealed by a complaint made by EPIC, the American privacy watchdog. Google follows shop purchases and links billions of transaction details to the personal data of internet users.

What's more, these giants are strengthening their grip on the market every day. Trying to avoid them is almost impossible: they form a chain of networks, whose purpose is to sell more by binding customers to them ever more closely. As soon as it had launched its Kindle e-readers, Amazon announced that it wanted to evolve towards a closed-loop system: a closed eco-system where people buy and do everything via a single platform. *The Everything Store*, as the biography of Jeff Bezos is titled.

In China and exceedingly beyond, Alibaba's and Tencent's payment apps are incredibly important because WeChat Pay and Alipay have gained access to all social domains. With its 'new retail' strategy, Alibaba wants to demolish the barriers between the real and the online world. Payments are made easy with Alipay, which is already used by 520 million people, also for physical transactions.

Tencent has grown in recent years into China's largest internet conglomerate according to market capitalization. Thanks to its WeChat app, it has a tremendously powerful platform, within which users can organize practically their entire lives: from banking to maintaining their social and business contacts, from booking a taxi ride to paying the energy bill.

By also focusing on mobile in-store payments, physical purchases and the associated user profiles can be mapped to a large extent. Alibaba and Tencent collect all information about a user in an ID portfolio. 'We know who they are, what they want and what they do not want,' CEO Daniel Zhang of Alibaba said in the Financial Times. After all, they listen and follow along on everyone's most intimate device: the smartphone.

Data is not only useful for these companies' own purposes, but also to sell to others for marketing purposes - usually at very steep prices. The more important the eco-system becomes, the higher the revenue from advertising. Today, there are already advertising agencies specialized in marketing on Amazon alone and the retail giant also has its own media branch, the Amazon Media Group. Product adverts are increasingly being enriched with content, such as recipes and detailed product information.

'The way your product is viewed on Amazon and in the Amazon community through ratings and reviews has a strong impact on the future of your brand,' says John Denny, e-commerce director of Bai Brands, an American drinks manufacturer and advertiser on Amazon. 'It is increasingly so that if you win on Amazon, you win the whole game. End of story. That is the world marketeers need to bear in mind.'

// In the future, even your vacuum cleaner will probably be passing on information to Amazon. //

Information from the physical world is also becoming more and more important. Smart devices know more about their users than we sometimes realize. This is one of the reasons why Amazon invests so much in hardware for people's homes, in imitation of its rivals Apple (Siri is to get an in-house speaker) and Google (with its smart thermostat Nest). Facebook (a video chat device is on the way) and Alibaba (with Tmail Genie) are following close behind.

In the future, even your vacuum cleaner will probably be passing on information to Amazon. Colin Angle, CEO of iRobot, the company behind the Roomba robot vacuum cleaner, has already revealed plans in this direction: the robot maps people's houses in order to work out its own routes for cleaning, but the sale of this data to the tech-giants like Amazon, Alphabet or Apple might be an interesting earning model for the future, according to Angle. Roomba is already working in conjunction with Amazon's Alexa and Google Assistant for the voice-activated operation of its devices.

'There's an entire ecosystem of things and services that the smart home can deliver, once you have a rich map [i.e. data] of the home that the user has allowed to be shared,' thinks Angle (Wolfe, 2017). At this stage, there are no concrete plans, Angle later corrected himself, but the idea remains open as a possibility.[13]

Once Amazon or Apple has a detailed map of the inside of every house, they will also know exactly how everybody lives and can make even more made-to-measure product offers. For example, they might recommend a range of sofas they already know will fit neatly into your living room. Or suggest that an extra cupboard might be useful in that corner in the hall, instead of all the junk that is currently lying there. Before long, the super-companies will know all there is to know about us.

The question is whether the Big Six need a vacuum cleaner to get to this position of power. Their own connected devices already allow them to see, hear and read more and more of what happens in our homes, both inside and out. In this respect, the ease of the services they provide seems more important to people than their privacy.

And did you know other brands and retailers are paying for all this? They are all connected in one way or another with Amazon, Google, Apple, Facebook or Alibaba and Tencent. How much budget do large brands invest in Adwords, virtual stores and apps? Or in 'cloud services'? Brands and retailers are the biggest sponsors of their current and future competitors, 'the Big Six'.

Faced with this concentration of data power, local brands and retailers are confronted by a serious information and knowledge imbalance. The only way they can compete with the giants is to focus on their own strengths: human contact, trust and specialization.

The internet of all things

Sensors linked to the internet are known by the generic term the 'Internet of Things' (IoT). The possibilities are limitless: digitally monitoring all movements in your shop or warehouse, tracking goods, directing warehouse robots, recognizing customers, and so much more. According to market researcher Gartner some 8.4 billion internet-connected devices were sold in 2017, not including PCs, tablets and telephones. This figure is expected to rise to 20 billion in the near future.

A large number of these devices will be used for logistical processes or to support the purchasing experience. But even sensors that are not directly employed for these purposes can still provide an added value in the form of data. This can range from measuring how many people are in a given space to tags with an NFC chip. Imec - the European research centre for nano-electronics and digital technology - has already developed a cheap and thin prototype of the latter. These could be integrated into the packaging of products to check trajectory and durability (shelf life).

All the data collected from these various touchpoints represents a valuable treasure trove of information for companies. It can tell them where, when and how much is sold, so that they can - amongst many other things - estimate accurately how much a new campaign will bring, detect fraud, determine the ideal price point or predict when a sales peak is approaching. All this information can be regarded as big data, but nowadays this information stream can also be analyzed in real time to offer customers a more personal service, such as an improved search function or recommendations based on previous purchases.

Since, supermarket chains have been making it easier to automate shopping in every possible way. For instance, by adding barcode scanners to their mobile app customers can scan, say, an empty pot of jam, which are then added automatically to their virtual shopping list. Not only do these apps subsequently remember everyone's favorite grocery products, often times they can also be voice-activated and are able to recognize rival products, suggest a comparable brand from the supermarket's own range or help you select products that fit your dietary choices.

Now reaching a next phase, we are seeing an increasing number of connected devices and products, which know when they need to be filled up, repaired or replaced. The idea of a fridge that knows what it contains and what it needs to re-order was once a classic element in futurist designs for the house of the future. Today, these fridges are a reality. Science fiction has become science fact.

The perfect bra

Sensors not only help to improve sales; they can also significantly improve the customer experience. Lingerie brand Lincherie has smart mirrors in its stores that can judge the perfect bra size. When women enter the fitting room they are digitally scanned (no tape measures involved). Using this data, the ideal size is determined by the smart mirror, which scans the body at no fewer than 140 points. The only thing that needs to be determined by the stylist is the bra's cut.

The scan makes a profile that can then be used in a personalized webshop, that only shows customers bras of the perfect size. This approach also means that the store doesn't need to keep a wide range of bras in stock. The customer can view the different models, but the order is made online (in the shop or elsewhere) and delivery is at home. 'This allows us to reach a new target group,' says Annelies Braeckman, retail manager for Europe at owner company Van de Velde. 'Young people sometimes find lingerie shops a bit high-threshold, but they are happy to buy online. That's why they come to us, because we're digital and different.'

Smart devices supply themselves

In the battle for the household products market, Amazon launched the Dash Button. This wireless button allows you to order a specific product with just a single press. If you put the button next to your washing machine, you can order washing powder. The order is added automatically to your digital shopping basket. All you then need to do is confirm your order and your powder is sent off to you with a minimum of delay. Smart purchase buttons of this kind have been made available in the US, Germany, Austria and the UK. By the start of 2017, Amazon had developed some 250 different buttons for domestic products as diverse as batteries, Colgate toothpaste, Red Bull and Trojan condoms, but today, they are already being antiquated by smarter, connected systems. As it turns out, Amazon Dash was merely foreplay.

It is only a small step before that same fridge immediately orders new bottles of milk and has them delivered to your home. With a glance at their smartphone, thanks to smart locks, people are able to open the front door for the courier, who puts the milk away in the correct place in the fridge, indicated to him by an RFID signal. The necessary technology is already available and in the yearsahead will become commonplace. Why should you waste time doing groceries if your fridge fills itself?

Once again, Amazon is at the forefront of this kind of automation, with its Dash Replenishment Service. Following on from its Dash buttons, the web retailer is making the technology available to the producers of electrical goods who are interested in developing smart devices. As such, washing machine manufacturer Whirlpool is collaborating with Amazon to make a smart top load washer and dryer: the machine calculates when your box of washing powder should be almost empty and orders a new one for you on your Amazon account. At Brother, they created something similar for toner for their printers, as did Brita for the filters used in their water purifiers.

Towards a 'replenishment economy'

This is leading to the creation of a large replenishment economy, which simply cuts retailers out of the equation. Amazon's Dash buttons are merely a precursor of this system, as is the making of orders by voice command via Alexa or Alibaba's TMall Genie or barcode scanners integrated in retailers' apps. They all make possible semi-automatic purchasing, whilst at the same time minutely mapping their consumers' purchasing behaviour. And by making purchasing intuitive and instant, the customer journey becomes as short as possible and the different 'moments of truth' that traditionally precede the final sale are encapsulated in the single press of a button.

Source: Google

FIGURE 12 · Moments of truth' in the sales trajectory

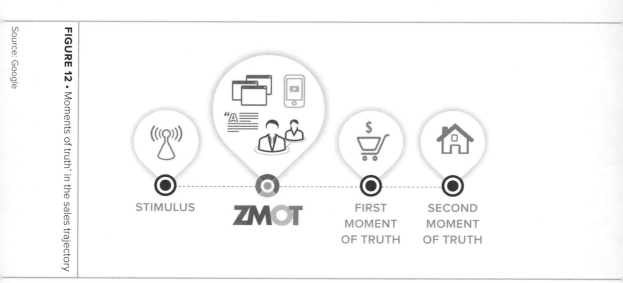

With the advent of the order button, the time span and the number of steps between the first stimulus and the purchase are reduced to a single short movement. With machine-to-machine ordering (for example, a printer that orders its own toner), all the moments of truth up to the second moment of truth fall away. In other words, up to the moment when the (unconsciously) purchased product is taken into use.

By always knowing what people will buy instead of what they probably or even possibly might buy, matters relating to supply and stock become a certainty rather than a risk. Stocks are no longer a calculated guess, but are guaranteed sales. Equally, in sellers' accounts stocks are no longer a cost: instead, they are generated turnover, even though the payment still needs to be made.

The more efficient this system becomes, the further it can be applied to other stages of the supply chain. In the replenishment economy, suppliers will only produce what they know they can sell, which reduces the risk of surpluses to almost zero and strengthens the producer's negotiating position viz à viz the retailers. True, retailers can still try to switch to an alternative product, but this is risky when consumers are already certain about what they want to buy.

// Why should you waste time doing groceries if your fridge fills itself? //

In a replenishment economy, the supply chain will also look very different. All the different steps will be taken with a concrete sale to the end user in mind. In time, 'make-to-stock' will disappear from the retail sector; everything will be 'made-to-order'. This removes the uncertainty from the chain, providing both suppliers and retailers with some much needed breathing space. The potential benefit is already clear to some brands and producers: Unilever bought the Dollar Shave Club, to which P&G responded by launching the Tide Wash Club. Supermarket chains attempt to counter Amazon Prime with meal boxes and subscription formulas of their own. And this is only the start.

There will inevitably be a competition war between brands and the electronics manufacturers, not only to reach the consumers, but also to reach their machines. What brand of washing power will the smart washing machine order? The new rat-race for brands will involve being the first to sign licensing agreements with the machine producers, but it is a race well worth winning: connected devices can potentially be the most loyal customers the brands have ever had.

The question for retailers is how they can play a role in this shortened chain, in which - yet again - there seems to be no obvious place for them. It is a question they would be foolish to ignore or underestimate. Doug Stephens, better known as the Retail Prophet, predicts (2017) that in the near future 40% of all sales will be machine-to-machine. Walmart is already preparing its answer and has applied for a patent for a system that makes it possible for smart, connected devices to reorder products when they are exhausted - at Walmart, of course.

Your virtual assistant looking over your shoulder

But the real future for wearables lies primarily in all-inclusive systems that will become our inseparable companions - like our smartphones today, only better. Rather than having a collection of gadgets, each with a different functionality, the ultimate wearable will get so close to you that it will actually become a part of you. We are evolving towards a technology geared to your voice and your movements, which, as a result, is so much more intuitive. This machine will become your personal assistant, looking over your shoulder, whispering into your ear, gazing into your eyes, helping, supporting, encouraging... You already carry Siri around in your pocket, but Alexa wants be in your living room.

At the moment, we know Alexa primarily through Amazon Echo, which on first acquaintance looks like nothing more than an internet-connected loudspeaker - but it is so much more than that. This speaker is manned by Alexa, a voice-operated personal assistant who does just about everything, from ordering a pizza to giving you the weather forecast and even dimming the lights in your house. Alexa is learning new functionalities every day, because Amazon has made its technology available to external developers, who are helping to create new applications. In the world of retail and FMCG, this includes Domino's Pizzas, Uber and Sonos, the loudspeaker brand. If you ask Alexa to order you a pizza, she orders it from Domino's. Sonos is developing its own speaker into which Alexa is integrated. Peapod from Ahold has also made an Amazon Echo application that allows you to order and replenish the products you need.

Voice assistants like Alexa quite literally give the internet... a voice. You can talk with them and they answer back. What they answer is partly programmed in advance by software developers, but Alexa also draws on the vast reservoir of data contained on the internet. If you have an iPhone, you have no doubt succumbed to the temptation of asking Siri about the meaning of life and whether she enjoys it. At a more practical level, you can also ask her the way to the nearest supermarket. For domestic applications, Google has developed Google Home and on Android telephones you can call up your Google voice assistant with 'OK Google'. IKEA has also started in this field, launching smart lighting that you can operate with Amazon Alexa, Google Home and Apple HomeKit.

The pace of innovation shows no signs of letting up. Amazon's products Echo Show and Look are already equipped with a camera, so that the devices cannot only hear users but also see them. In this way, for example, people can make selfies of their outfits on which Alexa will offer expert advice, or else give others (and Amazon) a peek into their wardrobe. In addition to video calls, it is also possible for the devices to see, for example, what people are cooking and provide 'live' expert advice from famous chefs.

The addition of a visual functionality has significantly expanded the possibilities offered by the virtual assistants, although this once again raises the issue of privacy. The assistant's cameras and microphones are always in operation and Amazon's claim that Alexa only listens and watches (and records) when she hears her name will be put to the test in a murder trial in which Amazon Echo has been called as a witness. Amazon claims that the Echo at the scene of the crime was on stand-by and was only playing music. Is this true? Or does the company really have recordings of what happened on the evening of the murder?

Technology: literally skin-deep?

Smart technology will soon become a part of our bodies. The day when we first start to install chips and sensors under our skin is getting closer and closer. Especially now that no less a person than Elon Musk, the visionary founder of Tesla, seems keen to get involved in this field. With Neuralink, he hopes to computerize the human brain, using artificial intelligence and implants to help people become smarter and more efficient.

// In Silicon Valley the whizz-kids are already working on the next step after smart, connected devices: smart, connected humans. //

But Musk by no means has the field to himself. In Silicon Valley the whizz-kids are already working on the next step after smart, connected devices: smart, connected humans. At the moment, wearables are the nearest to achieving this. Wearable technology is already available in the form of smart watches, smart glasses and smart cloths.

Of the wearables, the smart watch forms the largest group, but it remains a niche market in comparison with smartphones and tablets. It can count on little wide-spread enthusiasm amongst consumers and likewise in the retail environment. Smart devices that you can wear in your ear (hearables) are good for about 1% of the market, as are clothes enhanced with sensors. These are currently minimal percentages, but according to market analyst IDC (2017) these devices are none-theless just a beginning, a sign of things to come. Who knows what the future has in store...

Smart glasses help more than just your eyes

Smart glasses project information into your field of vision, but without depriving you of sight of your surroundings (augmented reality). This means that smart glasses can be a potentially useful companion whilst shopping, allowing you to ask for additional information or even for the identification of certain objects. In reality, however, we have not yet progressed that far. Although the technology already exists, very few smart glasses have yet been commercialized. The most well-known is Google Glass, which was available for sale a few years ago as a de-velopment model, but never really caught on.

Research continues but the big breakthrough has yet to be made. Interesting ex-periments are being carried out by Lenovo, Snapchat (sunglasses with a camera) and even Visa (sunglasses with a payment functionality). The Visa model looks exactly like ordinary sunglasses, except that a small chip is worked into one of the arms. To pay, all you need to do is hold the glasses above a terminal that is fitted with NFC technology. Unfortunately, the lack of any other function proba-bly means that the Visa glasses have little chance of success, but it again demon-strates what kind of applications will be possible in the near future. This was one of Visa's objectives. 'The idea is to show the market things you don't expect to see as payment devices - like sunglasses or perhaps even a ring,' And indeed, a com-pany in Hong Kong is now marketing a wedding ring that allows you to make con-tact-free payments.[14]

Talking underwear and other smart clothes

A little bit sexier (in all senses of the word) is the smart underwear designed by Billie Whitehouse, a designer specialized in connected clothing. For Durex she de-veloped a range of undergarments with sensors at all strategic places, which can be operated easily with a smartphone app. The idea? You get your partner to wear the lingerie, start up the app, and make the light of your life literally tremble with pleasure...

For people who prefer the calm of yoga to the excitement of bedroom athletics, Billie Whitehouse has also developed Nadi X, a pair of vibrating yoga pants that helps you to assume the right positions and maintain them with focus - and all for 300 dollars...

Or what to think of a bra you can talk to? The OMsignal Bra first saw the light of day in the American army, which wanted to provide smart underwear for its female soldiers. The sensors in the elasticated edging of the bra measure heart rate, body temperature and perspiration levels - and will do the same for any sportingly inclined woman who feels the need for (or can afford) such things.

For brands, wearables are not only a new market where they might potentially be able to achieve success in the future with an as yet unknown range of innovative products, but they might just as easily turn out to be a way to immerse consumers still deeper in the brand world through ever more intimate forms of communication with the individual customer.

Robots behind the scenes - and in front

Robots take over the warehouse

In e-commerce it is often efficiency that determines how profitable a company will be. In this respect, automation and robotization can play a key role. Amazon has focused for years on trying to create the best possible operational processes and now limits human contact with packages in their warehouses to a minimum. It achieves this with the help of robots, which have automated the tasks involved in getting products from storage racks into delivery lorries to such an extent that the aforementioned human contact has been reduced to less than a minute per order.

The Amazon warehouses contain thousands upon thousands of separate racks that can easily be found and lifted by self-propelled robots. These robot-carts, about the size of a lawn mower, then find their way quickly and easily to the human operative who is putting together the order. All the operative has to do is take the right product from the right rack, scan it, and put it in a plastic box. As soon as one rack has been dealt with, the next one arrives and the process is repeated until the order is completed. This not only results in time and productivity savings, because the human operatives no longer need to search among the racks to find what they need, but it also means the racks can be stacked closer together, so that more storage space is freed up. Although perhaps it does need to be mentioned that the distribution centre just described specializes in smaller products like smartphones, books and T-shirts.

The packer is automatically provided with a suitable box, already folded. He/she then adds the shock-proof protection to the contents and tapes the box closed. Even the right length of sticking tape is determined automatically. As soon as the box is ready for dispatch, it is placed on a kilometres-long conveyor belt until it reaches the right place, being labelled on the way with a barcode and the delivery details. Once it arrives at the right spot on the belt, it is pushed off (automatically, how else?), where a second human operative carries it to a waiting delivery van. From shelf to van: a seamlessly integrated process.

Nowadays, of course, the Amazon warehouses are by no means unique. There are plenty of companies that use fully automated carts and fork-lifts to move pallets packed with goods around their production halls and storage facilities.

 // They work more efficiently than people and are cheaper, but are mainly active behind the scenes. //

Robots take over the shop floor

Bearing in mind that within the next decade online sales will account for 20 to 25% of all retail turnover, physical stores can no longer confine themselves to a purely transactional role. But this presents retailers with something of a dilemma. On the one hand, they need to make savings on their retail operations, out of economic necessity. On the other hand, they need to invest in order to enhance their brand and shopping experiences. Faced with this delicate balancing act, the retailers might receive help from a not immediately obvious quarter: robots - or that at least is the conclusion of a study by the Roland Berger research bureau (2016). A robot now costs less than the annual salary of a shop assistant and this cost will continue to fall. So there is no doubt that robots are price-competitive - but what role can they play in a retail environment? Roland Berger sees four main applications.

The first is **goods management**: robots are very effective at checking, inventorying, and replenishing stocks on shelves and in warehouses. Robots can optimize logistical operations and minimize storage costs. They work more efficiently than people and are cheaper, but are mainly active behind the scenes. Where speed and convenience are the main priorities, we can reasonably expect to see fully robotized collection points, similar to those the American start-up Shotput is planning. The on-the-go supermarkets of the future will also be completely unmanned, with robots employed throughout the supply chain. Albert Heijn top man Wouter Kolk is already aware that this might be the fate of AH to go, while retail watcher Cate Trotter is convinced that even the discount supermarkets will eventually replace all their people with machines.

Robots like Pepper, Nao or Tiki are more than capable of welcoming customers, as well as entertaining them, providing them with product information, communicating special offers and serving as platforms for augmented and virtual reality applications. They are multilingual and their friendly appearance lowers the threshold for customers. A test with Pepper at Carrefour showed that the number of customer interactions with the robot was thirty times higher than with digital terminals.

Information robots can be particularly useful in large stores with a wide range of products, which are largely self-service and where specialized advice provided by qualified staff is of less importance. After two years of tests in California, the American DIY chain Lowe's has now given their cutely named LoweBots the freedom of their stores. These robots are multilingual and help handymen to find the things they need: ask or scan in your request and the LoweBot will take you to the right shelf. According to Lowe's, the bots are also there 'to help our flesh-and-blood staff': they can answer simple questions, allowing more time for their human colleagues to answer the complicated ones. LoweBots also monitor the inventory in real time.

For smaller shops with a limited range or in luxury stores, where customers have high expectations of the staff, robots are probably less suitable. However, they are well suited for the **movement and delivery of products** or the processing of automatic payments. Drones and the self-driving Starship robot have been tested by Metro, Tesco and many more. At Hointer, the robotized jeans store in Seattle, robots bring the products the customer has chosen to the fitting rooms. Result? The store has 50% lower staff costs, needs five times less floor space and customers try on three times more clothes.

The final and most innovative application is what Roland Berger calls **customer path analysis**. Robots can count the number of customers passing through the store, follow their trajectories, calculate the conversion rate and even analyze customer behaviour and emotions. This will finally allow retailers in physical stores to make the same kind of analyses that the online webshops have been making for years. Retailnext uses robotization for this kind of in-depth in-store analysis, whereas Digeiz employs robots to chart customer movements on the shop floor.

Some people find the reading of their emotions by sensors just a little bit creepy. In a shop, customers display a whole range of emotions, depending on what they want, what they find, the general ambiance, the special offers, etc. We convey these emotions through the miniscule and involuntary movement of our facial muscles. Robot sensors are getting better and better at recognizing these emotions and linking them to individuals. Emovu, by the American Eyeris company, analyzes emotions to offer more relevant products and experiences.

Whether robots will eventually play a significant role in retail is dependent on a number of factors. Shopping areas and warehouses will need to be adjusted to accommodate them. And people will have to learn to accept them as helpers and colleagues. A fun prospect? 'Affirmative!'

Drones: the future of delivery?

Drone technology continues to become more refined and these unmanned aircraft, usually quadcopters, are already being used for the delivery of goods. Walmart, Google and Amazon are all currently conducting drone tests. Under the name of Amazon Prime Air, Amazon made its first test delivery on 7 December 2016 in the vicinity of Cambridge, working in conjunction with the British government.

The package is loaded automatically onto the drone, which is then transported by a mini-rail track to a special take-off platform. The flight had a maximum duration of 13 minutes with a maximum load of up to 2.3 kilograms (5 pounds). Having made its delivery, the drone could return independently to its base. Even though the test was confined to a small group of customers within a radius of just a few kilometres from the fulfilment centre, retail stakeholders are far fom done testing the limits of this technology.

Notwithstanding the hurdles drones are still facing, among which government regulation restricting the commercial deployment of the technology, patent filings and experiments keep buzzing about. Delivery specialist DHL has successfully completed similar tests in Reit im Winkl (Germany) and is keen to continue its experimentation, whereas in the summer of 2016, 7-Eleven, America's largest chain of superettes, successfully completed its first commercial delivery with a drone. Likewise, Pizza chain Domino's is starting in New Zealand with DRU (Domino's Robotic Unit) deliveries and is negotiating with governments in several countries to make large-scale delivery by drone legal. This would allow the chain to significantly expand its action radius for home deliveries, as scooters are obviously limited in this respect, on the assumption that customers want their pizza delivered warm.

Bart Theys, a researcher at KU Leuven, built a hybrid drone, which takes off vertically like a quadcopter, but then turns its wings and flies horizontally like a fixed-wing drone. Yet, he believes that small and built-up countries, where delivery distances and times are relatively small, are not the ideal environment for a drone of this kind. 'It could be useful for deliveries between two fixed points, like a shuttle service for important matters. You can compare it with the old pneumatic tube dispatch system you used to find in large buildings. I don't really see an early application in retail. At the moment, it's only used as a promo-stunt or in emergency situations.'

In more vast regions, drones could however be a solution to reach remote and secluded areas. This is why JD.com aims to build the largest Chinese logistics network for drones, in agreement with the board of the Shaanxi province in central China and in collaboration with the Xi'an National Civil Aerospace Industrial Base. The drones might become able to transport up to a thousand kilos and have a radius of 300 kilometers via hundreds of different routes and drone stations. 'We have a network in mind so that in the future we can efficiently transport goods between cities and even between provinces', says Wang Zhenui, CEO of JD Logistics.

Chatbots are the new call centres

Chatbots are digital assistants used to improve the purchasing experience. They have been in existence for a number of years but it is only recently that they have been used in smart applications. The idea is that a consumer can ask a question in simple language and get help from the bot. In the past, they were used on retail websites as a supplement to the traditional search function, but today they are also integrated into popular chat applications like Facebook Messenger, Skype or WhatsApp. In this way, the consumer can complete an order in a familiar and trusted environment.

In an ideal world, a chatbot can inform your customers, note complaints and complete the purchasing process. Often, however, this is not the case; for example, because the customer asks things or says things that the chatbot does not (yet) understand. But even in those cases, the bots can still do a good deal of the necessary work. Until recently, you needed a person to deal with every part of every conversation. Today, the bot can ask and answer the first questions, only passing the call on to a human colleague if things become too complex.

Artificial intelligence will soon feel completely normal

Sooner or later, we will all be confronted with smart and self-learning systems, which know more than us and come across as being human. Artificial intelligence will be everywhere, from the assembly line to the check-out in your local supermarket. And we won't even know it, because that is the remarkable thing about AI: it all seems so natural and so real.

Chat with Burberry

British premium brand Burberry is ahead of its peers in terms of smart technology and data-driven personalization. It is striking that Burberry uses a clear omnichannel approach. 'Entering our stores is just like visiting our website', said ex-CEO Angela Ahrendts as early as in 2014.

As one of the first, Burberry equipped its London flagship store with interactive screens and gave all employees tablets, where they can not only find more product information but also information about the customer, based on his or her purchase history and social media activities. At the same time, products in the Burberry stores are also equipped with RFID labels and a Snapcode, which gives shoppers more information about the production and how to wear the item on their smartphone.

Burberry is eagerly experimenting with new and social media, as well, whether it is Snapchat, Apple TV or Instagram. For London Fashion Week 2016, Burberry launched its own chatbot, giving brand enthusiasts more information about the latest campaign, pre-production sketches and an interactive maze via a multiple choice 'conversation' on Facebook Messenger. Immediately after the fashion show, the new collection could also be bought right away (see-now-buy-now).

Since, the chatbot has been expanded with various customer services, as well as options to view and order the collections. Shoppers can even ask the bot to reserve a Uber ride to the nearest store.

Burberry is currently also working on an AI strategy, says David Harris, head of IT: 'We believe in the added value of artificial intelligence to create better products, faster and cheaper processes and more insightful analyzes. By renewing our products and customer experience, we confirm our position in the luxury market.'

For AI to really count as AI, it needs to pass what scientists call the Turing test: if people do not realize that they are talking to something non-human, the machine can be regarded as intelligent. In retail, you can find AI in various forms, more than you probably think - but that, as we have just said, is the nature of artificial intelligence. From chatbots to voice assistants and robots, it will change the face of retail beyond all recognition.

It is only a matter of time before your glasses tell you where you need to go, play soothing music if your heartbeat increases, warn you that the traffic light is at red, and reminds you that your mother's birthday is next week. That is the true nature of artificial intelligence. That is not how we currently see it portrayed, but that is nonetheless how we will experience it in real life in just a few years' time.

 // Artificial intelligence will be everywhere, from the assembly line to the check-out in your local supermarket. //

'The Future of Payments': payments in the near future

The smartphone is currently the third most popular device for making purchases online, after the PC and the tablet. According to the Mobile Shopping Focus Report from Demandware (2016), in the US and Europe smartphones are good for 45% of all web traffic, but only make 38% of all shopping baskets and are only used to complete 25% of payments for those baskets. These figures will probably rise as payment methods improve and when paying in a shop or for a parking ticket in this manner feels easier and more intuitive than is currently the case.

If there is one domain where digitalization will fundamentally change the lives of producers, retailers and consumers, it will be methods of payment. Cash is on the way out, although its disappearance is taking longer than some people expected. A study by the European Central Bank revealed that no less than three-quarters of all shop payments in the European Union are still made with cash. 'Even in this digital era, cash money remains of essential importance for our economy,' said ECB president Mario Draghi (Tanghe, 2017).

Even so, researchers at A.T. Kearney (2016) calculated that the number of non-cash payments will increase from 30% now to 40% by 2020. By that date, a fifth of all those non-cash transactions will be performed by alternative payment instruments, stimulated by the advent of further portable devices.

From bank card to smartphone
Nearly half of all transactions in the European Union are card payments (51.6% in 2017, according to the ECB), while almost all other types of payments are being

used less and less: credit payments, debit and checks all lost ground between 2012 and 2017. Except for one exception: payments by electronic currency rose from 1.6% in 2012 to 2.6% in 2017. The share of electronic money is therefore still limited, but it is increasing considerably. In the Euro area its usage already amounted to 4.1% of all transactions in that same year.

Thanks to the smartphone, as consumers increasingly opt for contactless payment with their debit card or their mobile phone. When they do so with money in an electronic wallet, such as PayPal, Google Wallet or even virtual currencies like Bit-coin, they pay with electronic money. According to the ECB, e-money is all money that is stored virtually.

Another use of e-money is to be found in contactless payments, where the cus-tomer does not even have to enter a pin code anymore but only need to have his payment card scanned or to swing with the right app in front of a payment ter-minal. A big step was taken in that area with the arrival of Android Pay, a digital wallet for smartphones that runs on the Google operating system. Just link your credit and bank cards to the app and off you go: you can make contactless pay-ments simply by passing your smartphone in front of one of the specially fitted pay terminals - although for purchases of more than 25 euros you do first need to unlock your phone to confirm the payment.

The arrival of Apple Pay is to be noted as well: according to research by Boston Retail Partners (2017), Apple has overtaken the market share of PayPal already, which has been the largest payment platform for some years. However, it remains the case that Android operates on more than 80% of the world's smartphones, whereas Apple Pay is only compatible with the iPhone and iPad. Not that Android Pay has the payment market all to itself. There are numerous other contactless payment systems, such as Seqr, which can be downloaded in sixteen countries and is usable at roughly 30 million payment points worldwide. The principle remains the same: you link your card to your smartphone, scan in the QR code, tick the right card and enter a pin code (if needed). Various other local and national apps, many of them started by banks, link your bank account instead of your bank card to an automatic payment system for participating retailers.

Soon with a selfie or a fingerprint

It is not just the e-commerce shops, but also the classic retailers who are interested in alternative payment systems that make secret codes, passwords and card readers unnecessary. They claim that too many customers pull out of the transaction at the payment phase. This frequently heard complaint has finally registered with the developers of payment systems: they are now working on payment methods that work with fingerprint recognition or biometrics.

In the Netherlands, MasterCard and ABN Amro launched a pilot programme to explore the potential of biometric payment. 'Measurable personal details were used to authorize a payment,' explains communications manager Isabelle Roels of MasterCard Benelux (Soenens, 2015). 'The most well-known example is a fingerprint, because that is unique to each person. But facial recognition is also possible.'

// As Bill Gates once said: 'Banking is necessary; banks aren't'. //

All a user needed to do was download the MasterCard Identity Check App and scan his fingerprint. People who preferred to pay with a selfie first needed to take a photograph of themselves with their smartphone. These details were then stored by the app, which used them as a reference when a payment needed to be made. Whoever ordered something online got a pop-up on their smartphone screen with a request to pay. Depending on the user's earlier preference, he could then either use his finger print or make a selfie. The payment would only be made if the MasterCard app recognized the print or the photo. The results of the trial in the Netherlands suggested that the test subjects were 'very enthusiastic' (Snyders, 2016): 93% said they would like to carry on making payments with fingerprint recognition; for selfie recognition, the figure was 77%. And MasterCard is only one of several companies carrying out similar experiments.

And why not with social media?

Facebook, Twitter, WhatsApp, Snapchat: why not indeed? As Bill Gates once said: 'Banking is necessary; banks aren't'. There have been rumours for some time that Facebook wants to add extensive payment options to its Messenger chat service. American users can already use the app to make money transfers to fellow users, but, according to the IT news site The Information, the company also wants to use the chat app for payments in shops. The website discovered commands in the app's source code like 'pay in person' and 'pay directly in Messenger when you pick up the item'. Mark Zuckerberg continues to insist that he does not see Facebook as a payment service, however: 'That is not the type of company we want to be, [but] we do work with all the other companies who do make payments'.[15]

The Israeli start-up PayKey is also working on a system to make possible the transfer of money to other people within your community of friends via conversations on Facebook or WhatsApp. If this is successful, there is nothing to stop retailers selling their products and having them paid through their own Facebook page.

If you want proof that social payment works, you need look no further than the success of social payment apps like Splitwise or Snapcash. With Snapcash one can easily send money to friends via Snapchat, all users need to do is link a debit card to their account. A swipe up in the chat feature of the social messaging app is all it takes to send money to peers.

Africa and Asia: a huge market of small users
There are many European initiatives for mobile payments, but none of them has yet become truly mainstream. Similar systems are, however, already mainstream in countries like China or Kenya. It is tempting to see the mobile revolution as a western product, yet it is precisely in regions where large-scale internet connections are seldom that m-commerce and mobile payments most flourish.

In China (as already mentioned), mobile payments are not simply the work of the banks and the American technology players. Amongst others, the popular WeChat chat service plays an important role. The time that Europeans spend on Facebook Messenger or WhatsApp is spent by the Chinese on WeChat and Line, but these latter two applications are far more exhaustive. WeChat is a chat platform supplemented with games, media and... payment options. WeChatPay makes it possible to send money to friends or make payments online and in physical stores.

Tencent, the company behind WeChat, also takes a cut from each transaction. The individual commissions are small, but they soon add up if you have millions of users. In January 2016 (a peak moment with the Chinese New Year), Tencent reported that it received around 300 million yuan - around 38 million euros - in transaction commissions. Moreover, this amount comes exclusively from China and South Africa, where the service is also available. Retailers can, however, receive payments worldwide, which allows them to place an extra focus on Asian and South African tourists. Increasingly, shop keepers in the West are offering WeChatPay as well, in order to accommodate Chinese buyers.

The CEO of Tencent has also made public that the company charges its commission at a rate of 0.1% of the transaction value. Although this charge has now been dropped for transactions between friends, there is still a processing charge when virtual currency is transferred to a real bank account, which is intended to encourage users to keep their virtual wallet well filled.

The fact that a chat application can become a new banking alternative has also attracted the interest of western entrepreneurs. Facebook has been trying to exchange payments and gifts through Messenger for years. Recently it focused its arrows on India. There are strong indications that WhatsApp, part of Facebook, is working on its own payment technology based on India's Unified Payments Interface. The Swedish Truecaller would also have plans in that direction.

And then there was blockchain...
You have probably already heard something about bitcoin, blockchain, cryptocurrency or virtual money. And you are probably going to hear a lot more, according to Peter Hinssen (2016), innovation consultant and technology trend-watcher: 'I believe that blockchain is the most important technological revolution since we discovered the World Wide Web in 1995.'

Blockchain is the technology that forms the basis of bitcoin, the most well-known of the virtual currencies - although all the other similar currencies work in broadly the same manner. Having said that, the exact method of its working is highly complex, which is why the banks are studying the technology behind it, with a view to making their own payment infrastructure safer and more secure.

Essentially, blockchain is a decentralized network of computers, which together keep a virtual ledger of transactions between certain parties via an encrypted virtual chain (the blockchain). With this system, transactions for which you currently need an intermediary (a bank or a paying agency) could be made in the near future directly between two individuals in all safety, even though those individuals do not know each other. All the system's value is locked in a database, which is spread over the system's users worldwide.

Created in 2008, Bitcoin wants to position itself as an alternative payment method. Today, the Bitcoin is still primarily an alternative form of investment, but in order to enable faster payment transactions the virtual currency split into Bitcoin and Bitcoin Cash at the end of 2017. Increasingly, companies and institutions are beginning to see the benefits of land- and bank-independent means of payment like these.

For example, in Brisbane Airport in Australia travelers can pay with cryptocurrencies, including Bitcoin, Ethereum and Dash, in the shops as well as at the terminal. The advantage: travelers do not need to have appropriate currency, do not suffer from exchange rates and simply need less money in their pockets.

The first online shopping mall where you can pay with virtual coins exclusively, opened its virtual doors in Singapore. The virtual shopping center, MegaX, is targeting young tech fanatics and only accepts Bitcoin or MGX coins, a currency of its own which raised 2.5 million US dollar to invest in the start-up of the shopping center during its first funding round.

The technology behind the system - the actual blockchain - has, however, been adopted by many large financial institutions, because this makes it possible to conduct large, complex and expensive transactions cheaper, more efficiently and more transparently. According to a report by Deloitte, the system will soon break through in other sectors. More venture capital is currently being pumped into companies active with the blockchain than was ever pumped into the emergence of the commercial internet back in 1996. What does this technology have in store for us in the years ahead? Time will tell - but the blockchain is here to stay.

Blockchain, the platform killer

As more and more innovative brands and retailers are discovering, blockchain technology has some very interesting opportunities in store for retail. Not only could it be a valuable aid for retailers, it could actually replace retailers as well.

Transparent chain: follow the chicken to your plate

A product's origin is easily traced thanks to blockchain: French supermarket group Carrefour is creating an entirely transparent supply chain for several of its product categories thanks to the blockchain technology. Every step of the supply chain, from its manufacturing to its processing conditions, is captured in a decentralized database and this allows customers to trace the entire route a product has followed onto their plate. One such example is that they can trace Carrefour's private label poultry meat's origins.

Food manufacturers Dole, Unilever, Nestlé and others are pursuing the same goal and that is why they are partnering with IBM to better map and track a product's movement in the supply chain, thanks to blockchain technology. Walmart also joined the IBM system and said in June 2017 that it was now able to track a mango's route in 2.2 days instead of 7 days.

Alibaba is also known to invest a lot in blockchain technology, particularly to combat counterfeit items. Thanks to the blockchain, no single individual person or supplier can adjust or create fake results, creating a fraud-proof system.

Take out the supermarket: from manufacturer straight to consumer

Russian start-up INS Ecosystem has plans to cut out the supermarket as the expensive middle man between manufacturer and consumer. Founders Peter Fedchenkov and Dmitry Zhulin, who also founded grocery delivery service Instamart, believe that their online platform could reduce grocery prices up to 30%.

FMCG-giants Unilever, Mars, Friesland Campina and Reckitt Benckiser have all signed collaboration deals, just like pharma manufacturers and more local food and non-food brands. Whether it is Durex or Gaviscon, they all believe in INS' decentralized e-commerce platform. Seven out of the twenty largest FMCG manufacturers have already expressed an interest to join the platform, the founders say. The short chain is not a novelty, INS Ecosystem admits, but the blockchain has enabled its application more than ever. Founder Peter Fedchenkov says the decentralized data system allows for safe, efficient and cheap trading between the manufacturer and the consumer, eliminating the supermarket as the go-between.

Why use blockchain? The technology, alongside smart contracts, allows for a new generation of platforms, according to the founders. It allows for more transparency in the supply chain and the use of its own virtual currency, the INS token, gives shoppers their own loyalty and reward program as well.

// Thanks to the blockchain, no single individual person or supplier can adjust or create fake results, creating a fraud-proof system. //

Even though customers can use other currencies as well, the marketing campaigns and the loyalty programs will all focus on the INS token. Compare it to an airline's 'air miles', but thanks to smart contracts in the blockchain (programs that automatically hands out tokens when required), this system is much more advanced, cheaper to use and more personalized. INS only demands a 1% fee on every transaction. The reason why the fee is so low, is because the system operates as independently and cheaply as possible. INS' intervention as platform aggregator is restricted to an absolute minimum, thanks to the decentralized blockchain technology.

Moscow and Amsterdam are the first to enjoy this new system: Moscow is the home town of the crypto enterprise and Amsterdam profits from the company's deal with PostNL, the Dutch postal service that will handle logistics and shipments in the Benelux as a third party. INS Ecosystem highly values the 'last mile' partner, because that is the actual touch point between the digital and physical world, between the platform and the consumer.

That same PostNL, however, is already running its own platform-based grocery service called Stockon. The service consists of automatic bi-weekly grocery deliveries, based on an adaptable yet fixed personal grocery list of staple goods. Just like with INS Ecosystem, none of the products on supply are owned by Stockon. They are instead given in consignment by producers and private label manufacturers. Blockchain would be a logical next step for the platform as well.

Amazon invests in crypto, could become a bank

Why hasn't Amazon taken up this technology yet? Rest assured, they are undoubtedly working on it. Amazon has already registered several domains referring to crypto currencies, possibly as a pre-emptive measure, but most likely because it has plans of its own. Blockchain could turn Amazon into an even more powerful ecosystem, just like INS Ecosystem is planning.

Its very own crypto currency, or virtual currency, would eliminate all of the possible exchange rate issues on the global market. It would no longer need a bank or external financing options, because it can create capital rounds for the currency itself and use it as an investor tool. Blockchain is designed to have no regulatory third party that can or needs to intervene. Cryptocurrencies are in fact deliberate boycotts of the traditional bank.

Moreover, Amazon could actually become a bank itself: more than half of surveyed Amazon shoppers (LendEDU 2018) would consider an Amazon coin, nearly 45% would open an account with the online giant. About 38% says it has an equal amount of trust in Amazon as in a bank and nearly 30% would even consider a mortgage at Amazon.

It would also considerably increase Amazon's power, considering it would not need anyone aside from a delivery service: Amazon could go from manufacturer to consumer, eliminating banks, wholesalers and supermarkets. If Amazon acquires a global logistical supplier next (or first), the Seattle-based retail giant will own every piece of the chain.

The entire chain, without interruption

In the long run, Amazon would not even need the many retailers and partners on its Marketplace anymore, because it would be able to present a limitless amount of products straight from the blockchain, from the manufacturer to the consumer. An enormous advantage of a blockchain-powered online platform is that it can work from a pull model, according to INS Ecosystem's founders.

It removes boundaries of communication between consumers and manufacturers, which is why the consumer can indicate what he needs. Retailers will no longer decide the product range, because the platforms wants to give consumers direct access to the manufacturers' entire product range. There are no practical limitations because the short chain does not result in expensive stocks and no time or resources are wasted in the supply chain.

The advantages for a manufacturer is the access to data straight from the consumer instead of through the retailer, lower retail channel costs and no need to take a retail margin into account. INS also points out that a blockchain platform will bring more smaller brands to the forefront, compared to their struggle to occupy shelves in stores. Amazon would most likely bring its own brands to the limelight, which would give it one straight line to the consumer, without interruption.

Millions of Amazon-like stores in the blockchain?

There has been no official confirmation that Amazon is working on its own crypto platform, but it is without a shadow of doubt thinking about it: especially since, aside from Russian INS Ecosystem, the mysterious Bezop crypto currency has also popped up. 'Cryptocommerce is an untapped universe and Bezop has set the tone', it claims.

The American blockchain entrepreneurs behind Bezop did not turn to Amazon founder Jeff Bezos for inspiration by chance: they want to use blockchain to create a worldwide marketplace where every retailer and manufacturer can offer goods to the consumer without the need to start their own web shop, the need to invest in a cash register or payment system (crypto currency handles everything) and without a third party (like Amazon, Alibaba or Zalando) regulating the platform and walking away with data or margins.

Bezop considers itself to be a 'decentralized peer-to-peer ecommerce order management and processing system, an autonomous buyer-seller protection service, and a simple value added tax (VAT) collection system - all powered by smart contracts and built on a decentralized blockchain network'. 'Build stunning Amazon-like stores for millions of businesses' is the company's slogan.

Even though Bezop is still in its infancy and is regularly criticized in the crypto community, the idea is valid, and surely giants like Amazon and Alibaba must be aware of that too. If Amazon invests in technology, then blockchain is the next logical step. It could be the end of the current marketplace platforms with retailers as external suppliers. Will blockchain kill the platforms?

'Future of the Store': experience has many meanings

The verticalization of retail is crippling the horizontal retailers and worldwide online competition is slowly strangling the smaller physical outlets. The number of empty shops in the high streets continues to increase, further impoverishing the cityscape with each passing month, while customers continue to 'showroom' to their heart's content.

Does physical space still have a value in retail? Of course it does - but it needs an update. The shops where you have to fight your way between rack after rack of goods, before dumping your overfull shopping basket next to a till operated by a surly cashier are certainly gone forever. And probably a good thing, too! We need to convert the classic sales space into a meeting place, stripped of everything inessential, where only service and experience remain. Human beings are social creatures in search of instant gratification. And that is what new retail must give them.

// Human beings are social creatures in search of instant gratification. //

In the near future, no-one will make the effort to get out of their armchair simply to buy their weekly supply of washing powder, toilet paper and coffee. They will do it online. This is the strength but also the weakness of e-commerce. By contrast, if you want to learn how to make fresh sushi, share it with your friends, select a few pieces of naturally caught fish to be delivered to your home later, while you first try on a few new pairs of shoes... For this kind of experience people are still willing to head on down to the city centre. Providing, of course, they don't need to search for a parking space or drag all their bags half way across town. People are looking for the value to be found in personal contact and service, but served in a rich technological sauce. Modern shopping needs to provide exceptional pleasure or exceptional entertainment that you can't find anywhere else - irrespective of whether your shop is a physical or a digital one.

Do we still need shops?

Customer experience (Murray, 2013) can be defined as the sum total of:

- the environment: the sensory aspects that people experience throughout the entirety of the customer journey;
- the engagement in the retail space: the way in which people are addressed, in all senses of the word and also in every phase of the customer journey;
- the selection of goods: the closeness of the match between the offer and the customer, and the distinctiveness of the offer in relation to its competitors.

Physical stores can certainly score heavily on the first two points. But with a careful selection of goods - an intelligently curated offer - shops in the high street can also compete with the online retailers on the third point as well. For decades, customers have been overwhelmed by an overdose of products and services, presented in an often impersonal, styleless and uninspiring setting. In the absence of helpful sales staff they were left to their own devices, hopelessly searching for hours for the needle they wanted in the shop's haystack - and this while time is now one of the modern consumer's most precious commodities.

Now that women are professionally as active as men and an endless range of tempting options are competing for our free time, people today want routine domestic matters to be completed as quickly and as pleasantly as possible. This applies equally to shopping. Shoppers want to have fun, preferably in a unique way that they will not forget in a hurry. The shopper does not simply want to see, touch and test a selection of products and services (environment), but wishes instead to be emotionally involved in the process (engagement), before giving his personal seal of approval (personalization). If all this can be offered in a setting where the 'wow' feeling is never far away, the retailer has a good chance of winning hearts and minds like never before.

When Steve Jobs presented his concept for the Apple stores, he said that his main objective was to create a shopping experience that would be as good as the products themselves. Anyone who has ever visited an Apple store will know exactly what he meant: the stylized, high-tech setting where you can pick up and try equally stylized products, assisted by friendly and knowledgeable staff in a manner you seldom find elsewhere. It is, as Jobs hoped, inspirational.

This is the key: to attract people, brands must inspire them. Again, this is something for which the physical store is well suited. Whereas in recent years it was often thought that the physical store was on its last legs, producers are increasingly starting to realize that they are actually an ideal channel to turn customers into fans. There is no better place to play on the customer's senses than on the shop floor. Investing in unique and high quality experiences in physical stores provides retailers with improved brand recognition, greater customer satisfaction and higher levels of customer trust. The turnover follows automatically.

In the past, you needed to use traditional and ever more expensive mass media to get your story across to the public, so that you could build up your brand awareness. Today, you can use a physical store to do exactly the same thing. In fact, this strategy is so convincing that even 'hardcore' online players like Zalando and Amazon are also playing the physical card.

Choosing between faster or slower

Design savants like Katelijn Quartier (UHasselt) and Cate Trotter (Insider Trends) agree: physical stores need to concentrate on one of two things and deliver: either ultra-efficiency or meaningful experience. Retailers and brands therefore face a straight choice. There is no middle ground. An Amazon Go supermarket is conceptualized to get people in and out as quickly as possible with precisely the items they need. The Just Walk Out system at Amazon Go allows for customers to just take anything from the store and leave the shop, automatically checking out and paying for their purchases. Its aim is to take 'run shopping' to a new level: convenience at its best.

Similar hyper-convenient stores are quickly popping up all over China and elsewhere in Asia. Apart from Alibaba's cash and cashier-free Hema supermarkets and similar cafeteria concept Tao Café using facial recognition, rival JD.com is pushing hard with both the till-free supermarket chain 7Fresh and the unmanned X-Mart stores. In Jakarta, Indonesia, for instance, JD.com opened the first large unmanned department store: situated in a mall, this particular X-Mart has a surface of 270 square meters, selling everything from snacks to fashion. All completely till-free, so customers can simply walk out still wearing the jeans they tried on.

One of the biggest advantages for the retailer? The cameras and sensors let JD.com track consumers' every move, providing them with ample data.

To play their convenience role to the fullest, technology can be an excellent ally. 'The side of retail that needs to speed up will be automated. Tasks that are repetitive and have no added value for the customer will eventually be taken over by hardware and software,' says Cate Trotter (2016). It seems she is right. Amazon bookstores are based almost entirely on technology and data. The shops are small and not much fun, but careful title selection ensures that each book is potentially relevant for the local public. Amazon knows its customers better than anyone and therefore knows what they want.

// Some shops can offer both a fast and a slow option, while still serving the same customers. //

'Strip the shopping experience of everything unnecessary,' advises Cate Trotter, 'so that only the essential remains.' By making a conscious choice between 'fun' and 'run', you can accurately assess the elements of your customer experience: what do people expect from your environment, your offer and the way they are approached? You don't go to Action shops because they are a thing of beauty or because the staff give such inspirational help; you go because they have the right assortment at the best price. Only 35% of their range is fixed; the rest is variable, which means the shopper needs to pop in regularly to find the best bargains. And bargain-hunting is also a form of experience. The same is true of other discount chains, from Aldi to Poundland and IKEA. People expect this convenience to be translated into fast service and an even faster check-out. What they are sacrificing (by spending some of their valuable time in an uninspiring environment) they want to get back in other ways.

Some shops can offer both a fast and a slow option, while still serving the same customers. Sometimes a shopper needs to get away in a hurry; sometimes he has time for a more relaxed look around. Smart brands make both these things possible, like the Starbucks in London where there is both a seated area with waiter service and a counter where you can quickly pick up your order, pre-paid online. In Texas, Target opened its first dual-entrance store: people in a hurry can enter the 'ease' side of the store, where online orders can be picked up or more instant items like groceries, last-minute gifts or cleaning supplies can be bought. Whoever wants a more high-end experience enters the 'inspiration' side, offering seasonal decor, beauty products and specialty brands in aisles with a department store look-and-feel.

Give shoppers the ultimate experience

Nike and Adidas are both seeking to provide a memorable high-tech experience in their flagship stores. At Adidas in New York, it is as if you are entering a real football stadium, complete with entrance tunnels and grandstands, where visitors can watch sports videos. Even so, for truly interested potential buyers the opportunity to test out the products on offer yields the biggest added value, so Adidas provides them with areas - not treadmills - where they can run, kick a ball or even do a little bit of cross fitness. Portable sensors analyze your stride pattern to make sure you get the perfect shoes, boots, etc.

In New York's SoHo district, Nike has taken things to the next level - almost literally - by fitting out its five-storey building as a sort of museum, but a highly interactive one (PSFK Labs, 2017). Each floor is devoted to a different sport, packed with the latest technological gadgetry, test zones and historical paraphernalia of the kind that drives fans of the brand wild. But the store is much more than just a fun location: quality service is central, including a ladies lounge with specialized staff and the opportunity to make an appointment with a Nike+ Expert to improve your sports routine.

Shops can either be bigger or smaller than in the past. It doesn't really matter. The days of calculating turnover per square metre are finished. What really counts now is total turnover, both online and offline. In this context, floor space in shops acquires a new significance. In the central shopping streets and malls where they still have big stores, the major brands create experience centres that make clever use of the available space to demonstrate their products, organize workshops, give training courses and generally entertain their visitors.

For its larger locations, the cosmetics brand Sephora has developed the concept of the Beauty TIP (Teach, Inspire, Play), in which technology and advice go hand in hand. Make-up fans can for instance try out new products with the help of augmented reality, applying different lipsticks and mascaras automatically to their reflection on a high-tech mirror. Of course, these mirrors also make it possible to instantly share your new look with your friends on social media. Whoever prefers an analogue approach can always follow 'classic' workshops or book a group session. Sephora was quick to see the benefits of AR to allow shoppers to test make-up without the need to wipe smears of their face every 30 seconds or to use lipsticks that have already been on 20 other pairs of lips. And if you can't make it to the store, you can still use the AR via the Sephora app. In other words, the same experience, irrespective of the channel. This is omnichannel; this is the future.

// The endless lines of shelves and racks are now for online; the products on the shelves and racks in physical stores need to be carefully chosen. //

However, space is not essential to provide a quality experience. The endless lines of shelves and racks from the past are now something you can find online, on the shop's internet terminals or tablets. The physical shop's shelves and racks now need to contain just the right number of carefully chosen products. 'The right product in the right place at the right time': that is the strategy of the classic American 'big-box' chain Target. Their New York shop is only a third of the size of other large stores, but its assortment is focused strongly on an urban public.

If you are not big, you need to be clever: variety and frequent rotation keep shoppers interested, curious and engaged. Shop-in-shops, pop-ups, capsule collections or just varying the range from time to time are all ways to keep customer experience at a high level. As already mentioned, this experience combines location, engagement and selection. Stores are becoming media and lifestyle hubs, where people like to be surprised. They are physical 'community centres', where kindred spirits can meet.

The shop as a medium
In recent years, multi-brand shops have unjustifiably been seen as being on their way out. Wrong! If they make a careful product selection and have a clear philos-

ophy that people can identify with, multi-brand stores can become lifestyle hubs where fans can find products and services that meet various needs.

In this sense, in omnichannel retail the physical store becomes a medium: a place where you can tell your story and one of the many touchpoints with your customer. In fact, a physical store becomes a kind of warehouse: a carefully curated repository of experience, where consumers can discover your (brand) values and participate in them in the best possible circumstances. It is a showcase where you can display the things you stand for as a company, where you show what is possible with your brand and where you enter into dialogue with customers on all these matters.

In this respect, the growth of new shopping concepts especially for men is a noticeable trend. Along with Bonobos, the American Todd Snyder brand is a trend-setting hub for trendy men in New York. In addition to the brand's clothing, their male customers can find a department with Aesop skin care products, a permanent pop-up store and a bespoke tailor. In 2017, they added a barber, a shoe-cleaner, a coffee bar and a restaurant. To further cultivate the group feeling, men can also attend special events in the store after closing time, such as a wine-tasting evening. As long as you have a story to tell, your store is a blank sheet limited in possibilities only by your creativity.

WOOD WOOD

Nothing beats the network at Wood Wood

The Danish fashion and lifestyle brand Wood Wood is a trendsetter in the world of streetwear. Wood Wood excels in co-creation: it regularly launches capule collections in collaboration with major brand names and has already collaborated with more than 50 partners such as Nike, Barbour, Eastpak and recently Champion. The capsule collection with Champion was first unveiled in the flagship store of the brand in London, while a previous collaboration with Disney was even launched at the renowned Colette in Paris, which gives Wood Wood international visibility and strength.

The brand itself has a webshop and six physical stores, two of which are in Berlin, three in Copenhagen and one in Aarhus, Denmark. Wood Wood offers in addition to its own collections and capsules many other brands in its own sales points, ranging from Asics to Comme des Garçons. While its own collections can be found internationally in multi-brand stores and even on Zalando, Wood Wood knows how to encourage people to keep coming to the stores.

Wood Wood breathes community: nothing is stronger than the network, this brand proves that like no other. The partially horizontal retailer continues to stimulate and surprise consumers with the many exclusive limited editions, and has now developed a close network of international friends and like-minded designers. With the launch events and other activities, it also brings that community to the physical shop floor.

For example, it invited the French tattoo artist FUZI UVTPK for a tattoo session in the Copenhagen flagship store. Wood Wood immediately coupled the launch of two exclusive wallet models with a drawing engraved in gold leaf to the style of FUZI UVTPK. The portfolios each had a circulation of only 33 pieces.

Pop-ups bring movement into shopping streets

An increasing number of retail experts are convinced that in the long term pop-ups can be the saviour of our shopping streets, even in major cities. Cate Trotter (2016) predicts, for example, that the high street of the future will be 'more flexible and therefore more interesting than ever before. High streets that are an exact replica of other high streets in other towns simply won't survive.' The comforting and familiar uniformity of the past needs to change. 'If we wish to continue stimulating the interest of the consumer, we need more variation. The simplest way to do this is to increase the number of pop-ups, so that the shopping streets look different every month. This means that whenever people pass they will find something new, so that they keep on coming back for more.'

// If we wish to continue stimulating the interest of the consumer, we need more variation. //

From being a cheap option to fill empty shops and offer starters a temporary test location, pop-up stores are evolving into a conscious and strategic part of the omnichannel mix for retailers and brands. Pop-ups are an ideal channel to surprise consumers by almost literally appearing out of nowhere under their nose. This is an excellent way to increase brand visibility. In particular, it is an excellent way for online players to increase their physical visibility, without the high costs of a permanent store and the extra complications that a true omnichannel model inevitably involves.

But not just the online players love pop-ups. Physical retailers are also seeing more and more benefits in their use. They can serve to focus the spotlight on a particular product group, or to reach other target groups, or expand their geographical reach. They can be a good way to experiment and try out new concepts. What's more, they fit in well with the 'transitory' spirit of the times, where everything needs to be fast and fleeting. The up-and-coming generation of consumers are digital natives and short-term concepts like pop-ups, which keep their finger on the pulse, better match the rhythm of their lives.

Louis Vuitton used pop-ups worldwide to launch its new Supreme collection. To create extra tension and buzz, the locations were kept a strict secret until just before the opening. The result was a storm of interest. Some people even spent nights sleeping in the street to be first into the shops, so much so that in the United States the company had to cancel some of their pop-ups for security reasons.

The fact that the pop-up concept looks like it is here to stay led a number of smart entrepreneurs to come up with a clever new idea. They developed a kind of marketplace on the internet that helps candidate retailers to look for the best location for their pop-ups in the most popular towns and cities. One of the results is the British We Are Pop Up, which specifically focuses on London and New York, and offers three formulas: from the classic 'full space' (an entire shop) to ShopShare, where different retailers work together, with each of them hiring space (a shelf, a rack, a corner, etc.) in accordance with their budget. If necessary, We Are Pop Up can even look for compatible retailers with complementary products.

As with all forms of retail, it is necessary to reinvent yourself on a regular basis. In this context, the temporary nature of the pop-up store is its strongest card: if done well, they surprise customers, make them curious, stimulate their interest and create buzz. Above all, it is important to monitor and maintain that element of surprise.

Micro-retail: small is beautiful

Until the turn of the century, 'big, biggest, best' was the golden rule in retail. However, increasing rental prices also pushed up the minimal requirement for turnover per square metre. When crisis hit in 2008 and the shoppers deserted the high street, downsizing quickly became the new creed.

What retailers surrendered in terms of square metres, they tried to win back through the curation of a more efficient offer, better suited both to customers and their surrounding environment. The opening of smaller local supermarkets in city centres by the big distribution chains was just the start. Nowadays, more and more retailers are focusing on convenience stores: even smaller than the local superettes and with an even more limited offer: no ten brands of washing powder or five of butter, but two at most.

Micro-retail is also slowly starting to gain ground in the non-food sectors. For example, in the Spanish city of Navarra IKEA has opened a store that is ten times smaller than what you would usually expect from the Swedish furniture giant. A third of the available space is focused on customers who come to collect their online orders. The store also sells a useful range of accessories, while customers can seek advice from helpful staff and place new orders from the interactive catalogue.

// Micro-retail is slowly starting to gain ground in the non-food sectors. //

The sports retailer Decathlon has also opened a series of small 120 square metre shops in branches of Asda, the British supermarket chain. The range is naturally smaller than in their flagship stores of 4,500 square metre, but they also give people advice, before recommending them to order online. Ordered products can then be delivered to their home or picked up from the Asda shop-in-shops.

That technology is the motor behind this trend is clearly proven by the French publishers Les Presses Universitaires. They opened a bookshop in the middle of Paris with more than three million titles in an area of just 72 square metres. Their secret? Printing on demand with the Espresso Book Machine. This remarkable device can print, bind and cover an entire book in a matter of minutes. It is like a book take-away. And while the customer is waiting, he can enjoy a cup of tea or coffee. The benefits are huge: no large shop, no stock and no overstocks, with customers treated to an experience the like of which they have probably never seen before.

Amazingly, things can get even smaller still! First prize goes to Pimkie, with its 'fashion minibars' in hotels. When they check in, the guests find that one of the cupboards in their room contains some items of clothing and accessories. If they see something they like, they can immediately wear it and pay for it when they leave. And if the clothes don't fit, a quick call to hotel reception will get the right size sent up to your room in a matter of minutes. It is a fun experience for the guests, a unique extra service for the hotel and the retailer has dozens of extra mini-shops in hotels in Brussels, Paris and Milan.

A shop is not an amusement park

Shops shouldn't be turned into amusement parks - although they often work to-gether with amusement parks and other amusement partners to make their shop-ping centres a destination, a trip for the whole family that offers maximum and varied entertainment over the longest period. This is logical. As the need for large physical shopping areas in every town and city declines, shopping centres will be-come scarcer and the distances shoppers need to travel greater.

To attract the maximum number of people, it is important to have a complete and multi-facetted offer. But retailers need to be careful they don't take things too far. It is a delicate balancing act to turn a physical store into an attractive and word-of-mouth inspiring environment without alienating shoppers or descending to the level of the empty forms of entertainment that a hype or gimmick can soon be-come, once they lose their initial impact.

M&M is a good example of the problem. Their flagship stores in London, New York and Las Vegas are tourist attractions in their own right. They are packed with all kinds of gadgets and paraphernalia celebrating the tasty chocolate treats. You can take part in a virtual race in an M&M car, take selfies with M&M figures, have personalized M&Ms printed or watch a 3D M&M film. In 2016, the London store had 5.3 million visitors, about the same as the Natural History Museum. Even so, the company is finding it hard to reach its sales targets, never mind make a profit. That being said, the flagship stores do what they are supposed to do: create visi-bility and advertising for the brand. But no-one in their right mind would risk the mad hustle and bustle of M&M World to actually buy M&Ms. In fact, standard size packs aren't even on sale there.

As M&M shows, this is a risky game to play. Young millennials are not really attracted by this kind of 'amusement arcade' approach. People's interests change, and they are changing faster all the time - as the once trendy brand of Abercrombie & Fitch discovered to their cost. In their heyday, their stores had people queuing up outside the door, primarily young girls anxious to get on a photograph with one of the semi-naked musclemen who served as glorified doormen. Inside, it was like trying to shop in a nightclub: loud music, dim lighting and an all-pervading perfume. In the meantime, shoppers voting with their feet have forced A&F to clean up their act: goodbye superficiality; hello diversity, purity and even daylight in their new store concept.

// Creating an experience does not mean overloading people with sensations. //

Creating an experience does not mean overloading people with sensations or that you need to turn your shop into the analogue equivalent of a computer game. In most product categories, it is the need for advice and the desire for good service that persuades people to make the effort to visit a physical store.

SONY
Sony Square NYC

Sony opened its first experience store on Times Square in New York. Under the motto 'igniting creativity and curiosity through extraordinary experiences', the shop is intended to serve as a test-lab to allow customers to make their acquaintance with Sony's latest products. The store organizes events - such as photo exhibitions taken with Sony cameras - designed to strengthen the Sony brand story.

The explicit intention is that the range in the store - there is a till and therefore an opportunity to buy, although this is not the main purpose of the Sony Square - should change regularly, with a new theme or product line every four to eight weeks. Of course, everything looks suitably high-tech, with operational Playstations, virtual reality demos and a mock living room where visitors can try out Sony's Internet of Things products. You can even borrow a camera for a tech-variant of a test drive.

But the strongest trump card of Sony Square NYC is its location. On Times Square it benefits from a constant stream of tourists. It requires no billboard advertising: the glitzy showroom is its own advertising. It attracts the crowds just by being there. But this can only work for a vertically integrated brand, because the store can never be profitable. Its purpose is purely marketing-oriented. Viewing this kind of experience store as a sales point is a capital mistake.

Phygital, live or omnichannel: it's all retail

During recent decades digital developments have completely changed the way we shop - and the younger generations in particular love it. Retailers are going to have to pull out all the stops if they want to combine the strengths of the physical store with the benefits of the digital world in such a way that the result is a unique shopping experience. It is not going to be easy!

It was this ambition that led to the emergence of 'phygital', also known as live retail or omnichannel. In short, the aim is to merge the physical and digital worlds into a single complementary whole. Simply combining a physical shop with an online shop is no longer sufficient. Nowadays, you need to bring together elements from both worlds to tell your own unique story through a wide range of different channels at the time and place when it will most appeal to the consumer and his specific needs.

A.S. Watson, the owner of the Kruidvat health and beauty retail chain , plans to invest 141 million euros in its physical stores. It intends to spend the bulk of this sum on technology, logistics and staff training, although a number of new outlets are also programmed. Sounds adventurous - perhaps even risky - in these online times? Malina Ngai Manlin, operational director at A.S. Watson, explains (Van Looveren, 2017): 'We were afraid that our online strategy would cannibalize the sales at our physical shops, but we then saw that customers who buy in both our online and our physical shops spend two and a half to three times more than customers who shop exclusively in the physical stores.'

// Where online, offline and mobile complement each other, customer satisfaction - and therefore their willingness to buy - increases. //

Until a few years ago, physical shops were thought to be on the point of extinction. We now know better. The only difference is that these shops will need to have become a lot smarter, to match the growing smartness of consumers (see the chapter on 'The Future of the Consumer'). Thanks to his smartphone, the new consumer is connected with the internet 24/7. In his head, the walls between online and offline have been torn down. Why, then, should there still be any difference between a webshop and a physical shop?

Media Markt Digital Store

Whoever is used to the Media Markt stores, with their carpet floors and piles of boxes, will be amazed when they visit the company's Digital Store. At just 400 square metre, it is the smallest Media Markt, but also the most futuristic. In the shop window proudly stands a robot, which drops the packages pre-ordered online into the shop's 'click & collect' unit. The power of automation: that is the clear message of the Media Markt Digital Store. Customers are surrounded by life-size screens on which virtual men and women flick through the range (5,000 items) with the help of touchscreens.

With the exception of one wall and one table with smartphones, tablets, some wearables and their accessories, the full assortment is hidden behind glass in a mini-warehouse. MM has invested heavily in engagement, explained Ferran Reverter, COO of the Media-Saturn Group and CEO of Media Markt Iberia at the RetailDetail Omnichannel Congress 2017. A giant screen with a VR device, (3D) printers you can use to print everything from posters to smartphone covers, a workshop area and a 3D visualization programme are intended to provide customers with the fun factor.

Of course, there is more to the Digital Store than that. There is a large service counter for business customers, a separate help desk for technical questions, counters for different specializations (informatics, photography, etc.) and two fast tracks for people who want to pick something up quickly and pay. The strength of the concept lies in the fact that the technology in the Digital Store has not pushed people into the background: a personalized, human service is still possible.

The store as showroom

Sometimes retailers get shoppers in their stores brazenly carrying their smartphones in their hands, taking one glance at something in the shop, instantly followed by a second glance at the phone. The staff know what this means: these people are showrooming. Shop assistants usually give showroomers a wide berth: the fear that the clearly well-informed and price-conscious customer will give them an embarrassing lecture is greater than their curiosity to know what he is actually looking for, never mind trying to check if he is comparing the right products and, if so, with which other retailer.

It irritates some retailers and their staff that shoppers now have the ability to arrive at their shop well informed and ready to compare prices. They often react with dismay and frustration. But they forget that the showroomer is still planning to make a purchase somewhere. So why not with them? This is a golden opportunity to try and convince a potential customer face to face.

Figures from the US show that half of all adults compare prices on the shop floor with the prices they can find online via their smartphone (IAB, 2016). Even so, most of the adult showroomers still opt to buy the product they want immediately in the physical store. However, the behaviour of younger showroomers is different: 70% of them compare prices in the store but then roughly the same proportion order the product they want on their smartphone or computer while still in the store. In other words, older people give the store where they are a better chance of making a sale than their younger counterparts, who often choose a rival store at a different location to make their purchase.

One thing however, is certain: a customer who is left to his own devices (no pun intended) and gets the feeling that none of the store staff are interested in helping him will turn around and walk straight out of the door. We know that customers like to see, feel and even smell products - so let them do it with a smile, a friendly word and a bit of advice. Where a customer decides to buy is largely determined by his experience in the shop.

Price is not the only thing that concerns the showroomer when he comes to the physical store, although this is often used as an excuse by retail managers for their falling sales. The majority of shoppers say that it is also about the completeness and clarity of the information they have been given. If they get any information at all on the shop floor, it is usually a paean of praise about the product in question. In contrast, online they learn about the product's less good qualities from the reviews of fellow-buyers.

In these circumstances, it is logical that the shopper wants to come to the store to see the product and perhaps even test it, before later placing his order online on the basis of the latest reviews and ratings. As long as the customer makes his order on the webshop of the retailer he visited, all's well that ends well. But that's not always the way it turns out: the competition online is fierce.

The fashion sector has responded to the showrooming phenomenon and even tries to exploit it to its own advantage. Some fashion retailers set up small showrooms where a selection of their garments are on display, so that customers can see them 'live'. They cannot buy anything in the showroom, but they can feel the fabric and check that the cut and the model matches what they want. It is then the task of the staff in the showroom to give the customer that little bit of extra service that will persuade him/her to instantly place an order. A shopper who is perfectly assisted when making his/her choice, is offered things that perfectly suit him/her, is provided with the necessary information about sizes, colours and materials, is well on the way to becoming a loyal and faithful fan of your brand. That is what customer experience is all about.

Making a first selection online allows the customer to consider all the options in the quiet of his own home, away from the hustle and bustle of the shop environment. This gives him the opportunity to approach the purchase in a more focused and targeted manner, so that he will be well informed and waste less time when he finally arrives at the physical store: win-win, both for the customer and the shop. The fear of retailers that in the future consumers will use their shops as nothing more than a showroom seems unfounded.

If retailers want to do something more than simply wait until the customer walks through the front door of their shop, this means they need to try and reach him through all the various channels at his disposal, to ensure that he has all the information he needs to weigh up his purchasing decision carefully. This is the only way you can guide the consumer to your shop to make his final decision and, hopefully, complete the sale. But that's not the end of the matter. Once the customer does arrive at a sales point (whether online or offline), it is the task of the retailer more than ever to try and surprise him with a unique shopping experience and exceptional service.

MADE.COM
Made.com: showrooming only

The British online furniture retailer Made.com is a disruptor in the interior sector. The company allows young talents to design items of furniture and then has them manufactured in China. Everything you can buy from Made.com was made for them especially and is exclusive. No intermediaries, no negotiations with brands or wholesalers, no expensive or dead stock. Just a strong data-driven and online business model. And an unusual one.

Their vision of a shop is similarly unusual. Made.com uses shops exclusively as showrooms. You cannot actually buy anything in them. Why? Online there is no way to tell how a sofa sits or how its fabric feels. But you can if you come to their showroom. And even if you don't make the effort to go, the fact that you can if you want to is reassuring and builds confidence. It is similar to the stone-though-the-window strategy of Coolblue.

In sectors where digitalization is not yet standard, physical contact points still have an added value. A stylish touchpoint that makes your brand story and culture tangible: that is all you need, nothing more. The Made.com showroom in London is not big, but the entire space is well equipped with touchscreens, tablets, QR codes and even 3D printed miniature models. Their largest showroom is in Paris, but you can't buy anything there, either! Pure branding.

Webrooming becomes click & collect

Webrooming is more or less the exact opposite of showrooming - and studies show that it is becoming increasingly popular. Three out of every four consumers now gather extensive information about products from a variety of media channels before finally going to a physical store to make their purchasing decision.

The food sector seems to be the exception to this trend. In 2014, 90% of Dutch consumers went to a physical supermarket to buy their food and drink. By 2020, it is estimated that 37% will also use an online channel for the same purpose. Thanks to click & collect, you can get your daily basket of groceries at the place and time of your choice. No more running up and down all those long supermarket aisles, no more waiting in those endless rows at the check-out, no more breaking your back as you lug it all to the car. The formula seems to be finding increasing favour with an increasing number of people.

// The fear of retailers that in the future consumers will use their shops as nothing more than showrooms seems unfounded. //

Moreover, click & collect is no longer something specifically confined to food. Nowadays, nearly all retailers with a webshop offer the possibility for customers to collect their online purchases in the nearest available store. This reduces delivery costs for both sides. However, the retailers need to make sure that the service at the collection points is faultless. Click & collect is not simply a way to get people in and out of your shop quickly. It is also an opportunity for cross-selling, upselling and additional impulse sales.

Human capital

One of the greatest strengths of the physical shop is and will continue to be its human capital. All the cute robots in the world won't change this. We may live in a world where technology plays a big role and is taking over human tasks one by one, but it still remains impossible to invent a technological application that can empathize with customers the way a flesh-and-blood person can. At the moment, it does not seem as if machines will be able to reproduce this golden human quality for quite some time to come - if ever.

People go shopping in part because it is a social activity. It provides interaction and generates emotions. These are things we seem to have forgotten, but now urgently need to revive. We need to stop thinking that retail staff are cheap, not worth training and that their only tasks are to fill up the shelves, keep the floor clean and add the price tickets to the goods in the shop.

True, they are currently the exception: the shop assistants who greet you with a warm word and a friendly smile. Nowadays, everyone is or seems to be so busy. Staff complements have been cut to a minimum; too many tasks need to be carried out by too few people, so that it is difficult to make time for the customer. In these circumstances, the customer is almost like an unwanted element and often gets the feeling he is being ignored when he asks for a little time, attention and help. The problem is that the staff do not have enough of the first to be able to give the second and the third.

In the future, shop staff, working in perfect and streamlined combination with technological advances, will have everything they need to make every customer a happy customer. That being said, helping customers in exactly the right way and giving them a fantastic shopping experience is an art and demands a set of basic qualities and skills for which people need training. If, as a retailer, you have devoted too little time and money to these things in the past, you need to change your strategy and you need to change it now. Don't regard it as a cost; regard it as an investment in a brighter future.

'Just a "satisfied" customer is not enough. A high Net Promoter Score demands "delight", the non-stop enchantment of a customer as a result of offering a highly pleasing and surprising experience,' says Kitty Koelemeijer of the Nyenrode Business University (Koelemeijer, 2017). Two factors are crucial for creating this 'delight': 'In the first place, it is the interaction with the shop personnel - friendliness, helpfulness, taking the time for customers, not being too pushy, and, if necessary, even bending the rules a little - which can provide either a fantastic or a terrible shopping experience. In addition, the product offer plays a role. Finding the right product at a surprising value-for-money price can be decisive.'

Doug Stephens, author of *Reengineering Retail* (2017), distinguishes between two types of staff retailers will need in the future if they wish to realize their ambitions: the retail technologist and the brand ambassador. The former will be the mastermind behind the scenes in a high-tech retail environment, where he does everything necessary to make the shopping experience of the customer run as smoothly and efficiently as possible. But in our part of the world, we will probably have greater need of the second profile that Stephens sketches: the brand ambassador.

The brand ambassador brings the brand to life on the shop floor. He stands fully behind his brand, is passionate about its products and knows them through and through. He succeeds in making a strong connection with the customer, so that he can involve him/her in the brand story. A retailer will be successful if he can turn a group of staff into a team of ambassadors.

For retailers and brands it is therefore crucial to be selective in their choice of staff. They need to give people opportunities and perspectives, and they need to train them until they become one with the philosophy, mission and vision of the shop. If they are allowed to take part in decision making, this creates motivation and encourages innovation. The age of the poorly educated, poorly paid shop assistant is over: human capital needs to be valued!

A new type of store employee is arising: the store employee as brand ambassador and expert. In an omnichannel environment, the personal approach and service provision must make the difference, so motivated staff is even more important in the future of shopping.

The educators of Lululemon

Lululemon, a now iconic American brand for yoga and sports apparel, treats its employees almost as if they were members of a cult. The interview by the HR department - the service 'human potential' - alone is unusual at Lululemon: candidates talk in informal group conversations - preferably seated on cushions on the floor - about themselves, their visions and their lifestyle. Typical job interview questions are not asked. Under the motto 'attract the best, scare the rest', the company expects employees to live and experience the brand culture every day.

To get them completely immersed in that culture, all employees go to a kind of reflection camp after a year, where much importance is attached to open communication and setting personal goals. It suits millennials, which are strongly value-oriented and attach great importance to self-development - even on the work floor. Lululemon asks all employees to share future goals and supports them in their implementation, even if it means leaving the company.

The staff is also expected to stay in its role as brand ambassadors: wherever they go, they represent Lululemon. Certainly in sports activities: sports, fitness or dance lessons are reimbursed by the employer; but employees are then expected to also spread the word about Lululemon.

The store staff are called 'educators': they are not sellers, but educators who can explain both the technical qualities of the products and advise on styling.

Smart cities work hand in hand with retail

The past few years are known as the years of the Retail Apocalypse. Shopping streets where you hardly see anyone, with more shops for rent or for sale than are actually in use... The appearance of our town and city centres is changing rapidly. Since 2010, GfK observes a sharply decreasing growth in the available retail space per inhabitant in Europe, due to store closures and a reorientation towards smaller retail centers in saturated markets.

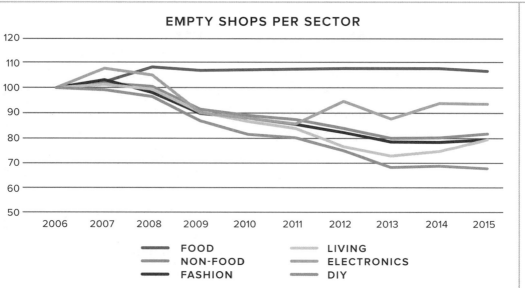

FIGURE 13 • Empty shops in the Netherlands (2016)

Source: Q&A/Locatus

Approximately 1.17 m² of retail space is available per inhabitant in the EU, a figure that has remained more or less stable in recent years (GfK 2017). However, a large shopping area does not mean much is being sold. On the contrary, it often results in the high street vacancy many cities are struggling with today. For example, in the saturated markets of the Netherlands and Belgium, one-tenth of all retail space is empty and the tide does not seem to turn (Locatus / PBL 2016).

For small indepent retailers, the situation is even more worrisome: in prime locations the rents are too high and even at the locations just below that level they increasingly have to compete against the chains (Bosteels 2016). In large malls and smaller cities or municipalities the problem gradually takes on dramatic proportions, regularly leaving a post-apocalyptic impression.

It is little wonder that local authorities are scratching their heads in puzzlement and that local trade associations are asking themselves with concern how they can lure shoppers back to the high street. But this challenge is really a fantastic opportunity for town halls and retailers to work together for the benefit of both.

High streets adapting to new reality

Underneath it all, new life is flourishing in the shopping streets. The productivity of shopping areas in Europe is slowly rising again. What is known as the Retail Apocalypse is thus the beginning of a new dynamic: in mature markets, online growth is slowing down and physical retail is gradually adapting to the new reality.

Although the number of commercial real estate projects remains considerably lower than during the retail boom of 2000 to 2012, new projects are appearing (GfK 2018). Large chains are once again expanding and online players build a physical presence, while loss-making businesses are closing their doors.

It is striking that the productivity of shopping areas has also risen again in recent years. Although the number of stores is declining, the total retail area remains fairly stable due to consolidation and the merging of several small stores into one large flagship store at Prime. Retail estate is on the move and is increasingly concentrating in one place — moving from the countryside to the cities, for instance. Stores that survive the so-called Apocalypse, see their turnover going upwards once again.

 // Location is a major factor in determining the right type of shop. //

Sometimes, what really needs to be done is reduce the number of available shop square metres. The Dutch city of Roosendaal reasoned that too much shop space is what leads to empty shops. Its solution? 'To start with, we needed to make a new and clearly defined city centre area within a ring road. A new spatial use plan was then drawn up for this centre, which is so flexible that entrepreneurs can do just about anything there. Opening new shops outside the ring road is now prohibited,' explains urban planner Riek Bakker (Hermanides, 2016). 'In this way, you create a scarcity. The idea is that retailers must either be in local shopping centres or the city centre. It is no longer allowed to try and find other, cheaper locations somewhere in between or on the edge of the city.'

Location is indeed a major factor in determining the right type of shop, as there are still significant geographical differences, not only within Western Europe, but also within individual countries. In larger, more widespread countries like Germany, where the distances are greater and the shop density lower, local players continue to have a more important role. As a result, we see an uneven development throughout Europe: there are increasingly larger differences between saturated markets, such as the Benelux, Austria and Scandinavia, and growth markets such as the Baltic States, Croatia and Poland, where the growth in surface area is much higher, but the productivity mostly lower (GfK, 2018).

In general, we are evolving towards greater urbanization, but there are still rural regions and intermediary zones between the two. In smaller centres the opening of flagship stores by brands is not really feasible, although brands do need local anchoring and visibility to stay 'top of mind'. So they still need shops in these centres and this is where the business model of many large brands - which are downsizing wholesale and focusing on online and their own shops - often breaks down. In the intermediary zones they again need to find retailers prepared to distribute their brands. In this respect, retail warehouses (along main roads or the edge of town) are a good compromise between absolute fun-shopping (a day's shopping in town) and run-shopping (quick in and out for the daily purchases).

Micro-retail also has potential advantages for shopping streets. Their lower surface area means lower rental costs (and, consequently, a lower required return per square metre), so that having your own shop at a top location once again becomes realistic for a larger number of retailers. A larger and more varied selection of unique shops in a shopping street will also attract more customers, who will also enjoy better service, since in micro-retail the focus in on interaction with consumers.

Pop-ups: fewer empty shops, more variation
The results of the various policies to combat high street unoccupancy will not be visible overnight. In these circumstances, the advent of pop-up stores is a godsend for the hard-pressed retail sector. The phenomenon of the 'temporary shop' has been on the rise for some time. Some of the initiators start a pop-up to test out a new concept; others see it as a springboard to later setting up a business of their own. If the pop-up works, they are off and running; if it fails, they have only lost a minimal investment. More and more established retailers also see pop-ups as handy outlets to quickly sell off surplus unsold stock.

Even the major retailers are now exploiting the pop-up concept. Aldi opened a pop-up store in the fashionable London district of Shoreditch to focus attention on its wine range - the first time the chain had opened a shop with just a single product. IKEA opened a pop-up restaurant in Paris, which, of course, made use of products from their own catalogue for the interior and ingredients for their menu that are also available in the store. Service providers have discovered the pop-up as a sales channel as well. New 'nomad' retail concepts rely even exclusively on occasional pop-up stores for their physical presence. Multinationals also see pop-ups as an ideal marketing instrument. Think of Samsung, which opened a pop-up in the Kalverstraat in Amsterdam exclusively to promote a single product: its Gear virtual reality glasses.

Transport and logistics: what to do with traffic?

Ask retail experts which criteria are crucial for making a good shopping city and you will generally get the same three answers: a varied range of shops, a varied range of non-shopping activities (bars and restaurants, events, tourist attractions, etc.) and, last but not least, good accessibility.

Parking: mobility as a service

When it comes to shopping, car parking often comes up as a discussion topic. Logically so, knowing that if you add up all the parking spaces in Europe, you end up with an area roughly half the size of Belgium. Hence, frequent arguments about the merits of free versus paying parking arise. While numerous retail organizations argue for free parking as a means to encourage consumers back to the city and combat the 'empty shop' phenomenon, those in academic circles say that things are not quite so simple.

'Shops and shopping centres must be attractive for visitors. Nowadays, shopping centres are destinations, places where people like to come and stay for a while. For the shops, of course, but also for the bars and restaurants, culture and other leisure activities. Visitors need to be motivated. If barriers are erected, like difficult access, poor parking facilities or expensive parking, visitors will be discouraged instead of encouraged and will go in search of other shopping centres were good parking is available, easy to reach and free,' says Cor Molenaar of the Erasmus University in Rotterdam (Parkeer 24, 2016).

However, paid parking can actually be one of the solutions for the problem of poor accessibility, according to UCLA Professor Donald Shoup. In New York, drivers need to spend an average of an hour driving around before they can find a parking space in the area where parking is free. In his book *The High Cost of Free Parking* (2011), he argues that making car owners pay a small fee for parking could eliminate this problem. How small is small? That will depend on demand. He favours a variable rate per location that ensures 15% of spaces will always be free, so that people do not need to waste so much time looking around.

'Parking is one of the most important instruments available to local authorities to manage (car) mobility. Making free parking available means that the city loses its control over the number of cars coming into the city centre each day. Moreover, free parking also leads to more "search traffic" and may result in more commuters coming to work by car, reducing the number of available spaces for other visitors still further,' thinks Giuliano Mingardo, a colleague of Molenaar at the Erasmus University in Rotterdam.

In other words, paid parking is about more than a straightforward source of income; it is about the efficient management of inner city space. The proceeds of parking can be used to further enhance the attractiveness of city centres. This is necessary, say urban planners, because there is really no such thing as free parking: someone always has to pick up the bill for the necessary infrastructure - and it is either the citizen or the consumer. Perhaps for these reasons, the number of cities where you can still park for free is relatively small. 'One of the reasons why local authorities are so often opposed to free parking in the city centre as a support measure for the retail sector is because there is no evidence that free parking has a direct positive impact on the number of customers and/or the level of turnover for retailers,' dixit Mingardo.

In an attempt to reconcile both positions, cities can try to make use of smart technology. The 270,000 inhabitants of the French city of Montpellier benefit from a smart parking solution. In order to make traffic more fluid and increase rotation in the retail heart of the city, Montpellier developed a Connected Parking system, with smart parking nodes registering which parking places are vacant, how long a car occupies a spot and other data, including the temperature of the roadway to signal the presence of ice sheets. With it comes an itinerary calculating app, integrating all transport modes (public, car, bike hire and parking), as well as predictive information about parking and bike availability.

Montpellier started by developing their smart city projects related to mobility, but later moved on to an encompassing Internet of Things network. As the Connected Parking is part of an open data approach, the information is available online for both citizens and companies, using it to create other smart city services. As such, a global vision has been developed including everything from mobility and commerce to water management and citizen health.

Alternatively, an adjusted infrastructure can also help to achieve lower traffic densities in city centres without negatively affecting retailers. To keep as many commuter vehicles out of the centre as possible, parking space outside of city centres can be offered at a significantly lower rate compared to parking spots in the heart of the city. Bus services are then run from the cheaper car parks to the centre. 'With a total parking concept for an entire city it is possible to maximize the use of the existing parking capacity more effectively. Collaborating with the local authorities about parking fees, accessibility, availability, connections to public transport, facilities for pedestrians and cyclists, etc. creates the best inclusive and integral solution for the right target groups at the right time,' according to Frank De Moor, CEO of the Q-Park parking company.

Cities and local administrations could collaborate more closely with the business world to treat mobility as a service, as is the case in Finland, where 23 organizations have bundled their data relating to mobility in the MAAS (Mobility as a Service) platform. The result is a mobile route planner app that takes account of every single transport option: private transport (car or bike), shared transport (car pooling, cycle hire), requestable transport (taxi, bell-bus) and public transport (train, tram, bus, ferry), all with real time information about the time the different trajectories take (Ballon 2016). The app can equally be used to pay any fees involved. Technology helps to serve the mobile man or woman in an ever less mobile traffic environment.

// Cities and local administrations need to collaborate more closely with the business world to treat mobility as a service. //

Hands-free shopping: the end of bag carrying

There are a number of new shopping concepts which show just how far some retailers are prepared to go for their customers. One good example is the American online fashion brand, Bonobos (which has since been taken over by no less an organization than Walmart). The brand was initially developed out of the founders' own hopeless search for comfortable and easy fitting trousers for men. It took account of the fact men are not generally avid shoppers and often have difficulty to find the right size or the perfect match.

With this in mind, they developed the Bonobos Guide Shop, a shop where you book an appointment with an expert one-to-one assistant who helps you to choose your clothes. As the icing on the cake, your choices are delivered direct to your home or office. There is no pressure, no hassle and, above all, no carrying of bags. Bonobos believe in the future of hands-free shopping.

Many other locations experiment with hands-free shopping. At Mall of the Emirates in Dubai, customers can drop off their shopping bags at a concierge service and pick them up later for free or have them delivered at home. Even less exclusive locations are investing in this service: in Westfield shopping center in London, shoppers can ask for a Hands-free Shopping Passport for 15 GBP. When shopping, they can leave up to 10 purchases at the shops themselves, after which someone collects them and keeps them in a safe checkout zone. If you use the valet service of the shopping center, you will even receive the bags directly in your car.

In more and more inner cities, similar systems are being tested, this way hoping to attract more people to the city centers. Here, purchases are delivered to lockers near public car parks at the edge of town. Shoppers can arrange for their bags to be delivered to one of these lockers and then pick them up when they return for their car, or have them delivered at home right away. Whoever buys from participating retailers, no longer has to traipse through the streets loaded like a pack mule.

Delivering differently

It is not only the traffic of residents, commuters, shoppers and tourists that is causing the streets of our inner cities to grind to a halt. We also need to find a way to deal more efficiently with logistical traffic if we want to keep our cities accessible. In the past, the problem was 'limited' to lorries making deliveries to high street shops, but in recent years the growth of e-commerce has intensified this problem and also led to a mushrooming of van traffic for the numerous deliveries to homes and offices. The only answer is that producers, retailers and city authorities must all make better use of smarter delivery technology.

What appeals most to the imagination are high-tech solutions, such as drones and self-driving cars. The latter have found fertile testing grounds in the US, where both Walmart and Kroger are trialling self-driving cars at the moment of writing. Whereas Walmart expects consumers to still drive along with an autonomous Google car to go pick up their grocery orders, Kroger aims to have self-driving vans driving around, delivering online orders from door to door. British online grocery service Ocado tested the same thing one year earlier.

But in the meantime, smart distribution systems could do just the trick. Q-Park in London has introduced refrigeration as part of its distribution and collection solutions, so that fresh produce can be delivered to its facilities at a central location before the rush hour, kept cool and then collected later by retailers when the traffic is lighter. According to the parking company, this not only reduces traffic but also congestion, exhaust emissions and the stress felt by couriers and retailers who otherwise need to battle their way through London's busy streets. Smart distribution also means producers', importers' and wholesalers' larger lorries deliver their goods to a depot on the outskirts of the city, where the different deliveries are split up before being taken into the centre by smaller, more manoeuvrable and, above all, more environmentally friendly vehicles. As such, the mobility solution currently receiving most attention, notwithstanding its inherent risks, must be cycle delivery.

The city centre as an open air shopping zone

Retail specialists repeatedly stress the distinction between convenience and experience. While the consumer tends to seek the former in retail parks on the edge of the city, for the latter he generally has two options: a shopping centre/mall or its open-air variant, the city centre. At the present time, the shopping centres seem to be much more popular in this respect than the cities.

'Shopping centres represent a challenge for the city centres first and foremost in terms of the experience they offer,' writes Ballon (2016). 'The key to this experience is to be found is a harmonious and well-coordinated customer journey: the process of orientation (where you are going to shop), the journey to get there (transport and parking), the shopping itself (walking around, searching for what you want, paying, having a rest along the way) and the journey home (mobility and after sales). Viewed in these terms, a shopping centre has more trump cards to play: it can more easily provide name visibility, its accessibility and cheap parking make it attractive, its clear signposting and routing make it easy to navigate, and a varied offer of shops and catering outlets under a single roof provide both interest and relaxation.'

In theory, city centres should be able to offer the same. More than that, this author is convinced that cities, providing they use smart technology in a smart way, can close the gap with shopping centres and even overtake them: 'Cities need to link their own experience strengths (authenticity, more independent stores, more variety and quality) to a cleverly managed and harmonious customer journey. This begins with smart mobility and parking, getting to know the customer better, and - via sensors, beacons and apps - the development of a customer route. This latter can either be omni-purpose or fully personalized: after the first or second shop, the smart systems already recognize patterns that reveal what kind of shopper you are and what you are looking for.'

// Cities need to link their experience strengths to a cleverly managed and harmonious customer journey. //

Increasingly, small-scale local initiatives are appearing, for example in cities that offer shoppers free wifi. In the Belgian provincial towns Roeselare and Oostende a Smart Citie app shows consumers, among other things, the way to the nearest car park (where, of course, they can pay with their smartphone). If the consumer enters a shop, he is immediately presented with a screen which details that shop's most interesting special offers. The app also serves as a customer card for every shop and enables consumers to make payments, appointments and orders.

More importantly, the local authorities in collaboration with the local retail sector have succeeded in putting the city back on the retail map thanks to the mobile app and, with the help of subsidies, attracting new shops back to the city centre. In a relatively short space of time, the small town of Roeselare was able to reduce the number of unoccupied shops and increased the number of shoppers in its main streets. As a result, the 'Roeselare model' was praised at an academic congress in London as an international example of how inner city decline can be turned around.

Even so, the digitalization of our cities remains a delicate question. The Google-holding Alphabet has set up Sidewalk Labs to do precisely that - digitalize cities - but has encountered opposition from 'vested interests, the political world and existing infrastructures' (Koelemeijer, 2017). For this reason, Sidewalk Labs is now considering the creation of its own digital city, where it can experiment on themes relating to mobility and parking, public transport, use of energy, security and privacy, all under the motto of 'technology cannot be held back!'[20]

'Future of Retail': to each their niche

Tabula rasa: the disappearance of the role of the classic retailer gives creative entrepreneurs the chance to begin with a blank sheet of paper. Out-of-the-box thinking is no longer just a bonus. If the whole box has been flattened, it becomes a necessity.

Because the pace of change is increasing dramatically and competition can materialize from almost anywhere in the world, it is no longer enough - as it was in the past - to change the course of your ship gradually. If you fail to innovate in time, fail to acquire a new dominance, you will be pushed aside without mercy. In today's markets, there is no second place. 'The winner takes it all...' (to borrow from ABBA) - and the loser isn't even 'standing small' anymore - he disappears entirely. Nokia, Blackberry, Yahoo, HHGregg and many others have learnt this hard lesson to their cost. Micro-multinationals are the new standard, rather than large and sluggish structures.

Having said this, achieving dominance is not beyond the bounds of possibility, if companies define their market accurately enough. The key thing is to become a leader in your own niche, and there are niches enough in this individualized world, where there are almost as many styles and opinions as there are people. For this reason, start-ups have been given a succession of remarkable opportunities in recent decades and smart whizz-kids have succeeded in making skilled and grateful use of the new rules of the game.

New businesses are rising from the ashes

According to the Deloitte Retail Volatility Index (2016), more and more new players have been stealing a slice of the market from the larger, classic retailers, either by surfing on the success of the major platforms or by developing their own unique business model. How can new or relatively small set-ups do well in the current hyper-competitive environment, where margins are so tight and prices under such pressure? Today's successful retailers are the brands who manage to avoid the bloodbath of the price wars and re-write the rules of the game to their own benefit. Younger retail companies benefit from the ease with which it is possible to start a business today, thanks to the internet and the number of empty shops in our high streets.

In current circumstances, local authorities and property owners are delighted if pop-up stores want to fill up some of the vacant premises that litter our city centres, while the web platforms can earn big money by allowing small-scale entrepreneurs or starters to make use of their massive infrastructure. Together (and according to Deloitte their strength lies in their number, not the power of individual players), they are further hollowing out the market of the stick-in-the-mud traditional players. Small-scale entrepreneurs and starters succeed by finding a niche that sets them apart. It is what lies in between the top and the bottom of the pyramid that gets cut out.

The Deloitte analysis of 80 stock-listed retailers in the US between 2010 and 2015 further revealed that only the brands that managed to differentiate themselves in terms of customer experience were able to significantly increase their turnover and their EBITDA (gross income) throughout the five-year period of the review. In particular, the brands that were able to provide the consumer with a strongly differentiating experience in combination with a strongly differentiating offer achieved double-digit growth.

Players who focused on price and convenience, but only gave a low added value for customer experience, saw their turnover increase marginally, but their EBITDA flat-lined or even fell back. Deloitte concluded from this that a memorable experience is a key factor for the new consumer.

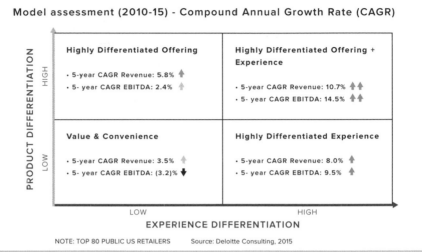

Model assessment (2010-15) - Compound Annual Growth Rate (CAGR)

PRODUCT DIFFERENTIATION
HIGH
LOW

Highly Differentiated Offering

• 5-year CAGR Revenue: 5.8% ↑
• 5- year CAGR EBITDA: 2.4% ↑

Highly Differentiated Offering + Experience

• 5-year CAGR Revenue: 10.7% ↑↑
• 5- year CAGR EBITDA: 14.5% ↑↑

Value & Convenience

• 5-year CAGR Revenue: 3.5% ↑
• 5- year CAGR EBITDA: (3.2)% ↓

Highly Differentiated Experience

• 5-year CAGR Revenue: 8.0% ↑
• 5- year CAGR EBITDA: 9.5% ↑

LOW   HIGH
EXPERIENCE DIFFERENTIATION

NOTE: TOP 80 PUBLIC US RETAILERS   Source: Deloitte Consulting, 2015

FIGURE 14 • Growth in relation to experience and offer

Source: Deloitte Retail Volatility Index

Why is this? There are three main reasons. Reason one: because the consumer is nowadays able to find everything he wants online, the added value of a basic offline offer - even at an advantageous price - without any extra 'experience' factor is too small. What's more, the online offer is unlimited, so that even an exceptionally broad or deep offline assortment is regarded as 'normal', unless it is coupled to an equally exceptional experience.

Let's admit it: where is the fun factor in a shop with boxes of shoes piled high against every wall? You'll probably leave the place with a headache, unless a competent assistant can help you to find what you want. No assistant? Then it's easier to go home and order online. With a few clicks you get to see dozens of shoes in your size and preferred colour, so that you can pick out your favourite. The high-resolution photos of each model tell you far more than all those closed boxes in the physical shop.

Reason two. Since the recession, low prices have become the norm. Purchasing power has fallen everywhere in the West and consumer confidence is at rock bottom. As a result, we have learnt to deal differently with consumption. 'Consume less' is now the message you increasingly hear and it shows that people are starting to think more carefully about their purchasing behaviour. They are not spending less; they are spending differently. They now prefer to spend their hard-earned cash on experiences and services, rather than products.

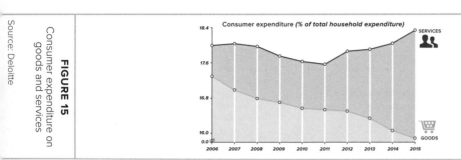

Source: Deloitte

FIGURE 15

Consumer expenditure on goods and services

Reason three. The modern consumer is satisfied with nothing less than excellence: excellent price, excellent quality or excellent experience. And because this modern consumer has become much more careful about what he spends in these austere times, the retailer needs to satisfy at least one of these three criteria if he wants to make a sale.

// It is no longer necessary to be in the same country as your customers or even your staff. //

The emergence of the micro-multinational

For the past 20 years, the economic tone has been set by the large multinationals. But we are now standing at the dawn of a new age: the age of the small multinational. Small, but oh-so dynamic. It is they who now determine the playing field. The possibilities for drop shipping, the availability of technology that connects the entire world and the limited resources that are necessary to start up a business have significantly reduced the entry threshold for new entrepreneurs. Nowadays, you can do a lot more with less. When WhatsApp was taken over by Facebook, it had just 55 employees. In other words, a small company. Yet, it had 450 million users.

Today's young people automatically think in global terms. For them, national boundaries no longer exist as barriers. As a result, it is no longer necessary to be in the same country as your customers or even your staff. One can be in China, while the other is in India. National borders are even falling away in C2C settings: as early as 2010, 85% of American eBay sellers reached at least five different countries. Platforms like Etsy and DaWanda make it possible for a jewellery maker in Greece to be found by customers from Albania to Alaska.

UNITED
WARDROBE
Global apps for second-hand fashion

On 15 January 2014, three Dutch students launched the United Wardrobe web platform, on which consumers can buy and sell second-hand clothing. The platform works like any other second-hand marketplace, only with a target audience of trendy 14 to 24 year olds.

By November 2017, United Wardrobe had 1.1 million users and about 750,000 product listings. After the Netherlands, the company is now active in Belgium and France, where it wants to invest further through influencer marketing and YouTube. At the end of 2017, it received an investment of one million euros, aiming to help it reach an international breakthrough. By the end of 2018, United Wardrobe wants to be bigger than at home in at least one market.

It is worth noting that before its capital injection, this micro-multinational ran its entire operation with just 15 full-time equivalents from an office in the old post building in Utrecht (an anti-squatting initiative from the local council), but saw itself being active in every European capital within seven years. The number of employees is now expected to grow from 25 to 250 over the next three years. In the meantime, however, the French United Wardrobe is still directed from Utrecht by phone, using a French-speaking manager.

A problem? No, an advantage, according to the entrepreneurs. The flexibility of the young team is part of United Wardrobe's competitive advantage. The fact that these bright young things are not really interested (yet) in a huge salary is also a plus. Because the company currently makes no profit - not that this worries the founders either! They share the same vision that has seen tech start-ups all around the world blossom in recent years: start small, scale up, attract investors, three or four years of strong growth, then sell up to one of the big players.

That big player could possibly be Depop, a very similar platform that was created in Italy in 2011. At the start of 2018, the digital vintage marketplace has reached some 8 million users, 80 employees, a head office in London and offices in Milan and New York, as well as a capital increase of no less than $ 20 million to conquer the United States. Depop now plans to win over the USA it with a number of physical stores.

Profit seems to be less highly prized than it once was. This, at least, seems to be the message from the platform giants, like Amazon and Uber. Although both are valued in billions, Uber still makes an operating loss and it is doubtful if Amazon will ever become profitable as a retailer. Some economists argue that current accounting principles need to be adjusted to better reflect the way value is created in a platform economy. Even so, cash flow and EBITDA (gross income) are still the main parameters that investors, banks and staff like to see.

How long will financiers be prepared to keep pumping money into companies that continue to pile up losses? And how long will it be before the continual carrying forward of debt is no longer an option? Sceptics point with a finger of doom at the internet bubble at the start of the new millennium. Optimists answer that today's internet technology is safely past the hype phase and has now reached sufficient maturity to reap its full benefit. But the reality remains: if the systems platforms like Amazon, Zalando or Alibaba ever go down, they are going to take an awful lot of other companies with them...

The platform economy: something for you?

Platforms bring us to the world of the peer-to-peer economy, where consumers sell to other consumers (C2C) and even to companies. The traditional pyramid in which goods travel downwards from the producer to the end user was already eroding before the most recent technological developments, but the boundaries between supply and demand have now fallen away completely. Still, this also offers new opportunities for brands and retailers. 'Listen to the wind of change'.

For example, more and more brands are encouraging the sharing and re-use of their products. Petit Bateau now has a second-hand platform where brand users can sell their unwanted clothes and undergarments to other users. In this way, they extend the life cycle of their products and make them more affordable for (young) families whose budgets are tight. At the same time, they show that their famous briefs and shirts can last for longer than a single generation.

This kind of sustainability initiative is very popular at the present time, but there are plenty of other ways to encourage the sharing economy in a manner that also allow brands and retailers to pick up a share of the rewards, either financially or in terms of enhancing their story and image. As a fashion retailer, why not ask your customers if they might be interested in designing accessories to match your out-fits, which you would manufacture and sell on their behalf under your brand flag? The possibilities are limitless.

In the United States, Rent the Runway gets swamped daily by fashion enthusiasts happy to rent designer looks instead of owning them. In the stores they are sub-merged in a world of luxury, fashion and service, getting the full designer store experience, yet without the price tag. Subscription models and rental concepts for fashion have been appearing elsewhere, but one of the most eye-catching initia-tives must be Lena, which since 2014 has been operating a 'clothing library', both online and offline. To keep the library viable, they also need to sell clothes. So if you like the dress you borrow, you can buy it. Lena's physical clothing library is in the Westerstraat in Amsterdam, but the company wants to reach customers throughout the country. To make this possible, Lena has also opened 'swap points' in collaboration with other initiatives in other towns. Customers can now collect or return their packages in other shops, lunchrooms, etc. In this way, Lena applies the system of 'drives' in fashion.

Platforms have many advantages for niche players. They are a great way to gain quick visibility and also allow small-scale retailers the freedom to define their own narrow market. Trying to create a one-stop shop as a local or even a national en-trepreneur in a world of platforms and e-commerce is neither useful nor feasible. But if you use them wisely, platforms offer the opportunity for smart specializa-tion, because even in a niche it is possible to develop sufficient critical mass to be profitable. Even so, you need to remain wary of the power and motives of the big system platforms: who is really the owner of your data and to what extent are you being given full access to it?

The (very) long tail
The emancipated shopper knows what he wants and thanks to search engines it has never been easier for him to find it. But this has benefits in the opposite direc-tion as well: even the producers who fail to score mega-hits still get the opportuni-ty to offer their products for sale. And because geographical limits no longer apply, their selling market is still sufficiently large to be viable.

Retailers and producers have traditionally focused their attention on the top of the demand curve, where sales and turnover are highest. However, Chris Anderson (2006) has shown that the advent of online retail has also given rise to the creation of a very long distribution tail: there is as much space (and demand) under this tail as under the curve's head. Anderson predicts that the Western economy in the 21st century will shift from mass consumption to niche consumption. However, it will be more difficult to meet this new type of demand, since it will involve an endless variety of products in very small quantities, which therefore in turn involves a high level of idle stock if you want to offer the right product to the right person at the right time. This is a risky business, unless you know as the producer/seller that there is a real demand for your product and you are able to keep your distribution and marketing costs sufficiently low to still be able to make a profit at the end of the day.

Search engines and search functions facilitate the search for products (the underside of the tail is highly fragmented) and increase the visibility of niche manufacturers and suppliers, which helps to substantially reduce the above mentioned marketing costs. In an e-commerce environment, the stock costs are also significantly lower than in physical stores, since use is made of centralized warehouses or - even more advantageous - drop shipping. Last but not least, big data makes it possible to more accurately assess the demand for niche goods, although this does require significant initial investment in the necessary technology for data analyses and enhanced search functionalities.

FIGURE 16 • The long tail-model

THE NEW MARKETPLACE

POPULARITY

Head

Long Tail

PRODUCTS

In pure physical retail space must provide a return - with turnover per square metre as the most common criteria - but online it is possible to expand your assortment with products that are less in demand. This extended range only becomes feasible when marketing and distribution costs fall - which is generally the case online. As a result, the head of the demand curve is made from the products you find in the shops, the bestsellers of the assortment, while the tail is made from the less immediately popular niche products on an endless virtual shelf.

// According to the inventor of the phrase 'long tail', we are set to move from a retail of hits to a retail of a million niches. //

According to the inventor of the phrase 'long tail', we are set to move from a retail of hits to a retail of a million niches. Even so, Anderson says that it will still be necessary to have both hits and niche products if you want to stay viable. In the individual niches the risk is high and the market limited. To balance this out, you need hits with low risk and a high rotation.

Thanks to scale and network effects, some players - and this brings us back to the platforms - will get increasingly stronger: the more they sell, the cheaper their selling becomes. Once the cost of their sales is low enough, they can do the same with low volumes products, thereby allowing themselves the luxury of an ever longer tail. Anderson refers to these players as 'aggregators': Amazon, Google, Alibaba, Netflix (to name but a few). These companies gather together niche players and products and make them findable.

This need for a balance between hits and niches works in favour of the omnichannel retailers: in their physical stores they can offer a range of 'hit' sellers to give them a solid basis, while online they offer a tail with less obviously popular sizes and products. In this way, a retail brand gains visibility and has a physical service point, but avoids the need for an expensive and non-viable stock. The Amazon bookstore in New York only has 3,000 titles in stock, while as long ago as 2004 Anderson was already noting that Amazon had identified 130,000 best-selling books and concluded that these 130,000 were only responsible for half of total book sales. The other half? The long tail.

The outdoor chain A.S.Adventure, active in France, Belgium and in Germany through the McTrek chain, offers additional versions of its products and less popular sizes online via a system of drop shipping in collaboration with the brand suppliers. 'Thanks to our scale and our years of retail experience, we have been able to conclude partnerships with some brands, so that we are able to offer their full assortment online, with extra colours and extra sizes. As a result, we can also offer our unique shopping experience to customers who are a little larger or smaller than average, but without the need for us to buy a large stock. In other words, win-win for customer, retailer and brand,' explains e-commerce manager Thomas Vaarten (Neerman, 2017).

The question is whether the customer who wants a more loose-fitting pair of jeans is willing to wait patiently until they arrive with a delivery van. H&M was heavily criticized when it launched a campaign with a plus-sized model but only offered the collection for sale online.[21]

The service retailer

Niches and hyper-specialization

After an era of oversaturation in a mass market filled with big boxes and identical rows of shops with scarcely any variety in their offer, today's shopper wants more authenticity, more originality and - in keeping with the life style of the younger generations - more individuality. It's back to the future for shopping!

Suddenly, second-hand shops are back in vogue and people are once again buying vegetables at their local farmers' market. Those in the middle ground, however, are going through tough times. Off-license chains have been forced to close down, even though new specialized liquor stores are being opened every day, both online and offline. These new stores cleverly exploit the gin hype and the ripening interest in quality whiskey, both of which betray a growing feeling of nostalgia among many modern shoppers - a feeling to which the shops respond with an atmosphere (experience) that recalls the 'lost' craft skills of yesteryear. Similarly, the German chain of 'traditional' department stores Kaufhof has been balancing on the edge of bankruptcy, while premium department stores such as KaDeWe now embrace both luxury and technology, allowing it to keep its attraction among foreign and native customers alike.

Another interesting - example involves the unconventional lingerie brand La Fille d'O - worn by stars like Rihanna and Madonna. Although the 2008 crisis, the resultant fierce increase in competition and falling margins forced many designers out of business, Murielle Scherre at La Fille d'O decided to face up the challenge through expansion. She opened a second store in her Belgian home market and a sales point in the US, as well as launching her first apparel collection. Yet, this was expansion without concessions: as far as possible La Fille d'O lingerie is still designed and manufactured locally in the brand's own typically uncompromising and transparent style. Scherre also prefers to avoid the interference of investors, relying on crowdfunding for financing.

Of course, niche doesn't always have to mean premium. If Lidl now likes to call itself a fresh-food discounter instead of a discounter, this is also a form of specialization and differentiation. Moreover, smart technology has reduced the entry barriers to enterprise to an absolute minimum. Anyone who wants to start up their own business can now do so in less than a day. And not just online. Pop-up stores have reduced the physical threshold as well.

Towards a wide-ranging package of services

Bed manufacturer Auping is experimenting with the leasing of mattresses, both for hotels and personal use. In this way, worn mattresses are returned to the maker for reuse, instead of ending up on the rubbish dump. As a result, by 2020 Auping expects its production to be fully sustainable. By remaining in control of its raw materials, it has converted itself from being a mattress producer into a near circular business model. At the same time, this also means an evolution towards a service model. At Auping the product is no longer central; this position has been assumed by its sleeping comfort service. Actual ownership of a mattress is now secondary.

The electrical giant Philips, working with architect Thomas Rau, has done something similar with the lighting plan for Rau's offices. Rau isn't bothered about bulbs and lamps, which are obviously Philips' speciality: he just wants light. As an architect, he needs so many hours of light in his offices each year and he doesn't care how he gets it. The technical side of things does not matter to him. He is not interested in products. He is interested in light - and that's all he wants to pay for. In response to which, Philips came up with a 'luminous' idea: Pay-per-Lux, where people pay for the lighting point, but not for the possession of the lamp, bulb, armature, etc. In short, it is a subscription for light - and it turns Philips from being exclusively a manufacturer into part service provider.

Thomas Rau's request was primarily concerned with sustainability, but it also perfectly matches the ethos of the new generations, for whom possession for possession's sake has little added value. Demanding and always in a hurry, the contemporary shopper insists upon and expects service. Large retailers like the German Metro group understand this and know that meeting people's human needs in a sustainable manner is now more important than the counter-productive pushing of their products. Or as CEO Olaf Koch (Snoeck, 2015) puts it: 'People are the key, not the goods. We want to evolve from a company that produces goods to a company that provides services.'

 // People are the key, not the goods. //

As a service provider, it is possible to put the thumbscrew pressure of price wars behind you. Your unique selling proposition (USP) is no longer the lowest price, but the provision of the best solution for your customer's needs. This is the kind of convenience for which people are willing to pay. This means that in Metro's new service-focused model their source of profits will switch from the sale of products to the sale of services. In other words, away from products where the margins are wafer thin towards a new source of income in services where the margins give a much better return.

Service can also be a way to differentiate yourself from other players, certainly in markets where it is no longer possible to achieve any further differentiation at the product level because of price pressure, lack of innovation or consumer disinterest. Viewed in this context, the delivery subscriptions of Starbucks (your daily coffee fix delivered at your doorstep), Amazon, Walmart and even Lancôme (never a day without perfume) are a service, as are the meal boxes launched by Carrefour, Tesco and Kroger.

The growth potential in a service and human-oriented model also shifts towards securing a greater share of wallet with existing customers, because success is no longer a matter of increasing market share at the product level, but of satisfying the wishes of customers at every possible level. As a result, the market is no longer the product category, but rather the people you reach. For brands and retailers, this is a clever way to keep expanding in western markets that are essentially saturated.

It also explains, for example, why Zalando launched Zalon, a personal shopping service, where people can buy complete outfits instead of individual items. Zalando wants to profile itself as a service provider attuned to the needs of its shoppers, with the aim of winning a bigger share of the space in their bedroom cupboards. Or how about servicing with a of sustainability : Filippa K Lease offers the collections of the luxury brand for rent. 'Lending clothes, like exchange and upcycling, is in the lift. Filippa K Lease is part of our wider ambition to make fashion inspired by timeless simplicity with a minimal footprint,' or so they say.[22]

A service model also provides brands with a model to cut the retailer out of the distribution chain. Nike was one of the first to transform itself from a maker of sports clothes *pur sang* into a services and technology company. In addition to its clothes, the company now binds its customers with its apps, training and instructional videos, expert guidance, events for brand fans and even its own pop-up fitness centres. The result: almost 30% of Nike turnover now comes from direct sales to the consumer, in comparison with just 19% in 2014.

Dutch startup Dobbi collects your dirty laundry at home and brings it back cleaned and folded. PostNL and Henkel cooperate in the company, which wants to be a new disruptor. The company functions as a platform, in line with the many platforms such as Airbnb and Uber that are emerging in every branch: it only uses existing laundries and dry cleaners. Detergent producer Henkel not only supplies the products, it also invests financially in the start-up. The brand producer sees Dobbi as a new way to reach the consumer directly, without needing the supermarket as an intermediary, and thus also to attract direct detergent sales.

Service formulas are a relevant route for brands: similarly, Unilever invests in the online cleaning platform Helpling. The brand manufacturer matches consumers with cleaners ('Helplings'), who are sponsored by Unilever to use the brand's

THE FUTURE OF SHOPPING

cleaning products. The Helpling cleaners will obviously ensure that the right set of cleaning products is available at their clients' homes at all times. This is a valuable new sales and insights channel for Unilever, which is trying to gain back shoppers from the large digital sales platforms and wants to break through the power of retailers, who are increasingly focusing on their own brands.

It used to be the door-to-door salesman, tomorrow it might be the cleaning lady who sells Henkel and Unilever at people's doorsteps. Such services can also be a good way for retailers to gain the trust of consumers, however. For example, after Amazon, Albert Heijn is also experimenting with a smart lock system, enabling grocery delivery couriers and service providers alike to enter people's homes and become their most trusted and most important household partner.

Even so, many other brands focused on service still opt for a solid local anchoring and the proximity of retail partners in preference to direct service provision. Today, it is retailers like Darty, Expert and even discounter Media Markt who deliver and install the vast majority of household electrical goods. And even when a brand like Miele does open its own consumer webshop, it is still the company's retail partners who do the delivery and installation.

C2B: the consumer shows business the way

'Let the buyers determine the product,' says Saskia Van Uffelen, CEO of Ericsson Belux (Neerman, 2017): 'We still determine the product offer, but it needs to be radically the other way around. Why don't we let the consumer make his own product? It is absurd that the consumer, who knows exactly what he wants and how he wants it, should not be allowed to direct the entire product process.'

Of course, this is the way it has always been, but indirectly. Things that people want are made and sold. Things that people don't want, aren't. But that is a pretty roundabout way of doing things. Today it can all be more direct: the relationship between brand and buyer is now two-way traffic. Via social media, reviews, crowdsourcing actions and various other channels, consumers now enter into regular and open dialogue with companies, in which they are not afraid to express their views and wishes. In this way, consumers can create value for a company, through which a consumer-to-business model (C2B) is developed.

188

From filling in a survey form for a small reward to selling self-made stock photos to the company, there are a thousand and one different interactions that can help to bring about a reversal of the traditional value chain. This again proves that the consumer is no longer at the bottom of that chain. Consumers are becoming mini-companies in their own right. They can make or develop things for brands, from generating publicity as an influencer to creatively customizing existing brand products or co-creating new ones.

Alibaba's Jack Ma has long believed in a shift towards a C2B market (Corbin, 2014), in which everything will be based on 'customization', the adjustment of products to reflect the personal needs of individual customers. The competitive battle will no longer be about price, but about value, even online. Jack Ma is convinced that today's shoppers have very specific needs. Ideally, he would like to sell 10,000 different shirts in styles chosen by the buyer rather than 10,000 of the same shirts in the same style. According to the Chinese Jeff Bezos, big data and logistical excellence make this theoretically possible. It is the future of retail.

We are evolving towards a future of personalized service and sales. On sites like Priceline.com, travellers in the US can already state the price they are willing to pay for their holiday accommodation. They make an offer and then it is up to the hotels to respond to their wishes through a bidding process. The site promises: 'We will find you a room in a hotel willing to agree to your price'. A model of this kind, based on a reverse offer, is a perfect example of how the C2B economy works: the consumers determine the rules and parameters of the offer, while the companies rush around trying to satisfy the conditions of that offer.

This 'inverted' relationship, where the consumer shapes the company's behaviour rather than the other way around, is becoming ever more firmly embedded in the value chain. In the years ahead, we will see a proliferation of made-to-order products. And when 3D-printers reach the phase of full maturity, even the 'made' aspect will fall away, with people simply buying the design (unless they made it themselves) and the materials.

Users are getting an increasingly larger say in business models, in part because they are more outspoken than in the past and now demand this role, but also because the human-oriented brands can see the value of their input. Why? Because it sells. 80% of Nike's online shoe sales are personalized with NIKEiD. Via the company website or app, or using a touchscreen in some of their stores, sportsmen and women can chose the model, colours and even the fabrics of some parts of the sports shoes of their choice. The result is a unique piece of footwear: no two are alike. Competitors Vans, Adidas and Reebok now offer a comparable service.

In a similar vein, the Australian Shoes of Prey company is making a furore amongst female lovers of fashion shoes. The brand dispatches its high quality, made-to-measure products worldwide within two weeks. CEO Michael Fox promises that in 20 years' time all clothes and shoes will be made in this personalized way, with mass production in the sector being consigned to the dustbin of history. One of the main benefits of this collaborative process with the customer is the elimination of stock. Millions of possible models are only made once they have been ordered. There is no such thing as surplus or exhausted stock. The pre-payment of orders means there is always money circulating in the company, whereas in the past cash was often locked up in a huge stock.

In the luxury segment you can now find many cross-overs that offer both expensive made-to-measure haute couture and ready-to-wear boutique collections. For example, brands like Jimmy Choo and Fendi now have an option to personalize shoes and handbags. And at the opposite end of the spectrum, even the mass retailers are getting in on the game! Marks & Spenser, the classic of all classic British department stores, has recently introduced the personalization of shirts for men, from the material right down to the type of collar and buttons. True, this is mass personalization, yet even so it goes a long way towards meeting the wishes of demanding shoppers who want the products they buy with their hard-earned cash to fit them like a glove - or even better.

 // Retailers like Walmart and Metro have opened the hunting season on start-ups. //

The new commandment: co-creation
You can no longer do it alone. If you wish to continue innovating, you need innovative people. Re-inventing the wheel is impossible, even for Elon Musk and Jeff Bezos. More than ever before, standing still is the same as moving backwards, es-

pecially now that margins are wafer thin and products can go out of fashion almost overnight. For this reason, co-creation between companies has assumed a vital new importance.

If you don't have the knowledge in-house you must find it somewhere else. If you don't have the right technology, you must buy it or share it. In this context, retailers like Walmart and Metro have opened the hunting season on start-ups. These retail giants are now constantly searching for high-tech and other companies that can make their business model more efficient or their range of services wider. This is the only way they can compete with their rivals who already have technology more firmly embedded in their DNA. It explains, for example, why Metro acquired a participation in the German start-up Deutsche Technikberatung, which provides technical support to home users and small companies. The start-up first saw the light of day as part of the Spacelab Accelerator programme of Media-Saturn, which aimed to stimulate and recruit innovative young companies of precisely this kind.

Walmart pulled a similar (perhaps even bigger) surprise when it bought Jet.com, an online discounter. With the help of internet start-ups like Jet, Walmart hopes to learn the secrets of omnichannel retail and, with a little luck, teach Amazon a lesson or two, since the ex-largest retailer in the world is now significantly expanding its online activities. Walmart is also targeting the fashion sector, with the acquisition of Shoebuy.com, Modcloth.com and Bonobos. From Bonobos it can certainly learn a lot about customer service in new retail, as we saw in the chapter on 'The Future of the Store'. It is in this same strategic light that we need to see Ahold Delhaize's efforts to take over the loss-making online retail platform Bol.com at almost any cost.

Long-standing retailers can also work together, by opening shops next to each other, allowing each other corners and shop-in-shops in each other's premises, or by grouping purchases. Instead of regarding this kind of collaboration as a kind of 'Trojan horse', with the fear of cannibalization it entails, retailers must see it as a form of transparency and mutual strengthening.

Starbucks has a long-standing tradition of setting up shop within locations of Barnes & Noble bookstores, but for two or more actual retailers to share space, is

The logic behind these alliances always boils down to joining forces for better conditions from suppliers. Nonetheless, the growth of the hard discount competition by Aldi and Lidl, as well as the threatening impact of Amazon and Alibaba, are definitely playing in the background. Whether it is purchasing alliances, acquisitions, mergers (i.e. Sainsbury's and Asda in the UK) or more temporary collaborations, retailers are ready to do anything to keep the 'Big Six' out.

Or else, they just dive in head first: Parisian supermarket chain Monoprix makes part of its offer available on Amazon Prime Now, Amazon's grocery delivery service. Also in France, some time after Alibaba and Auchan became partners, rivals Tencent and Carrefour teamed up, resulting in future tech innovation on Carrefour's home turf and the launch of a high-tech supermarket formula 'Le Marché' in China, where customers can pay with face recognition at unmanned checkouts. UK grocer Morrison's, on the other hand, collaborates with Amazon to deliver groceries in the London area within less than one hour.

With the 'old' retail mindset, where brands thought of customers as something to be 'owned' and stores wanted to be one-stop shops with the largest part of the customer's wallet in their control, it was difficult to think in terms of this kind of co-operation. Co-operation requires an open view of the market, in which each competitor is not necessarily an enemy and the consumer is not the exclusive property of any one brand. Consolidation is just as important if you want to have sufficient weight to put into the scale as a differentiating factor. At the same time, by entering into more loose confederations, rather than immediately insisting on mergers and takeovers, companies can create dynamic, creative and innovative networks instead of larger (and often less flexible) retail mastodons.

 // Innovating and testing things together is a possible way to avoid tensions between retailers and brands, certainly in the food market. //

A-brands get it on with retailers

As the realization grows that a price-based offer is no longer good enough to cut the mustard, brand producers and retailers will start looking for ways to generate value together. This collaboration can take different forms and in the future will no doubt display ever greater degrees of creativity. In the supply chain, for instance, we can already see examples of both upstream (retailer Alibaba buying white goods manufacturer Haier) and downstream (lens producer Essilor buying the Canadian lens retailer Coastal Contacts) takeovers. In addition, more and more collaborations are taking place in the form of shop-in-shops, exclusivity agreements and co-creation. If you can't beat them, join them!

Electro giant Best Buy managed to save itself from total meltdown by allowing other trendsetting brands space in its stores: Sony, Samsung, Apple, Microsoft and the like were each given an 'experience area' where people could test their products and create their own brand universe. It is interesting that these brand shops were also manned by personnel from the manufacturers. This meant that customers were able to talk to real product experts, rather than the Best Buy staff, who tend to be jacks of all trades but masters of none. Of course, it also means a massive salary saving: Best Buy offers a great experience and quality service to its shoppers, but needs to make no investment at all.

Exclusive content collaborations are also enjoying an increasing degree of success and fit well with the current idea of the shop as a medium or curator. The capsule collections that leading fashion houses make for H&M have been among the few things in large retail in recent years for which the public has really gone wild. For both parties it is an opportunity to reach a different kind of target group and recruit them as loyal customers. In that regard, it also makes sense for large labels such as Barbour, Eastpak and Champion to enter into partnerships with the smaller Danish streetwear brand Wood Wood: the capule collections position the brands as more avant-garde and trendsetting, which also gives them street credibility towards the authenticity-seeking shopper .

Research & development can also be collaborative

Innovating and testing things together is a possible way to avoid tensions between retailers and brands, certainly in the food market. Expensive above-the-line campaigns (mass campaigns via traditional media) by brand producers no longer have the effect they once did. Nowadays, people trust those who are close to them and enter into dialogue with them - and that is the retailers, with whom they come into direct contact.

But that obviously puts the retailers in a position of power. In order to continue offering the best products at the best prices in the most competitive way, retailers often develop private labels, which makes their offer even more relevant and increases their margins. As a result, A-brands see their sales fall and their budgets for innovation and marketing fall correspondingly. This motivates the retailers to invest still further in their own products.

The brand producers feel themselves trapped by these developments and attempt to reach consumers directly. However, there are only a limited number of love brands for which people are prepared to make an exception. In food, these are the A-brands that nearly every retailer adds to his range, such as Coca-Cola and Nutella. For other brands, it soon becomes clear that trying to get to the consumer directly is not as easy as they thought. Just like the middle is being forced out in retail, this is now the fate of the B-brands.

As a result, the only way to remain relevant is to focus even more intensively on research and development. If this can be done as a collaborative venture between brands and retailers, they will soon see that there is a huge amount of information and expertise they can exchange. By working closely together to develop new products and/or services, they can differentiate themselves from their direct competitors and search for solutions to real problems. In short, they become genuine partners.

Many retailers co-create with their private label suppliers. Together, they look at the categories and products where they can make their house brand more than a simple copy-paste on the A-brand at a lower price. Think, for example, of the ranges of fresh meals offered by supermarkets based on the recipes of star-rated chefs: these are a co-creation between the retailer, the chef and the producer.

To this day, examples of co-creation between retailers and A-brands are more difficult to find, given the often tense relationships between both parties, but the development of a whole new chocolate range for the Carrefour supermarkets in close collaboration with Mondelez (the producer of Côte d'Or and Milka) is one that springs to mind.

Co-creation is also possible between retailers, brands and their end users. At its innovation centre, the Spanish Mercadona chain of supermarkets often makes use of customer ideas, who they call *los jefes* (the chefs). Together, they develop recipes for the Hacendado and Deliplus house brands. An example? When Mercadona asked customers to test possible recipes for a new traditionally made tomato sauce, one of the testers put forward her own recipe as an alternative. The test panel thought it was the best recipe of all and it is now on sale in Mercadona stores.

Outside the food sector, LEGO is a shining example of crowdsourcing. In the LEGO Ideas online community fans can post their own ideas and assess each other's designs, the most popular of which are then brought to market.

'The Future of Marketing': made-to-measure at micro level

Making your dream target public love your dream product at the ideal moment with the ideal made-to-measure message: it is the fantasy of every advertiser and marketeer. But in today's market it is a tough call and the type of advertiser or marketeer who can make it happen still needs to be invented. Don Draper 2.0.

Developing an advertising and marketing strategy in our globalized online world cannot be compared with the way things were done in recent decades. It is no longer enough for marketing directors and their advertising bureaus simply to come up with few catchy slogans and some glitzy ads. Consultation and collaboration with their target public is essential if they want to build a strong brand identity. And media houses need to become experts in all the possible new channels by which people can now be reached.

The future is made-to-measure, because every shopper is unique. He has his own wishes and needs, which he wants to have met at a very specific moment in the way that best suits him. In other words, time, place and channels are all involved. Extensive research has given marketeers greater insight into people's motivations, while technological innovations and evolutions make it possible to focus on these motivations in a more targeted way.

The aphrodisiac that will make a customer search for (rather than block) a brand contains a number of essential ingredients. In their report *Future of Advertising 2016*, trend bureau PSFK identified various core elements.

- People are and will continue to be crazy for immediate **rewards**, both material and immaterial.
- An offer that **satisfies a specific need** of the customer.
- The customer expects that his loyalty will be rewarded with fun **extras**.
- If a brand offers **amusement** or confers a certain **status** on the user, he will be more easily tempted to keep on coming back time after time.
- This applies equally for brands that are **innovative** and give their public a unique and exclusive experience.
- Timing is key: if a brand has the right recipe but offers its aphrodisiac at the wrong moment, when the customer is not in the mood, all its efforts will be wasted.

Brand fans help to make the story

If you want made-to-measure marketing, your content - the story around the brand - plays a key role. Unlike the past, this story is no longer unilateral or universal, but needs to be based instead on two-way traffic. 70% of people say that they prefer to learn about a product through content (Montini, 2015) rather than via traditional adverts. They quickly see who is worthy of their trust and is offering them what they want.

In an era of information overload, people only pick up the things that register with them at a deeper, emotional level. The rest is filtered out by our overstimulated brain. So if you want to get your message across to the shopper of the future, you need to be creative. Nothing works better to attract people's attention than a surprise - and technological 'tricks' can be great for doing just that.

For example, beer brand Desperados picked up augmented reality in France for a limited edition series. The packaging was designed in collaboration with street artist Matthieu Dagorn: anyone who scanned the product label with the Desperados app, brought a virtual animation artwork to life, created by Dagorn. To create it, he used a physical décor to which he added virtual moving lines and dashes of color using Google Tilt Brush, a VR headset and hand controllers.

With its Oreo Dunk Challenge, the Oreo biscuit brand literally took things a stage further - a lot further, in fact. Sweet tooths could launch a virtual biscuit into space! The idea was to scan a photo of a real Oreo into your tablet or smartphone and then catapult it away from the earth with a well-timed swinging movement of the arm. Via Google Earth, brand fans could then follow the orbit of 'their' biscuit around the planet, with the landing in a glass of milk - the dunk - being shown in Google Street View.

The biscuit orbit was part of a wider campaign to socially and physically activate brand fans through different channels. Consumers were, of course, encouraged (via prizes) to share their 'dunk' on Twitter, Instagram and Facebook. There was even a special Oreo photo filter on Snapchat. The inventiveness and interactiveness of the campaign was surprising, and turned it into a big success. And that success will also have long-term benefits: the community used the app extensively and provided Oreo with masses of big data. So the brand wins twice. Fans love to be immersed into the world of their favourite brands and will remain loyal to them as long as they are special and, preferably, a little bit exclusive. Feeling special makes people feel good, and brands that can do so are onto a winner. How? Out with storytelling; in with storydoing.

In the summer of 2016, Adidas launched its Creator Studio, an online platform where football fans could design a shirt for the players of their favourite team. The designs competed against each other in the Battle Mode and the winners were worn by players as their club's official third shirt during the 2017/2018 football season. For each club a selection of the top 100 shirt designs with the most votes was compiled, from which the players of the team chose a winner. The participating clubs included world famous names like Real Madrid, Manchester United and Juventus. During the first week alone several thousand designs were submitted. 'Creator Studio offers fans a unique chance to be part of the history of some of the greatest football clubs in the world, something that has never happened before,' said Markus Baumann, General Manager Football at Adidas (Castillo, 2016).

// The community around the brand is an important strategic pillar in future-proof marketing. //

The community around the brand is an important strategic pillar in future-proof marketing. The Adidas example shows that fans like to help write the story of their favourite brands. There is a high correlation between the feeling of control a consumer has over an advert and their willingness to accept that advert. So the message is clear: involve your fans in the development of your story line and let them decide at least some of its direction. In other words, give them a leading role in your bestseller. Perhaps even the starring role. Why not?

The TV commercials for the 2016 'back to school' campaign of the American retailer Target were all written, acted and directed by school children. Who knows better how to appeal to children than other children, reasoned Target? And they were right. The result was a touching series of 15 second video clips in which kids showed their peers how to make new friends at school and how to solve other practical problems that affect many pupils. Children in the starring role, both literally and figuratively.

'Influencer marketing': the new stars

The ideas and objectives of fans can be an extra and fruitful source of inspiration to allow a brand to grow, and at a much lower cost than a traditional advertising campaign. Nowadays, everyone has channels through which they can express themselves and a network of contacts who might be susceptible to his/her opinions. These networks can be big or small, but they all have an influence on the people around them at their own level. The boundary between consumers and commercial partners is already becoming blurred. Everyone can be both a buyer and a seller, and via network platforms like Uber and Etsy every customer can also be both a marketeer and a receiver of your message, the influencer and the influenced.

For Generation Z, the networks of bloggers, video bloggers, Instagrammers and the like have much more influence than the TV and pop stars used in 'classic' advertising. Because they are ordinary people, today's new online stars come across as being more credible and more trustworthy, at least in the eyes of the young. They live like they live, eat what they eat and buy what they buy. And perhaps most important of all: everyone can become an influencer. For the Oreo Dunk Challenge, the brand engaged a number of influencers to encourage people to take part: an attempt by Instagrammer Danielle Jonas to dunk an Oreo while running on a treadmill attracted more than 400,000 views (Julius, 2017).

Influencer marketing will increasingly take the place of mass marketing and with the help of big data will become systematically more focused and specific. As innovative marketing expert Lamarque writes in her book *Influencers* (2017), micro-influencers with 750 to 1,500 followers deserve a central place in most influence marketing plans. It is above all these micro-influencers who can achieve the brands' ultimate objective: an impact on purchasing behaviour.

In contrast, famous celebrities are macro-influencers, who, according to Lamarque, are more suited to mass communication than to targeted influencer marketing. Collaboration in this case is essentially a question of (usually expensive) sponsoring, like the life-long deal between LeBron James and Nike. But is there still really any point in having overpaid sports stars appear in candy bar adverts, when foodies - who are close to their network and cost a fraction of the price - can share innovative dessert recipes involving its use?

Sustainable relations and sustainable business
Fans like to see their own thoughts and feelings mirrored in the values that a brand projects. They want to see their own lifestyle reflected back at them. A brand that invests in the passions and values of its customers lays the basis for a sustainable relationship, irrespective of whether the product is Freetrade certified, ecologically responsible, organically grown, hand-made or whatever.

The Dutch chocolate brand Tony's Chocolonely is extremely popular and trendy on its home turf and beyond. However, the brand refuses to pay for advertising. It does have a marketing director, who has developed the Tony's Chocolonely Friends strategy. The chocolate maker believes that when people hear its story they will be so impressed that they will automatically want to spread the story further. This means that Tony's Chocolonely needs to get its story to as many people as possible to get the ball rolling. With this in mind, the company offers its fans ready-made and convenient tools, such as a lecture package (downloaded on average 600 times each week). It also encourages staff to tell their version of the brand story in Tony Talks, short films which are then shared on social media. The communication approach consists of three simple steps: 'Tony's makes aware', 'Tony's sets the example' and 'Good examples are followed'.

Tony's Chocolonely is an example of a company that believes in the power of 'storydoing', which takes thing a stage further than 'storytelling'. As the name implies, you need to do more than just tell your story; you need to live that story in your actions every single day. Having management live and breathe the story does not suffice; staff and customers must be inspired as well. This implies the need for a strong brand ambassador mentality among a group of remarkably loyal and strident fans.

Retail can no longer be defined as the straightforward sale of products. People nowadays go in search of all kinds of information, tips and tricks that can help them to achieve their own personal objectives. A company that shares its knowledge with its customers, communicates openly and transparently, and shows itself to be an expert in its field, will attract their attention and win their trust.

 // People are searching for Instagram-worthy experiences that give them social capital. //

The shop as advertising space

'The shop experience can be something more than just a way to spend money.' These are the words of Rachel Shechtman, who has put the term 'retail media' firmly on the retail map with her STORY store concept in New York. According to Shechtman, retail is an ideal media channel, which can initiate meaningful dialogue between customers and brands.

To prove her point, she developed an unconventional business model based on the publishing world: brands pay her for space in her store, even if not a single product passes the check-out. At STORY, brands are sponsors, who provide products in exchange for a contact moment with the consumer. Shechtman effectively sells advertising space in what has become a kind of walk-through magazine.

To prove her success: department store chain Macy's ended up acquiring the concept store, recruiting Schechtman as Macy's' brand experience officer. The entrepreneur is expected to enrich the stores' experiences and to help bring brand activations to the department stores, even calling the appointment an important step in its path to renewed growth.

STORY is a magazine, a gallery and a shop all rolled into one. Every few months, the store is emptied and a new theme installed, such as Wellness, Love and Fresh. There are no fixed collections or product ranges. Each time, the content is new and specific. As a result, the STORY model is sometimes described as being 'curated shopping': the shop owner acts as a curator, carefully putting together a range of 'exhibits', just like an exhibition in a museum. The products are treated as part of the story.

The customer experience is based on three C's: content, community and commerce. 'If you look at what people do in a shop, you see social interaction, a voyage of discovery and a purchasing process. We try to give our shopping experience a format that allows us to offer more than one thing: we provide information about all our brands, organize events and, of course, encourage our customers to buy!' dixit Schechtman.

STORY's income is dependent on the brands, not the number of people who buy things in the store. Immediate consumption - right then and there - is not the objective. It often happens that shoppers leave STORY and go and buy the products they have seen in the brand flagship stores. It is all the same to Schechtman, as long as her customers - the brands - are happy. Instead of placing the focus on product sales, which is what usually happens in retail, she has switched the emphasis to the servicing of brands.

The same thing happens online. More and more shops are being conceived as dynamic platforms, with blogs, social media support and a strong focus on content experience, in keeping with the search of the modern consumer for something more than material consumption. And since marketing is evolving from storytelling to storydoing, this increases the potential for branded commercial experiences.

People are searching for Instagram-worthy experiences that give them social capital. So when marketing goes omnichannel, it must remember not to lose sight of the physical space. Everything can be an experience location, from a smart mirror in a fitting room to a smart lift in a multi-storey car park. Why shouldn't your brand sponsor chairs at a trendy hairdressing salon, where you can perhaps also create a relaxation corner, so that people can try your refreshments, gadgets or care products while they are waiting to have their hair done?

Of course, anyone who persuades brands to pay simply for the display of their products (or sometimes just their name) must always be able to offer something in return. The return on marketing campaigns is always a delicate matter, which in the shopping environment of the future will largely be settled by data. 'We base all our stories on a list of demands we get from our sponsor brand. Since these differ from sponsor to sponsor, ranging from content creation to research and development, we let the demands decide our angle of approach. In this way, we can offer a specific, tailor-made experience, which gives them the guarantee of a good return,' explains the STORY boss.

At the moment, there is more certainty about the return online than offline, simply because there is more data online to quantify it. However, efforts are being made to develop new technology that will also help the offline measuring process. STORY is already active in the data gathering field inside their store and works with heat maps to show which zones and/or products were most visited and also which were most picked up. Likewise at Spacified, the participating brands are rewarded with information in the form of demographic data obtained from customer counters, cameras and wifi tracking (also see the chapter on 'The Future of Technology'). That being said, the analysis of customer behaviour in an offline environment still meets (for the time being) with greater resistance than its analysis online.

Brands that view things in larger terms than simply hiring part of someone else's floor space can always opt for their own flagship stores and brand shops, as we discussed at the start of the book. But sometimes you never know where these temporary or part stores are going to lead. For example, the pop-up ice-cream parlours of the Magnum brand began as a temporary brand activation stunt but were such a success that they have been developed into a large chain of permanent Magnum Pleasure Stores. Responding to the personalization trend, the stores allow you to create your own unique Magnum ice-cream from a variety of toppings and decorations. The shops are not directly operated by the brand owner, Unilever, but by a local catering distributer, who sees this retail outlet as a useful sideline.

DAS TESTKAUFHAUS

Feedback Factory, the world's first startup supermarket

Berlin houses the world's first startup supermarket Feedback Factory - originally named Kaufhaus des Testens, or KaDeTe, but the famous German department store KaDeWe did not appreciate the nudge - that only sells products that are not yet, or barely, available in retail or wholesale.

The physical marketplace gives start-up brands and companies the chance to get in touch with both consumers and buyers. Here, starting brands from all possible sectors can trial selling their goods to consumers. However, selling is only one part of it: this marketplace also offers market research.

Comparable to STORY in New York, Feedback Factory builds networks and links companies to each other by targeting three target groups. Consumers can try out and buy new, innovative products, while contributing to 'live' market research for the startups. Buyers for retail chains then gain access to the sales figures and market research insights to choose the right products for their stores. Finally, the start-ups are given both the opportunity to reach the consumer and to be picked up by buyers and investors.

As a startup network, Feedback Factory is constantly on the lookout for new partners. This is how ProSiebenSat.1 Accelerator already joined in, the investment vehicle of a German television group that supports startups through media and advertising campaigns. Feedback Factory does not rule out the possibility of becoming an incubator itself.

Timing is everything

Even the most wonderful story in the world will be a complete waste of time and effort if it reaches the people for whom it is intended at the wrong time. Today, many of us are almost constantly online. As a result, today's customer journey, certainly in comparison with the past, has a much more fragmented look. Purchasing decisions that used to be made at one or two moments - for example, in a shop or at an info session - are now the product of hundreds of different moments at various points along the customer pathway.

Google divides this pathway into what it calls 'moments of truth' (see the chapter on 'Towards a replenishment economy'), which today take the form of a continuous loop rather than a linear straight line. Every moment in the customer loop is now so short and fleeting that they have become micro-moments (Google, 2015). Whether they want to place an order or are merely searching for information, people want to find what they are looking for instantly. Mobile devices have made this possible. If something springs into our mind, we grab our smartphone and seconds later our curiosity is satisfied. What's more, this is a trend that will intensify as technology gets closer to our person (wearables) and becomes more intuitive (speech-directed digital assistants).

A micro-moment is characterized by intention (people consciously seek contact), context (it is preceded by a thought) and immediacy (it must happen now, not later). These are the moments when people reach for their phone to find what they want or need. During these brief contact moments, companies must be present, useful and fast. Google distinguishes four different types of micro-moment (Gozin, 2017):

- I want to know something.
- I want to go somewhere.
- I want to buy something.
- I want to do something.

People come into contact with brands for short periods and at different times. It is up to the brands (and retailers) to be ready to exploit these moments with short, impactful and interesting messages. Only then might people be willing to devote a few seconds of their precious time and highly prized attention to what the brand wants to say. But if there is no instant 'wow', they will hit the close button.

According to Google, people expect above all that experiences are relevant, personal and helpful. This is the only way they can play a meaningful role in people's day-to-day lives. With 'I want to know something' and 'I want to do something' moments, people are usually searching for honest and objective information. They are in the orientation phase and possibly still far away from the first moment of truth, the moment when they decide to make a purchase. Brands who respond truthfully to this request - and to nothing else, because that's all he wants at the moment, and he wants it fast! - will already score points in the user's perception. If, however, the user is in a sales moment, he must be able to find the correct 'specs' at a product level with equal speed and efficiency.

If companies opt to reach their target group via the smartphone, they would be wise to make best use of the data available to them about the customer's circumstances (time of day, location, etc.) at the moment they want to interact with him. This is the only way to provide him with the information he needs at the moment he needs it.

The above paragraphs should make clear that existing media such as television, smartphones and social media all still have an important role to play for marketeers. Those who choose TV as a medium are well advised to integrate their brand and its story directly into relevant amusement programmes, in a manner that so arouses the curiosity of consumers that they are prompted to seek further contact away from the television screen.

In addition, new technologies also offer numerous opportunities to get closer to brand fans. Social media is not the platform to bother consumers with message after unwanted message, but it is the perfect tool for one-to-one communication with a fan. Chatting is no longer a-commercial but allows companies to keep a finger on the pulse of what is happening when problems or questions about their brand arise. Alertness and a problem-solving approach will help to keep your company 'top of mind', so that confidence in your brand grows. Deploying the necessary technology that makes it possible for fans to keep in contact with each other is essential if you want to build any community — and therefore also a community around your brand.

Self-evidently, products and packaging are also part of the brand story. Technological innovations now make it feasible to integrate additional product information, benefits, recipes and other extras, which shoppers can discover with their smartphone. Aids such as augmented reality and virtual reality open up new perspectives to immerse consumers in your brand world and to provide them with unique experiences that have never been possible before.

It is clear that the coming of age of the digital world inevitably means that marketing and advertising need to undergo a radical change of course. The fundamental changes in society in recent years have also revolutionized the way brands need to relate to their customers and also the rules of the game by which this relationship is governed. Ignore these new rules at your peril!

'The Future of the Supply Chain': the challenge of efficient delivery

The circular economy

Many different ecological problems are putting the linear economic model under pressure. This model presupposes a value chain that begins with natural resources (raw materials to make products) and ends with waste matter (products that have reached the end of their useful life and have no value). Governments around the world are doing their best to ensure the optimum recycling and the most effective treatment of this waste matter, but everyone agrees that something now needs to be done to reduce the size of the waste mountain.

// An ecological way of thinking is no longer the preserve of a group of moral crusaders wearing goat-wool socks. //

An ecological way of thinking is no longer the preserve of a group of moral crusaders wearing goat-wool socks, as the broad public success of the products of companies like Ecover (owned today by SC Johnson) demonstrates. Founded in 1980 in a warehouse with walls covered in paintings of flowers and CND symbols, the company has evolved into an efficient professional organization with hyper-modern facilities. Today, Ecover is the largest producer of environmentally friendly cleaning products in the world. It was (and still is) a company far ahead of its time, with a clear vision that it was not afraid to broadcast, day in day out. It is living proof that 'storydoing' works.

Closing the loop

The life cycle of products needs to be extended to the maximum possible extent and, where possible, replaced by a life circle. Closing the loop is not only the most socially responsible model, but also the most economically interesting one.

The reuse of 'old' raw materials from the recycling of worn-out or broken end products offers an alternative for the repeat purchase of 'new' raw materials. Electronics retailers have already been offering bonuses for quite some time to people who hand in their old smartphone when they are buying a new one, but now clothing stores like H&M are also putting forward marketing and sales arguments that old clothes should be returned to them for recycling.

Gunter Pauli, the ex-CEO of Ecover and author of *The Blue Economy* (2010), leaves no one in any doubt that this ecological approach is a sustainable economic model. In terms of business potential, Pauli understandably points to the possibility of your company profiling itself as an innovator (Snoeck, 2014). In an era where differentiation is a central task for any brand or company that wants to be successful, this is a useful trump card to have, but it is supplemented by the economic advantages of a more optimized and less wasteful production chain. In a circular economy the residual value of a product for the first time becomes positive (because it is reusable) instead of negative (because waste costs money to dispose of).

Cradle-to-cradle

C&A was the first global retailer to launch fully waste-free t-shirts with its 'Cradle to Cradle Certified Gold' t-shirt collection. The shirts are completely reusable and 100% bio-degradable: you could just throw it on the compost heap in your garden. What's more, the collection is available in two models and 17 different colours, and is made entirely from organically grown cotton. C&A sees the collection as the next logical step in its sustainability strategy, since the budget fashion chain claims already to be one of the biggest buyers of organically grown cotton in the world.

For companies to obtain cradle-to-cradle certification, an independent analysis of their entire production chain is made: from a toxicological analysis of the raw materials used, through water and energy use, to the social conditions of production. To be able to guarantee a 'no waste' solution, it is crucial that thought is devoted to every aspect of the production process and its sustainability as early as the drawing board phase.

'What distinguishes cradle-to-cradle is the fact that it is a resolutely positive approach,' explains Frans Beckers of EPEA, which helps companies to apply the cradle-to-cradle methodology in concrete terms (*RetailDetail Magazine*, 2014). 'We return to basics, to the core of the design process in order to create products that are, in essence, sustainable. At the present time, companies are largely engaged in passive recycling: it is only after a product comes to the end of its life that they look to find a solution for the waste and limit the damage it can cause. But you can also practice an active form of recycling, by already thinking during the design stage about how the component elements can be reused later on without any loss of quality.'

Lengthening the chain
Cradle-to-cradle is a good way to close the loop, but it is not yet a watertight system and may take some time to become so. For the time being, extending the life cycle of products and lengthening the chain of the linear economy as far as possible is still a sensible alternative strategy. Claus Skytte, founder of Resecond, the first exchange store for clothes, identified eight phases in the classic linear economy (Skytte & Dreier, 2015):

- research;
- innovation;
- financing;
- production;
- distribution;
- retail;
- consumption;
- destruction.

He aims to replace this final step - destruction - with three additional phases:
- optimized consumption;
- sharing;
- recycling.

More and more initiatives are attempting to extend the life cycle of products through sharing and recycling. Just outside Stockholm in Sweden, you can find the world's first recycling shopping centre: ReTuna. ReTuna Återbruksgalleria (to give it its full name) only sells products that have been donated by people and have been repaired or reconfigured by teams of local authority workers. 'Sustainability is not about restraining yourself and living less; it is about doing more with the things we already have available,' say the founders.

All the donated items are spread over 14 different shops in the centre according to product category. Amongst other things, you can find an electrical goods shop, a furniture store and a restaurant with organic food. All the retailers in the centre are committed to working in an environmentally-friendly manner and all the new products for sale (right down to the food in the restaurant) must be organic and/or climate-friendly.

Jules Clarysse
pure bath & kitchen
A new and sustainable start

Towel manufacturer Jules Clarysse has been awarded a cradle-to-cradle certificate for a number of items in its product line. The fact that the company survived the fall-out of the economic crisis was in large part due to its circular strategy. When the price-consciousness of its mainly private label customers reached new heights and cotton prices also soared as a result of poor harvests, the management decided to radically change course. It opted to play the sustainability card and before long was making towels from recycled jeans material.

The company developed a production line based on what it called 'post consumer textile' - in other words, material that had already been through consumer hands. This differentiation was its salvation and today Jules Clarysse is the only remaining towelling manufacturer in Belgium and a European pioneer, trading all over the world.

Take this idea a stage further and you end up with the not-so-fresh market, like the pop-up Oz Harvest Market in Australia, which sells food exclusively rescued from the rubbish dump or donated by catering outlets, but which is still perfectly edible. The buyers set their own prices, giving what they can or what they think is fair. 'Social grocers' of this kind are not a new phenomenon, but in these harsher modern times are coming to stand more in the centre of society than on its fringes.

MUD JEANS
COTTON LEASE

Mud Jeans leases jeans

Mud Jeans applies the circular economy to fashion. Although the Dutch jeans company has not managed to close the loop completely, it still goes a long way towards it by consistently recycling its jeans. To encourage people not to leave unused or worn-out jeans hanging in their cupboards, in 2013 the company launched its award-winning Lease-A-Jeans programme, which made it possible for people to rent jeans instead of buying them. After an agreed period, you either bring the jeans back to the store or else you buy them. Even then, the buyers are encouraged, when the jeans finally wear out, to return them to the store for recycling instead of just throwing them away. What is possible for mattresses (see Auping earlier in this book) is also possible for clothes.

Short chain

While producers and retailers on the consumer side are busy trying to lengthen the life cycle of products, they are also equally busy trying to shorten the supply chain. For example, to make their business model in personalized shoes possible, Shoes of Prey felt obliged to take production into its own hands. In this way, it was able to cut its delivery times to customers from ten weeks to just one week - one of its key selling points. By opening its own factory in China, Shoes of Prey was able to optimize its processes for its personalization model, which had seemed so difficult to achieve in factories not under its direct control. 'Manufacturers rely on volume with the tiniest of margins, so for them it is incredibly difficult to adjust to something out of the ordinary. But personalization on a large scale is not possible without a strong underlying production process,' explains CEO Michael Fox.

Retailers and brands understand that it can work to their advantage if they can cut links out of the supply chain, especially if you need to compete with the big 'fast-fashion' players like Zara and H&M. In reality, of course, it is usually the fast-fashion players who set the standard for the short chain in the clothing industry. Speed has become the norm, especially since today's shoppers are more impatient than ever. Speed supremo is the Japanese Uniqlo, which has shortened the production process from design table to shop shelf to an amazing 13 days! (Van Looveren, 2017). This just pips Zara, which also regularly manages the same feat in two weeks.

// In the battle for the crucial 'last mile', physical stores are also coming back into the picture. //

Speed is just one of the benefits from a shortened supply chain. Nearly all new business plans in retail and FMCG make use of the same idea: by eliminating some of the links in the chain, brands can get better control over their supply, whilst at the same time cutting costs and increasing margins. Thanks to its streamlined vertical integration, Made.com can monitor things at close range and react to any situation rapidly, allowing them to work with maximum flexibility, says Damien Poelhekke (Van Looveren, 2016), director for Belgium and the Netherlands: 'Using historical data, we can see exactly what expected output should be. We look at these details weekly, so that we can assess our stock, monitor trends and adjust our purchasing quickly, if necessary. That is the advantage of the short supply chain in our model. We launch at lot of new collections, but we can also quickly terminate a collection if it is not selling well'. Note that big data is essential to this process.

The shift of retailers towards private labels is also a common feature in efforts to shorten the chain, with the intention of creating a (more) direct supply flow, while from the opposite direction FMCG manufacturers are also climbing higher up the chain to knock out expensive or slow-moving links. In the food industry, a shorter chain also has a clear emotional value for the end consumer. Perhaps for this combination of reasons, the model is becoming increasingly popular.

The battle for the last mile

The shopper wants to receive his purchases quickly and efficiently. The most recent competitive battle in online retail is therefore the battle for the last mile. In the world of omnichannel, whoever makes it first to the customer's home for the final delivery, almost quite literally has a foot in the door.

However, the issues relating to delivery are more complex than merely getting packages *linea recta* to someone's doorstep. What's more, retailers need to do everything possible to keep delivery costs as low as possible; otherwise, the convenience they offer will eat even further into their already meagre margins.

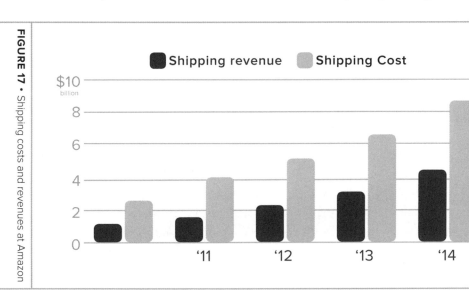

FIGURE 17 · Shipping costs and revenues at Amazon

Returns as a necessary evil

Regular returns are another drain on a retailer's profitability. In 2013, the Zalando management admitted that the returns percentage was somewhere around 50% (Evert e.a., 2013). Since then, they (and most others) have stubbornly refused to comment further on the matter, but in online retail, at least 30% of purchases are indeed returned, calculates Alec Minnema, who at the start of 2017 obtained his doctorate from the State University of Groningen with a thesis on this subject.

The cost of returns averages 12.5% of the sale price. This not only includes the dispatch costs, but also the cost of the processing, the repacking and the fact that some goods are no longer in a condition to be resold, which is a particular problem in the fashion industry, where the return rate is highest (35%) and the longevity of goods shortest.

Given these figures, it is little wonder that companies are investing heavily in technical solutions for smart and virtual fitting rooms or 'try-on' software. For example, the start-up Curvetips screens the clothing on websites using artificial intelligence and only shows customers the items that suit and fit them, based on their personal profile. This leads to higher conversions and lower returns.

Even so, it is also important to keep on investing in free returns, according to research by Minnema (Minnema, 2017). A cost-free return policy results in more sales, because people perceive less risk. As a result, people are more inclined to recommend the webshop to others. Minnema suggests that it is also a good idea to map and analyze the return behaviour of individual customers. Although most companies do not make use of 'return by' dates, profits increase by an average of 20% when they do.

With same day delivery and instant returns, Zalando wants to push up its convenience levels even higher. In collaboration with its logistical service providers in different European cities, such as London and Paris, it offers an option for customers to try on their deliveries on arrival and have them collected half an hour later if they decide not to buy them. 'Today, convenience is the customer's main concern. Deliveries and returns are both key moments, since they have a direct impact on purchasing behaviour and customer loyalty,' dixit Pingki Houang, CEO of Stuart France, Zalando's courier service in France (Merieau, 2016).

Retailers become logistical service providers

The question then becomes how to organize your logistics as efficiently as possible to keep the costs as manageable as possible: with your own courier service or by outsourcing? Doing it yourself is still prohibitively expensive, say most omnichannel retailers. But Amazon thinks differently and is systematically taking over elements of the logistical process. From using its own planes to the bringing of its purchases from the Chinese interior to the country's ports, Amazon now wants full control of the logistical chain. This centralization is cheaper for the online giant, but is also a way to keep all aspects of their business internal, keep out prying eyes and ensuring contact with the consumer.

American rival Walmart (partly) thinks the same and is going to use its own retail staff as couriers for the delivery of online orders. The staff will deliver packages to people's homes while they are on their way to or from work. This isn't the fastest method of delivery, but it is certainly the cheapest and most personal. While the Walmart employee is at the customer's home, it is possible to make direct contact. This can be useful to offer other Walmart services or gather information that Walmart can use in future. For a retailer with a wide-ranging assortment like Walmart, this is an opportunity to do cross-selling on the doorstep or perhaps even to pick up the customer's shopping list for next week! It also appeals to the type of customer who misses personal contact in our online world. Effectively, Walmart is turning its own staff into offline brand ambassadors. But for this reason it should be seen as part of their salaried job, and not just an unpaid extra they are expected to do for free. Once again: value your human capital (see the chapter on 'The Future of the Store').

For the elderly and people in need of care, a messenger service can also fulfil another role: checking to see that everything is okay. As the group of older people living longer at home continues to grow, there is clearly a market for couriers who can also play an additional care role. In the US, Jersey Post has developed the free Call and Check programme, whereby postal staff call in weekly or in some cases even daily on the elderly customers on their round. In the Netherlands, Wageningen University and the Ding Dong meals service are trialling a scheme that links the delivery of daily groceries and medicines to the provision of medical and dietary advice. And even the local franchise holders of many supermarkets are now doing something similar, by keeping a friendly eye on their more vulnerable customers when they deliver meals to their homes, just like the village grocer of 50 years ago. 'Back to the future for shopping'.

The Dutch online food delivery service Picnic takes things a step further, by not only dealing entirely with its own logistics, but also making deliveries for other retailers! 'We are going to the customer's house anyway, so why not take along the book he ordered from Amersfoort as well. We are also happy to collect the returns of other webshops,' explains Picnic (Te Pas, 2016).

Fulfilment: a fulfilling business model

Large web retailers like Amazon, Bol.com and Zalando offer such sharp prices and have such huge marketing costs that their products hardly make any profit at all. As a result, they search for other forms of income, including marketing and advertising for the partners on their platform, but also the fulfilment of the logistical needs of these partners.

Zalando, for example, has developed Zalando Fulfilment Solutions, which gives fashion brands access to Zalando's logistical infrastructure and knowledge. Within a logistical network of eight fulfilment centres in five different countries, Zalando is already providing the logistical services for international fashion groups like Bestseller, Elvi, EVITA, Motion Fashion and Surf4Shoes. 'With this service, Zalando takes over the order processing for our partners from the moment of ordering until any eventual returns. This initiative is complementary to the digital services that the Zalando platform already offers, such as Brand Solutions or Zalando Media Solutions,' says the company's own website.

The Zalando platform wants to be 'a management system for the fashion world', providing different options to bring together different kinds of fashion brands and meet their various needs. 'It not only offers digital services such as data analysis and advertising, but from now on also fulfilment solutions, so that it becomes an integral part of the business strategy of brand partners and retailers,' according to Jan Bartels, VP Logistics Product at Zalando (Bentvelsen, 2017).

Likewise, JD.com handles logistics for other retailers and brands in China. JD.com has struck a deal with Unilever to move its products, both food and non-food, to warehouses and stores in more remote parts of China. Earlier, French brand producer Danone set up the same type of partnership with JD.com. In a move to differentiate from Alibaba, the Chinese company is banking heavily on logistics: with over 500 warehouses it promises to deliver over 90 percent of orders on the same or next day, even in the most hard-to-reach regions of China.

It was nonetheless Alibaba that first pioneered this integrated approach and it now seems that the western platforms are converting themselves in the image of the Chinese model, suggesting they are trying to beat the Chinese at their own game - which will not be easy.

Shops doubling as distribution centres: is the future omni?

In the battle for the crucial 'last mile', physical stores are also coming back into the picture: as well as being contact and marketing points, they are also local supply points. Omnichannel presents retailers with a serious logistical challenge, in which the bar for stock management is being set ever higher. Try explaining to shoppers who order something in a store that they have to wait a few days for the delivery of their product, when you know the webshops are offering the same product with same-day delivery. It just won't wash.

In an effort to tackle this problem, more and more companies are setting up hybrid distribution networks. Physical stores with an attached distribution centre can serve a double purpose as both a service point and a logistical hub, where shoppers can come both to ask questions and to collect their packages, and perhaps even try them and, if necessary, return them. In this way, an aspect of the online revolution that is generally regarded as a disadvantageous and unnecessary cost can actually be turned into an asset - providing you can calculate your stock accurately using big data analysis.

In the UK, the former post-order company Argos has transformed itself into a real omnichannel pioneer. With 750 stores, it is one of the largest retailers in British high streets and it continues to open new branches (albeit after a drastic restructuring). Argos now focuses on micro-stores and smaller shops in a 'hub-and-spoke' distribution model. The hub store is a large store on the edge of a large city and the spoke stores are smaller stores in the city centre and smaller surrounding towns. As well as being a store in its own right, each hub acts as a supply depot that can provision an average of four to six spoke stores within a matter of hours. In this way, the retailer wins twice: it is not necessary to keep stocks of every product in every store but Argos can still promise its customers same-day delivery.

The combination of fulfilment centre and retail store is becoming increasingly common. The electrical goods giant Best Buy and the Amazon Prime Now hubs both make use of the system. But the real pioneer in this field is the Russian e-commerce leader Ulmart, which has three large distribution centres outside cities supplying forty urban fulfilment centres. These Kiber markets are open day and night, and customers can either collect packages ordered online or else order directly on site. The order is processed immediately and the buyers can track its progress digitally in real time. The Ulmart fulfilment centres can usually deliver most products to a customer's home within two hours, and there is even an option to pay in cash, which is what most Russians prefer.

// In the battle for the crucial 'last mile', physical stores are also coming back into the picture. //

The spreading of stocks is an important trend, that most leading retail companies are starting to apply. Increasingly, the product range is distributed over a growing number of supply points. As such, the creation of hybrid distribution networks brings the products closer to the consumer. Thanks to the availability of big data, these types of connected logistics become possible.

Instead of keeping central stock, distributed networks help retailers keep tight control over the supply decision-making process and especially ensures them speed and flexibility: products are only put into the chain if there is demand. Limiting the inventory in the stores, hub and spoke spreads risks and costs, while also providing a more efficient omnichannel customer service.

The world-leading fashion company Inditex, known from brands such as Zara and Massimo Dutti, plans to integrate its entire stock, both online and offline. CEO Pablo Isla has indicated that the complete integration of the storage rooms in stores and online is a very important strategic point for the fast fashion company.

If an item is no longer available online but still is present in stores, it can be delivered directly to the customer from any store that carries stock. With the ship-from-store service Zara not only wants to serve customers faster, which is an important factor in the competition with online giants like Asos, but it also wants to achieve better control over stocks. By using the physical stores as a logistics hub, it can also remain more relevant and up to date.

Brands can use the strategy of integrating logistics as well, by leveraging inventory at their retail clients stores and web shops. This is the idea behind Miinto, a Danish fashion platform that wants reduce overproduction and waste in fashion, while at the same time supporting local independent store keepers. Overstock in physical stores is a big problem in the fashion industry, as H&M proved when it had to report a serious profit drop due to large quantities of unsold stock in 2017.

Fastest or best?

In the US, there is currently a race between Amazon and Walmart to see who can serve their online customers the fastest. In response to the Amazon Fresh collection points, where members of Amazon Prime can already collect their products just 15 minutes after ordering them, Walmart has introduced automated collection points that are open around the clock. These kiosks can hold up to 30,000 products, including cooled and frozen food and drink.

The modern customer's expectation that he can collect his packages when and where he likes is something that causes many logistics experts sleepless nights. In response, they have developed a variety of creative initiatives: from drones that follow you by GPS and literally drop the package into your hands to hyper-loops through which products - and even people - can be transported at lightning speed. But for the time being these are just ideas. In practice, we are seeing the emergence of more and more locker systems at convenient locations, shared neighbourhood delivery boxes and the delivery of packages 'on the go' by GPS tracking. In the near future, the time when we had to be at home or at work to receive our packages will be no more than a distant memory.

In particular, GPS tracking is coming to the fore in the race to get goods to the shopper as quickly as possible. Parcel company Parcify uses GPS data on the customer's smartphone to locate them precisely, so that their couriers can even deliver to a moving target - as long as it is not moving faster than 3 mph! In other words, fine for walking shoppers, but not much use for anyone else (yet).

Not walking? No problem! Cars can also transmit signals, so that couriers can find them and leave your package in the boot. With Volvo In-Car Delivery, logistics companies can gain one-time access to your boot using a digital key, following which you will get a text message to say the delivery has taken place. In partnership with DHL and Audi, Amazon has also carried out boot delivery trials in Munich, although with this system the driver still needed to let the delivery company know via an app where his car was parked. And if you are fortunate enough to have a Daimler smart car, you can use it as either a delivery or a return point.

In the future, robots and drones will again be the replacements for (expensive) human couriers. Many tests are taking place, with varying degrees of seriousness and success, but the robot of Tesco Now is already capable of making deliveries in London within an hour. It can do this completely independently, within a five mile radius of any Tesco supermarket. You can follow the robot's progress by app and they are protected against theft en route. It is certainly a more environmentally-friendly option than the many delivery vans and refrigerated trucks that currently clog our streets and foul our air. As pollution regulations and traffic restrictions are tightened, such robots seem to offer companies a win-win solution: cheaper and cleaner. Does this perhaps mean that the gig economy is in danger? And what about when 3D printers really take off?

Any idea you can think of, no matter how bizarre, has probably already been patented by Amazon. Letting people select the bus or train on which they want their package delivered while commuting to work? Amazon is looking into it. Keeping drivers and transporters in perpetual motion? They've got that covered as well. One patent even suggests that in future Amazon wants to keep complete mobile fulfilment centres on the road. If the company can then predict with sufficient accuracy what people in that area are going to buy, products can be dropped off almost as soon as they are ordered, or perhaps even before. The replenishment economy (see the chapter on 'The Future of Technology') may be closer than we think.

'Future of the Supermarket': will the supermarket survive the 21st century?

Customers were amazed when they entered the first Delhaize store in Brussels, Belgium, on 18 December 1957. It was the first supermarket on the European mainland and, at 400 square metre, was at least ten times bigger than the grocer's shops that people were used to. With its 3,000 references, it also sold ten times more products. Shoppers needed to use a cart instead of a basket and they stared goggle-eyed at the neon lighting, the flashy in-store advertising and the huge piles of tins and packages in all shapes and sizes. Above all, the sale of pre-packed meat was revolutionary. The opening of the store also provoked a storm of protest in some quarters: the local retailers felt threatened. And rightly so, as events proved: the supermarket soon became the dominant distribution concept for food.

The inspiration for Delhaize came from the US, where the Piggly Wiggly stores of entrepreneur Clarence Saunders had introduced the self-service concept as long ago as 1916, while the first supermarket proper was opened in New York City in 1930 under the name King Kullen (after its founder, Michael J. Cullen). With its area of 560 square metre, a spacious parking and a strategy of shifting large volumes at low prices, this model was already displaying most of the features that we still associate with supermarkets today.

Supermarkets have essentially changed little since their big breakthrough in the 1960s. The stores got bigger, their assortment of products grew, and new technology made its appearance to speed things up, like the electric cash register, the scanning of bar codes and (later) self-scanning. There were also variations, both large and small, on the same supermarket theme, ranging from hard discount to hypermarket. But the basic concept remained essentially the same: customers were offered the possibility to do all their food shopping in a single visit under a single roof at low prices never previously seen, now made possible by cost management and economies of scale.

Is this model now reaching the end of the road? Several chains have already been forced to close or to restructure. Food producers are being compelled to cut back and relocate, while farmers are now often selling their vegetables and meat at a loss. In addition, the classic supermarket model is being challenged by new models of food production and distribution. As in all other sectors, the advent of internet technology is playing a key role. Although the market share of online food sales remains relatively low, it is growing rapidly and putting the traditional balance of power in the sector under greater pressure, a trend enhanced by social factors like an ageing population, urbanization and mobility.

 // In addition, the classic supermarket model is being challenged by new models of production and distribution in food.

The rise of the sharing economy (think of free distribution groups and public allotments) is eating away at the foundations of our food system. Increasingly aware consumers are turning their back on industrialization and renewing their search for 'real' food. Farmers and producers are now selling their wares directly to the consumer; they don't need the supermarket anymore. Specialized shops are also starting to make their reappearance, both online and offline. The emphasis is shifting from selling products to selling meal solutions, so that the distinction between food retail and foodservice is becoming ever more blurred.

Shoppers have more options than ever before and are making choices. As a result, shopping behaviour is becoming increasingly fragmented. The supermarket as the one-stop shop is starting to feel the pinch. The confrontational question in the title of this chapter needs to be asked: will the supermarket survive the 21st century?

The end of the lowest price?

From its earliest days, the lowest price was always the big attraction of supermarkets. The self-service model increased productivity and economies of scale yielded purchasing discounts. As more and more supermarket players appeared on the market, the promise of the lowest price was no longer enough, so that supermarkets started adding new products and services to differentiate themselves.

Marketing students are taught that you need to make a choice to position your brand correctly. If you want to offer the lowest price, you can't have the best range of products as well. If you invest in attractive stores, they can't be the cheapest. The formula for the first international successes of Aldi was simple: as a discounter, you can promise the lowest prices, in return for which the customer has to accept poor service, bare shelves and a limited assortment. In contrast, full-service supermarkets offered more choice, fresh products and well-trained, customer-friendly staff in a pleasant shopping environment, all made possible by higher prices. There was no need to panic on either side: the market was still not saturated, so that there was still room for growth through expansion, without the competitors really getting in each other's way.

The classic model of the Wheel of Retail, whereby new competitors enter the market at a low price level that gradually becomes more refined, only began to change at the end of the 1980s and the start of the 1990s. By then, the market was saturated and competition for market share was fierce. Everywhere, new supermarkets were appearing that seemed to challenge the existing price versus service dichotomy - and scored heavily as a result. This is what retail consultant Hans Eysink Smeets (2014) calls the 'no compromise' trend (see Figure 18). The winners succeeded in throwing the compromise between price and service overboard - a model that was applied with equal success by some non-food retailers, as witnessed by the rapid rise of fast-fashion chains like H&M, Zara or Primark.

The UK saw the spectacular growth of Tesco, which combined low prices with a full assortment, a qualitative offer of fresh produce, and well-trained, helpful staff. Belgium had Colruyt; in the Netherlands, Jumbo started 'Zeven Zekerheden' (Seven Certainties); in France, the rise of E. Leclerc was unstoppable; in Spain, the winner was Mercadona... The logic was always the same: the customer is no longer willing to accept compromise so we need to offer low prices, a complete range and top service. All these players quickly conquered market share and forced the competition to respond.

And that is precisely what the competition did. During the past decade almost everyone has tried to imitate the successful 'no-compromise' players. Everyone wants to be in the top right-hand quadrant of the graphic. Aldi and Lidl have increased their levels of service, thereby moving to the right. They have also added fresh produce and A-brands to their offer and upgraded their shops, allowing them to widen their customer circle still further. In contrast, traditional service players like Delhaize and Carrefour in Belgium or Albert Heijn in the Netherlands have invested more in price reduction in an attempt to move upwards in the graphic, but with varying success.

The consequences of the 'no compromise' strategy have been harsh: everyone now competes with everyone else in an increasingly shrinking market. This has resulted in savage price and promotion wars, in which no holds are barred and no prisoners are taken. Margins have been pared to the bone and suppliers presented with ultimatums they cannot refuse. Among others, Tesco, Carrefour, Sainsbury's, Cora and Rewe have all undergone painful restructurings as a result. Is there no way out of this damaging spiral of price wars?

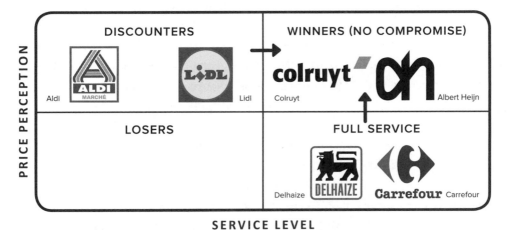

FIGURE 18 • Price versus service: the 'no compromise' model

These developments have certainly allowed room for new players to establish a differentiating positioning for themselves. Whole Foods, Eataly, Waitrose and the many new fresh markets have muscled in on the bottom-right quadrant. Low-end retailers like Action have moved into the top-left. Many online initiatives - think of Hello Fresh - are also staking a claim in the bottom-right. It is still open to discussion whether there is room for online discount concepts in this model, but this hasn't stopped Aldi UK from opening a wine webshop and Lidl from launching non-food webshops in several countries.

In his book *Penetration* (2015) marketing professor Marcel Corstjens asks why supermarket chains fail to turn the beneficial purchasing conditions they can impose on their suppliers into decent margins and profits. The profitability of the large food retailers is significantly lower than the large brand producers, while at the same time the producers are constantly complaining about the retailers' abuse of power in demanding ever lower prices. According to Professor Corstjens, there is something here that does not add up. If the retailers are so powerful, why aren't they richer?

Corstjens calls this the Robin Hood syndrome. Just like Robin Hood stole from the rich to give to the poor, so the food retailers demand lower prices from the producers that they can pass on to their shoppers. Retailers have power over their producers, but not over their customers. Because consumers tend to see little difference between the different retailers, they are happy to switch from one supermarket to another. Retailers know this and therefore opt for the quickest and easiest form of differentiation: price competition. Even though they also know that price can only offer them a competitive advantage for a very short period, soon to be eliminated by the price response of rival chains.

// Supermarket chains are compelled to attract as large a public as possible, but this make differentiation extremely difficult. //

The business model of the supermarket is characterized by high fixed costs and low margins. Whether there are ten or a hundred and ten shoppers in a supermarket makes no difference to expenditure on premises, operations and staff. Supermarket chains are therefore compelled to try and attract as large a public as possible to make profit from their narrow margins - but this makes differentiation extremely difficult. In contrast to the brand producers, they cannot afford to aim at specific shopper segments. True, they develop additional services, but this demands investment. Even if you are successful, the idea is instantly copied by your rivals. Moreover, research shows that shoppers are only reluctantly prepared to pay for a better supermarket shopping experience. So is differentiation really a viable alternative for food retailers?

In search of differentiation

The consumer's choice of shop is determined in the first instance by proximity. People shop in their own neighbourhood or on their way to work or school. In the mature and densely populated societies of Western Europe, this usually means a choice between four or five supermarkets. The nearest doesn't always win but the fifth supermarket will need some pretty convincing arguments to persuade shoppers to pass the other four. So although it goes against their nature, supermarkets have no other option than to make a choice of their own. Nobody can be the best in everything. A sharp price will remain a minimum, but the challenge consists in developing additional services for which the shopper is willing to pay, which aren't too easy for rivals to copy and for which the necessary investment can soon be earned back.

If supermarkets are competing with each other on an increasingly smaller playing field, space will inevitably be created elsewhere, both at the top and the bottom of the market, and perhaps even at its sides. This is where differentiating players have the opportunity to make a difference. Let's have a look at some of the possibilities.

Differentiation on price

Received wisdom says that 'only one can be the cheapest'. Even so, in most markets a number of different price-fighters are battling it out with each other. Aldi and Lidl are active in most European countries and are often joined by local discounters, such as Dia in Spain, Biedronka in Poland and BIM in Turkey. This works, because in the first instance price is a matter of perception - and perception does not always match reality. A strong price image can be the result of smart communication and clever promotional stunts, but it does not necessarily guarantee the lowest price on every product every day.

This makes the unique positioning of the Belgian discounter Colruyt all the more remarkable. They really do guarantee the lowest price on every product every day. Colruyt always reacts to price reductions by competitors, even their temporary promotions. But the chain doesn't have the purchasing power of Aldi and Lidl, nor even of its regional rivals, like Carrefour, Ahold Delhaize or Metro.

Colruyt can only make good its price promises by having a super-efficient, cost-focused organization and a smart approach to local price setting. Nevertheless, it is open to question whether this strategy is viable in the long run, certainly in a world where online barriers are falling away. Perhaps the chain is already starting to recognize this: today you can see them attempting to differentiate with an innovative private label policy and with new shop formulas that do not compete on price: Okay, Bio-Planet, Spar, CRU...

Premiumization

In a strong, price-driven market retailers search for ways to differentiate themselves with (perceived) quality that allows them to set a higher price. However, this involves a difficult balancing act between market penetration (to be profitable, supermarkets need to reach the largest possible public) and segmentation (not everyone is willing or able to pay higher prices).

The example of Delhaize illustrates just how difficult this balancing act can be. With a market share of 24%, Delhaize is not a niche player: the chain wants to reach all consumers with an offer that is superior in terms of choice and quality to the average Belgian supermarket. The result of this positioning is a less favourable price image. But attempts to sharpen this price image are not without risks of their own. When the retailer switched to a cost and price-cutting strategy in the wake of the 2008 financial crisis, supported by a reduced range, this actually led to a loss of market share, as dissatisfied customers moved elsewhere. In the meantime, the chain has returned to its original quality positioning and now counts on the know-how of merger partner Ahold to become more efficient.

Successful premium concepts in food are generally characterized by a limited market penetration. For example, British Waitrose, with its up-market positioning, needs to be satisfied with just sixth place and a market share of 5%. Similarly, Amazon's Whole Foods Market is also a niche player (or has been until now), notwithstanding a strong reputation in the US and the UK. In Belgium, Carrefour operates a luxury delicatessen-supermarket under the name Rob the Gourmet's Market, but with only a single outlet.

The historic French grocery chain Hédiard even came to the brink of bankruptcy in 2013, but made a fresh start thanks to a takeover by the Austrian investment group Do & Co. Since then, the luxury house has been reorganizing for many years, hoping to reverse the tide of accumulating losses with a new commercial strategy. Its new owner continues to believe in the potential of the Paris icon despite its current reality.

Even so, here and there you can still see the established supermarket chains toying with the idea of the premium concept, frequently at locations where price is assumed to play a less important role, like tourist zones or areas of greater purchasing power.

Carrefour *express* The innovation drive of Carrefour

Carrefour is experimenting with new shop formulas throughout Europe and seems to be aiming primarily for the top of the market. For example, in Madrid the retailer has opened a premium version of its local neighbourhood concept Carrefour Express. The store is located in an exclusive shopping street, la Calle de José Ortega y Gasset, among luxury brands like Armani, Chanel, Dior and Hugo Boss. The Express has an area of just 160 m² and sells 3,700 references, with an emphasis on fresh products. You can find both gastronomic products and ordinary groceries. It is a compact version of the Carrefour Gourmet concept, which was recently launched with a number of outlets in Italy. And this Italian Carrefour Gourmet formula is in turn a luxurious version of the Market concept, aimed at foodies with a selection of regional products and world cuisine.

Carrefour's Market at the Saint-Michel metro station in Paris again seems to have many elements of the Gourmet formula: an 'urban chic' store with wooden furnishings and counters for the sale of fresh goods, a focus on organic and healthy food, a well-stocked wine section and a delivery service. But the Gourmet insignia is nowhere to be seen. Carrefour Poland has also opened a premium Market in Warsaw, an innovative supermarket, with high-tech features such as a ripening room and a smoking room in the meat department and centrifuges so that customers can press juice from the fruit they have selected in the fresh section.

Moreover, in a well-to-do district of Brussels , Carrefour has opened a High-life version of its Market concept. This is a store with a more overtly 'upscale' positioning, where fresh again plays a key role. The design is modern and authentic, with warm materials like wood and brick. Shoppers can discover several novelties, such as ripened meat in the on-site ripening room, a top-end wine section, a good selection of organic products and new references that cannot be found in other Carrefour Market outlets.

'Convenience' is the answer

For a long time it seemed as though the large hypermarkets would completely force the traditional small local shop out of the market. But it didn't happen. On the contrary, today the proximity store is undergoing something of a revival. Societal factors such as urbanization, an ageing population, individualism and mobility issues are stimulating shopper demand for close-at-hand stores with long opening hours and a wide range of products and services at competitive prices. The large retailers have now rolled out this kind of store in nearly every European country: Carrefour Express, Tesco Express, Daily Monop', etc.

// Today the proximity store is undergoing something of a revival. //

Price is not the most important driver for these neighbourhood stores. Special promotions are less relevant than location, accessibility, speed, service and a range of products that responds to the needs of both local customers and passers-by: a meal service, home delivery, a collection point for washing and ironing, a package service, a dry cleaner's, shoe repairs, a photo service. In this way, convenience stores can re-establish their position in every town and village, reassuming their role at the centre of local life. Just like in the old days, yet very different.

BLUE BOX
City store supplies plumber

One of the novelties in the Carrefour Market Urbano, opened in the centre of Turin, is the Blue Box service centre. The fact that you can print off your photos here or arrange online for your washing to be done is no longer so remarkable. What is unusual is the fact that between nine in the morning and nine in the evening Carrefour puts a range of tradesmen at the disposal of its customers. You need a quick repair to your boiler or air-conditioning? Or perhaps an electrician or a locksmith? Blue Box can help. For this service Carrefour works together with Europ Assistance and wants to add more options in the future, such as child minding.

Convenience also means speed. The worst part of any visit to the shops is queuing up at the check-out to pay. It is no surprise that retailers try to make this moment as quick and as painless as possible. Franprix, the neighbourhood shop formula of the French Casino group, is testing a new payment system where shoppers can simply pay between the aisles of products. The staff are all equipped with a scanner, a tablet and a payment terminal, all portable. At Franprix, queuing looks set to become a thing of the past.

Local as the new normal

Each local district is different. There are differences in purchasing power, cultural background, average age and family composition, as discussed in the chapter on 'The Future of the Store'. It is only by better understanding and responding to the needs of their local communities that local supermarkets and neighbourhood stores will be able to differentiate themselves from their rivals and avoid the bloodbath of price competition. For example, if there are lots of businesses in your district, you had better make sure you have a lunchtime sandwich service.

Centrally directed chains sometimes find it difficult to give their local managers the necessary autonomy to make this possible. Independent retailers find it easier to think in terms of local requirements, almost as second nature. They are much closer to their customers, which is why franchises are often more effective at a local level than branch stores.

A noticeable recent trend is the rapid rise of regional products in both large and small supermarkets. In this way, chains underline their local anchoring by entering into partnerships with local producers to set themselves apart from the crowd and create goodwill with their clientele. Many shops now have a separate section with regional products, like in the local projects operated by Carrefour Belgium. This retailer drew up a charter that offered small producers the necessary guarantees in their business relations with the big chain and it also granted its shop managers considerable freedom in selecting and contacting these producers. The aim was to attract a different kind of customer (tourists, foodies, etc) - and it worked.

Supermarkets probably see schemes of this kind as a way to arm themselves against growing consumer interest in what is known as the short chain. Stores that are supplied directly from local producers know exactly where their products come from and where their money goes - and so do their customers. Social and ecological awareness both play a part in this rising trend: food teams, farmer's markets, fresh vegetable packs, packaging-free shops, online farmhouse stores: the number of initiatives continues to grow. However, this inevitably also creams off a (currently) small percentage of the supermarkets' turnover.

An eye for the multicultural shopper?
Although the people in our major cities come from many different ethnic back-grounds, very few traditional supermarkets seem to devote much attention to the multicultural shopper. They perhaps have half a shelf of halal products, but not much more than that. As a result, nearly all Muslims do part of their shopping in ethnic stores. Consequently, this channel is currently fragmented and lacking in professionalism, although in some countries specialized chains are starting to ap-pear, like Yassa Store in France. These retailers exploit the opportunities the larger chains continue to ignore.

In these new ethnic chains you hardly ever see western brands. They are not need-ed, since newcomers from abroad have never had an affinity with these brands. Instead, they offer bulk packs of products like spices and dates, which are interest-ing for the large families and group of friends more typical in ethnic communities. The experience in these stores is also different. They are places where people meet and talk. Consequently, they have a market feel of a kind that is largely lacking (for now) in traditional supermarkets.

Does this mean that ethnic shoppers never visit traditional supermarkets? Of course not. They are price-sensitive and often shop at discounters and supermar-kets that have strong special action campaigns. Also influencing their choice of supermarkets, is whether they can see staff wearing headscarves, which makes Muslim shoppers feel more welcome.

Some retailers are finally starting to respond to the expectations of their ethnic customers in a more focused manner. This is the case with the Auchan hyper-markets in France and Cora in Belgium, while in the Netherlands Albert Heijn and Jumbo now adjust their range to reflect the diversity of each market location. Will other chains follow? After all, ethnic communities form a large segment of the population with growing purchasing power. Surely supermarkets and brand producers will not leave all these potential customers untouched?

'Blurring': the ultimate differentiator?

'Don't sell products, sell solutions.' This is the new mantra in (food) retail. If a shopper is hungry, you can sell him the ingredients to cook for himself, meal components or full meals that he can warm up at home, ready-to-eat snacks that he can eat on the move, or even invite him to take a table and enjoy one of your meals at your on-site catering facility.

More and more supermarkets are testing the food service concept. With its announcement that a dozen or so of its branches will soon open coffee bars or restaurants, Albert Heijn is not the first (and won't be the last) supermarket chain to explore where the boundary between retail and catering properly lies. People call this 'blurring': retail will become food service; food service will become retail. The distinction will disappear. In US, they prefer the term 'grocerant' - a contraction of 'grocer' and 'restaurant'.

In other words, we are talking about a worldwide trend. Or is it just another new buzzword? Blurring is, of course, nothing new. Food stores and eateries first started appearing in petrol stations in the 1980s, leading to the wider idea of 'food on the go' as a solution for busy mobile professionals who need a quick snack, salad or sandwich. This offer has become more refined over the years. Whereas it was initially the food service companies who met the needs of these nomadic customers, the food retailers have now also discovered their potential. As a result, they have developed a number of convenience concepts with sandwiches and meals, such as M&S Simply Food, AH to go and Foodmarkt City by Jumbo.

// Shoppers no longer think in terms of channels. They expect the instant and complete satisfaction of their needs at every moment and place. //

The logic behind the concept is clear: try to serve impulsive consumers at all possible moments, including when they want to eat. Shoppers no longer think in terms of channels. They expect the instant and complete satisfaction of their needs at every moment and place. Each meal or snack that you can 'steal' from caterers as a retailer means extra turnover.

Supermarkets have realized that they are not only competing with each other for market share, but also with everyone else who sells food: the snack bar, the tank station, the office restaurant. In this battle for 'share of stomach' every euro counts, especially when you think that the margins are bigger than on sales of the large FMCG brands. As a result, the offer of ready-made meals in supermarkets has exploded since the 1990s.

In recent years, an additional element has been added: experience. Through offering a unique shopping experience, supermarkets want to avoid purely price-based competition by differentiating themselves from their rivals. In particular, they see experience as a weapon against e-commerce. You can't have a pleasant meal out on the internet. This kind of experience explains why shopping centres are also investing in a wider and more varied range of catering opportunities: non-food sectors can also see the value of food service elements as a way to differentiate and generate extra turnover: a hairdresser's with a coffee bar, a fashion shop with a wine bar. And how many of us are attracted to IKEA by the prospect of a portion of their delicious *Köttbullar*?

The frontier between food service and retail is still open
Can an in-store catering outlet really be decisive in the battle for 'share of stomach' or is it just a fun gimmick? Sushi stands are becoming an increasingly common sight in branches of Delhaize, Carrefour and Intermarché. Carrefour also has a Carrefour Café and a *pizzaiolo* in some of its revamped pilot hypermarkets. Makro has had its own self-service restaurant as long as the company has existed, but not integrated into the store concept.

In the Netherlands, Jumbo Foodmarkt was responsible for a blurring hype when it was launched back in 2013. Their store concept integrates different catering elements, ranging from pizza and pasta to grill dishes and Asian specialities. Shoppers can eat on site or buy to take away, according to a 'make it, take it, eat it' philosophy. In the pizzeria, for example, you can immediately eat the pizzas made in front of you, or take them home, or buy the ingredients to make them yourself.

Ever since, almost every other Dutch supermarket chain has felt obliged to develop its own food service concept. Plus and Dekamarkt World of Food soon followed. Albert Heijn waited a little longer and only began in 2017 with two integrated catering and food service concepts in existing Albert Heijn stores: Deli Kitchen and Bakery Café. In Bakery Café, located at the entrance to the supermarket, staff prepare fresh meals, ranging from salads to pizzas, grilled chicken and spareribs. Customers can put together their own meals and can eat them either on site or at home. A seated area is an essential part of both concepts.

Carrefour

Carrefour Express 'Urban Life'

Food retailers are also exploring the possibilities of blurring elsewhere in Europe. Carrefour has opened a convenience store in Milan that combines a co-working area, a lounge bar and a restaurant. This is the Carrefour Express 'Urban Life' concept. Is it a neighbourhood shop where people can also go for breakfast, a light lunch or a relaxing drink? Or is it a catering outlet where people can also do their shopping? Clearly, it is intended to be a bit of both.

Whatever else it is, the store is certainly not big: just 120 m² on two floors. On the ground floor, customers can make use of the cafeteria for a wide selection of breakfast products, desserts, snacks, pizza and freshly made sushi. There are also take-away meals, traditionally made ice-cream, a salad bar and a juice corner. Consume on the spot or take everything home: the choice is yours.

But the main innovation, according to Carrefour, is on the upper floor. In the co-working area-cum-lounge bar, people can sit in the comfortable sofas to work, relax, sample one of the 200 international beers or have a bite to eat. The store is open from seven in the morning until ten at night and in keeping with a fine Italian tradition there is a 'happy hour' between six and nine o'clock.

Even Real, the struggling German hypermarket chain of the Metro Group, unveiled a spectacular new shopping formula at the end of 2016, based on a fresh food experience in combination with the latest food technology. The name on the store front reads 'Markthalle Krefeld', with a much smaller 'Real' underneath. An extensive catering offer is central to the concept of this new hypermarket, which has a sales area of 11,500 square metre.. Shoppers can enjoy the delights of the 110-seat piazza or the 70-seat winter garden, in both of which they can eat. The menus vary with the season and the diners can watch while their meals are prepared. The emphasis is very much on 'fresh': a salad bar, pizzeria, oyster bar, sushi, grill, vegetarian, organic, a fresh bakery, a coffee roasting house, a wine bar...

Trend-watchers see a huge potential for blurring concepts in food, in part because the millennials and even more recent generations have a different attitude towards food-related matters than their predecessors. They cook less for themselves, although they still find quality, authenticity and experience important. Suitably adjusted casual dining concepts focusing on taste and health score well with this group. The proof: 'healthy' fast-food chains like Exki and Le Pain Quotidien are achieving international success.

It is important for supermarkets to try and cash in on at least a part of these instant consumption moments. Whether they should do this with a full in-store restaurant concept or by offering a range of ready-made meals and installing salad bars, sushi stands and the like is dependent on a number of variable factors. But every major food retailer - including Amazon - now offers a meal-in-a-box concept in response to the rise of HelloFresh.

FMCG finally online?

Can digitalization cause a revolution in the food market, just like it has caused a revolution in the worlds of music, literature and electronics? At the moment, the online share in food is limited: just 1% in Belgium, less than 2% in the Netherlands and the US, but almost 5% in France, nearly 7% in the UK and even more than 16% in South Korea, according to figures by Kantar Worldpanel (Roger, 2016).

The large supermarket chains are hesitating to commit fully to investment in e-commerce. They are involved in fierce competition battles with each other and are faced with the problems of low margins and high fixed costs. They are also the owners of considerable real estate (shops and distribution centres) that needs to continue making a profit. For this reason, they fear that e-commerce will put their existing model at risk. They don't want to cannibalize their own business!

This explains why digital innovation in food retail is not fully implemented by the existing well-known retailers, but by 'outsiders' like Amazon and Peapod in the US, Ocado in the UK or Picnic in the Netherlands. These are companies that do not carry the burden of a century-long history, thousands of permanent staff and a valuable real estate portfolio.

 // The 'convenience' argument alone is not enough. //

Pure play or omnichannel?

In order to make the breakthrough in food, the e-commerce model will need to offer today's supermarket customers significant benefits. The convenience argument alone (the saving of a tedious and time-consuming visit to the shops) is not enough. Food online will need to offer a better and a wider assortment at advantageous prices and with smooth collection or delivery. Just like Zalando does with shoes and Amazon and Alibaba do with just about everything.

This raises the inevitable question: is this also possible with food? Today, you can find supermarkets and convenience stores in almost every street. They have long opening hours and offer a complete range of products at competitive prices. Their supply system has proven its value over decades. So how can you make this model redundant?

There are two fundamentally different strategies in pure retail. Pure players believe that the online model is the future and that they can build a profitable business without the need for brick premises. The cost benefit of having no expensive real estate can then be passed on to the consumer in the form of low prices. New digital applications will also make it possible for them to deliver to consumers quicker and more efficiently than ever before.

Although most of the pure players are currently losing money, they place their faith in the belief that they will be able to develop scale with sufficient speed to reach a tipping point. They rely on the fact that online shoppers are generally more loyal and order more per visit than offline shoppers. For their purchasing, they generally work with established retail organizations, because they do not (yet) have sufficient purchasing power of their own. In this respect, Amazon is the exception.

Does Picnic mean the end of the supermarket?

Two thresholds are holding back the breakthrough of online shopping, according to Joris Beckers, the co-founder of the Dutch online Picnic supermarket. The overall price, because home delivery is expensive, and the long waiting time, because it is difficult to calculate the exact moment of delivery. 'For this reason, we developed a model to address these two problems: a new and fully cooled food chain. We don't have shops; we have smart delivery wagons.' (Twinkle, 2016). The positioning of these wagons can be followed by shoppers on their smartphone, so that they know exactly when their groceries, still nice and cool, will arrive at their front door of their office or home.

The Dutch online supermarket Picnic is a good example of the pure play approach. If you can believe their co-founder, Joris Beckers, Picnic will do for food what Zalando did for fashion. The company was launched in September 2015 in Amersfoort, since when it has rolled out activities throughout the Netherlands. Consumers can order their requirements via an app and their shopping is delivered free of charge to their home by electric-powered wagons. Picnic promises the lowest price for all its products. 'Each night we check 50,000 different prices,' they claim.

This is a remarkable and eye-catching offer. Most online supermarkets opt for a 'click & collect' system, add service costs and give no price guarantee. Setting up an e-commerce business is an expensive matter and food margins are wafer thin. But you can also see it differently, says Beckers: 'Our rivals are dependent on the 5% of customers who are prepared to pay for delivery. We target the other 95%.'

Most of the established supermarket players have yet to be convinced by the pure approach. They see more value in an omnichannel model that combines 'bricks' and 'clicks'. They assume that physical stores will continue to be of great importance for food retail, but also wish to build up a presence in the various alternative channels, including an online option that is complementary to their existing shop organization. In other words, the shopper gets a choice between the old way with a shopping basket in a store and the new way on a computer with delivery at home.

Nearly all today's supermarkets, both large and small, are now omnichannel, some with more conviction than others. The French market, for example, has almost no pure players, because all the major chains decided early on to move into e-commerce. As a result, the country was quickly filled with collection points (or 'drives' as they are known), where consumers can pick up their orders quickly and easily. In consequence, the market share of online in French food retail is rising at a faster rate than in many other countries.

Is this model viable? It is inevitable that an increase in the profitability of e-commerce will put the physical stores under pressure. In time, this may force the omnichannel players to close or downsize some of their supermarkets, or even to thoroughly revise the existing supermarket concept as we know it. Perhaps part of the current shopping space will be reserved for the preparation and collection of routine online deliveries, possibly in combination with inspiration shops and/or catering options.

Collect or deliver?
The reason why supermarkets prefer to invest in collection points is simple: delivery is very expensive. The costs of the 'last mile' are difficult to control, while shoppers have become used to the idea of home delivery in other sectors.

Supermarkets often begin with a very low-threshold form of e-commerce: the orders are prepared in-house by a member of the store staff walking along the shelves and putting products into a basket, just like a normal shopper would do. This requires only minimal investment and works quite well, up to the moment when the service becomes popular, at which point all those staff running around the store become more of a liability than an asset. Supermarkets are not distribution centres: on a large scale, the picking process cannot be efficient.

This requires the creation of a specific distribution centre for e-commerce collection points. These so-called 'dark stores' can supply the collection points more effectively and even make possible a degree of home delivery. This is how most of the 'drive' concepts in France now work, although there are still some hypermarkets where online orders are pulled from the shelves.

A similar system operates for the Bavarian online customers of the German supermarket chain Edeka. They can collect their orders at a time of their choosing (both day or night) from cooled lockers on the car park of the E-Centre supermarket in Gaimersheim. These automatic lockers are reminiscent of the lockers used by the mail-order companies, but with the difference that they have three different temperature compartments, which makes them suitable for dry, fresh and frozen products. Customers pick a time slot for collection when they place their orders online. There is now an additional test area for lockers at Munich airport and at two Unimarkt supermarkets in Austria.

In the meantime, several physical retailers are also experimenting with schemes that will make home delivery more feasible, some of which don't even require the customer to be there. For example, the American Kroger is partnering Uber in a project for super-fast delivery of this kind. As well as the difference in logistical cost, the need for the customer to be at home to receive his delivery has always been the strongest argument in favour of collection points, certainly when fresh or frozen produce is involved. Even so, Amazon Fresh, and the British Ocado have both recently proven the viability of the delivery model. And its popularity is increasing all the time. A survey carried out in 2016 by Delhaize in Belgium revealed that the interest among consumers for home delivery was much greater than originally thought. As a result, they launched a service which has since been moderately successful, notwithstanding the 9.95 euros delivery change.

Delivering directly to your fridge

ICA, the largest Swedish supermarket, was one of the first to trial a new e-commerce concept whereby fresh food was delivered directly into the customer's fridge, even if he is not a home, all made possible by smart locks.

The project was a collaboration between ICA, the PostNord postal service and the smart home start-up Glue. Glue has developed the Glue Smart Lock, an intelligent digital lock that the owner can operate at distance with his smartphone. The main advantage to the customer is that he doesn't need to stay at home to open the door to receive his delivery.

When the courier arrives, the customer is sent a coded text message to open his front door. The courier then enters the house and neatly puts away everything in fridge and cupboards. The courier texts the customer again when he leaves, so that the door can be properly locked.

ICA tested the concept in the summer of 2016 with forty or so families in Stockholm. The retailer expects that the online share of the food market will grow to 38% in the near future. 'With this development, we want to investigate the possibilities for home shopping,' says Anders Svensson, the CEO of ICA. 'The service makes the lives of our customers easier.' Today, Amazon, Albert Heijn and other retailers are trying the exact same thing.

Easier ordering

E-commerce players not only try to make the collection moment as easy as possible for their shoppers. They want to do the same with their ordering process. The Amazon Dash buttons quite literally require no more than a single press to order a new pack of washing powder or toilet paper. The Amazon Dash Replenishment Service (DRS) takes things another stage further: this re-orders products automatically when it knows your supply of something is running low. Or at least it does for people who have a compatible General Electric washing machine. Even so, it gives some idea of the potential impact of smart homes and the Internet of Things on retail.

French retailers simplify their ordering process for their consumers by providing them with scanners they can use at home to scan products that are nearly empty. This is a quick and easy way to put together your shopping list. Carrefour, Auchan and Intermarché all have their own variant of this system. Albert Heijn tested such a home scanner in the Netherlands, but the scanning function can be even more easily built into an app, according to the practice of more and more European supermarket formats. The scan function is now a basic component in almost all new apps.

Subscription services for routine replacements also seem to be an option worth exploring further: the Dollar Shave Club already exists, as do services for cat food, coffee and breakfast cereals (MyMuesli), to name but a few. Other new services are being launched every day. These are products that the same people buy in the same quantities at the same regular intervals. In the food sector, the meal boxes of HelloFresh are trendsetting, although as we have seen in the section on 'blurring' they are quickly being copied by their pure player rivals (Blue Apron, Smartmat, etc.) and by the regular supermarket chains. So why not automate their delivery at an interesting discount rate? The supplier is then guaranteed a loyal clientele and a predictable turnover, while the consumer is relieved of a tedious task.

// The growth of e-commerce offers brands the possibility to approach customers directly. //

Will brands also become e-tailers?

The growth of e-commerce offers brands the possibility to approach customers directly. It is not without good reason that the classic FMCG brands are green with envy of Nespresso. Nestlé has succeeded in creating a business worth millions with this brand, which is not dependent on retailers to reach consumers. It uses its own distribution channels, as well as both online and physical stores.

The system offers plenty of advantages, including a higher reaction speed by having full control over the logistical chain and the assortment. No difficult negotiations with buyers, no introduction and folder charges, no risk of being scrapped from product lists. Above all, direct contact with the consumer. Although this also means that the brand will have to tolerate direct competition in the supermarkets, since Nespresso, to continue with our example, no longer has the exclusive right to make its little aluminium cups and therefore finds itself obliged to gradually relax the selective criteria of its distribution model.

Even so, can Nespresso serve as an inspirational example for other FMCG brands? Perhaps it can, under the motto of 'eliminate the middle man'. Consider, for example, at the recent purchase of the Dollar Shave Club by Unilever at a relatively high price. This subscription service for shaving products deals directly with the end user and therefore has no need of retailers. Rival Procter & Gamble has responded with the Tide Wash Club in the US, which home delivers capsules of Tide washing powder at regular intervals. In Chicago it has also rolled out Tide Spin, which makes it possible for consumers to have their washing collected for cleaning by courier via an app. Internally, the company refers to this as the 'Uberization' of washing. In a very different sector, e-commerce now constitutes 6% of the turnover of the cosmetics producer L'Oréal and it is above all in the 'luxury' category that the group sees the most potential for growth.

In Germany, Nespresso food giant Nestlé has also developed the Nestlé Marktplatz webshop, where consumers cannot only find information and take part in competitions, but also order products from the wide Nestlé range. According to the company, these are mainly products that are difficult to find in supermarkets, but a quick visit to their website also shows Galaxy chocolate, jars of Nescafé Gold and tins of Quality Street sweets, none of which are actually what you can call collector's items. Fresh and deep-freeze products are, however, not (yet) available.

The breakthrough of mobile internet and smartphone apps makes it increasingly easy for strong brands to approach consumers directly. And the temptation to do so is great. That being said, many companies are still in two minds. Direct sales sound appealing, but it is not easy to make the distribution model viable. Besides, shoppers will not readily give up the convenience of one-stop shopping at their local supermarket, whether online or offline.

In addition, the strategy is not without risk. Retailers could be stimulated to respond negatively when suppliers suddenly become competitors - and their power over the brands is still considerable. Brands that are dependent for 90% of their sales on supermarkets have much more to lose than to gain. As a result, they will hesitate before playing the e-commerce card in full.

But this does not stop the brands from trying to gain more knowledge about online purchasing behaviour. Some of them even conclude partnerships with major online retailers. What's more, for completely new initiatives the online boulevard of opportunity is still wide open. This explains why multinationals like Unilever and P&G are investing with increasing frequency in digital start-ups. Club formulas, subscription services, ordering apps: the large brand manufacturers are exploring all the options thoroughly.

What will the supermarket of tomorrow look like?

Most observers agree that the physical supermarket is unlikely to disappear from the streetscape in the near future. However, they will undergo a transformation resulting from the impact of e-commerce on both their business model and customer expectations. There is a risk that there will be too many stores, so that some will probably close, while those that remain will become smaller. For many routine purchases, the physical store no longer has an added value in an era where it is possible to order products efficiently online or through a subscription service. This will force food retailers to make some harsh choices.

The first signs are already visible today. Large hypermarkets have lost market share in recent years because they want to be all things to all men and have suffered too much under competition from offline 'category killers' (players who become dominant through systematically undermining the market price, like Zooplus) and from online competitors.

The new concepts that players like Carrefour and Makro are rolling out today are more focused on categories where a memorable experience and inspiration play a more crucial role; for example, fresh food and decoration. For volume purchases, Carrefour has also introduced a touchscreen at the entrances to its store, so that your crates of beer and bumper-packs of soft-drinks are waiting for you at the end of your visit. In a different vein, Makro has decided to outsource its entire electrical goods department to Media Markt. The modern supermarket is now an inspiration platform and a collection point - and everyone is experimenting with all the options. Best examples must nonetheless be Alibaba's and JD's hightech super-markets, discussed earlier in this book.

What it's really all about: data!

Why do retailers, technology companies and brand producers continue to invest large sums in a business model that is loss-making and currently shows little sign of being able to turn that into significant profit? Because e-commerce yields something that you cannot find in the financial accounts of these companies: data. Knowledge of the consumer and his/her purchasing behaviour. In-depth knowledge that goes much further than what retailers have hitherto been able to collect using their loyalty card and till receipt analyses.

Amazon might have begun as an online bookstore, but today it sells just about everything to hundreds of millions of people. The company possesses huge data-bases recording online shopping behaviour, which it couples to far-reaching and systematic investigation. Now that the company is also opening physical stores and is building up significant market share in daily purchases through its Whole Food outlets, the scale of this knowledge is increasing exponentially. To such an extent that a large part of customer purchasing behaviour is now predictable. It is no coincidence that the Amazon Go concept is built around an app. Why? Because it produces data. Platforms like HelloFresh, the Dollar Shave Club and the online activities of L'Oréal all have the same primary objective: collecting data and ex-ploiting it - as does Netflix in its own sector.

This is also the reason why Amazon wants to connect with leading FMCG brands, so that it can persuade them to review their business model. Instead of continuing to invest in trade relations with the large supermarket chains, it wants to convince them that e-commerce is the future. If they join forces with Amazon, so the argu-ment goes, they will be better able to serve consumers efficiently within the hour, saving them a tedious journey to the supermarket. In the meantime, Amazon will collect further huge amounts of data relating to large-volume sales of daily con-sumables. Knowledge is power.

// In the meantime, Amazon collects huge amounts of data relating to large-scale volume sales of daily consumables. Knowledge is power. //

Traditional retailers need to survive in the market without having the powerful platforms of an Amazon or Alibaba at their disposal. Fighting with unequal weapons? That depends. In this respect, it is interesting to note a recent initiative by a relatively small retailer who understands how the game works. Colruyt, the Belgian supermarket, has been building a local retail empire for some time that is not simply limited to daily purchases (with Colruyt, OKay, Spar and Bio-Planet), but has been expanded to include living, toys, household and electrical goods and even fashion, with shops and webshops as Dreamland, Dreambaby, ColliShop or ZEB. Colruyt customers have a single Xtra loyalty card and a single account for all the group's shops and webshops. As a result, no company knows more about Belgian consumers than Colruyt, not even Amazon, Facebook or Google. Sure, Belgium is a small market, but their tactic still offers Colruyt significant growth potential. And there is nothing to stop small local retailers around the world from doing the same, allowing them to exploit the intimacy of their local circle of customers to their advantage. In this way, it is not necessarily game, set and match to Amazon or Alibaba.

What will the supermarket of tomorrow sell?

It is not only the concept of the supermarket that will be the subject of fierce discussion in the years ahead. The products that fill our shelves will also see significant change, not only in terms of 'what' but also in terms of 'how' they get there. As we saw in the chapter on 'The Future of the Consumer', what we eat must become healthier and more sustainable. This is an area where technological evolutions can have a serious impact on making this possible.

Made-to-measure food

In recent decades, most of the large food producers have focused on the development of tempting, tasty, affordable and accessible products. Things that are hard for the consumer to resist. In part, they achieved this by standardizing products through the clever dosing of sugar, salt and fat - and it was something they did extremely well. You can now find this kind of temptation almost everywhere.

However, the huge social costs of this strategy are now becoming increasingly evident, so that popular demand for greater regulation is becoming louder and louder. People, it is argued, need to be protected from themselves, in the manner that has already happened for tobacco and alcohol. If the food industry itself takes no action, the government will be forced to step in and impose limitations, which is the solution favoured by the World Health Organization. In the meantime, different countries and cities are already experimenting with variants of a sugar and/or fat tax.

Of course, not all individuals have the same dietary requirements. It depends on your physique, your level of physical activity and even your DNA. Nowadays, people with allergies and intolerances can find an ever-growing number of sales points to abundantly cater to their specific food needs: gluten-free, lactose-free, sugar-free, etc. Likewise, people's dietary requirements vary with the different stages of their lives. We find it completely normal to see shelf upon shelf of baby food in our supermarkets, but in the future it may become equally commonplace to see shelves for seniors or women in the menopause. And in the even more distant future, it is not beyond the bounds of possibility that scientifically-based advice will lead to the development of made-to-measure food specifically geared to your personal DNA profile.

In search of sustainable proteins

In order to feed our ever-growing world population, we already need more than one earth at existing rates of consumption. The demand for animal protein continues to increase as and where prosperity increases, but the seas are overfished and meat production is neither ecologically sound or efficient. We need to do things better, say the scientists.

For each 150 grams of steak on your plate, a cow has consumed a kilogram of fodder and used 2,500 litres of water. If we carry on like this, it will be impossible to supply even people's most basic food needs. So what can we do? The production of cultured (or in-vitro) meat would result in an 80-90% reduction in greenhouse gas emissions, require 45% less energy, 90% less water and 99% less land. Moreover, there would be no need for a single animal to be slaughtered.

The leading expert in this field is Professor Mark Post of the University of Maastricht. In 2013, he was the first to succeed in multiplying the cells of the muscle tissue of a cow to create a hamburger of 'real' meat. This first artificial hamburger cost some 250,000 euros to develop, but Post believes the production cost can be cut to 11 euros in just a matter of years. His company Mosa Meat wants to cultivate 'animal-free meat' in huge bio-reactors, similar to the way that some cheeses are currently made. He is receiving financial support for his project from (amongst others) Sergey Brin, one of the founders of Google.

// For each 150 grams of steak on your plate, a cow has consumed a kilogram of fodder and used 2,500 litres of water. //	

In many supermarkets today you can also find numerous products based on insects. These include snacks, spreads and meat substitutes based on crickets, locusts, mealworms and buffalo worms. Insects have a high nutritional value, are easy to cultivate, require little space, convert their own food intake efficiently into edible proteins and require only a limited emission of greenhouse gases to produce them in massive quantities. After a first hype in 2014, when many supermarkets and caterers embraced this new segment wholeheartedly, the sales figures fell back disappointingly, so that these wholesome products are now sadly starting to disappear from some shelves. Were the prices too high or were shoppers simply not convinced?

Another possible alternative is the use of insects as animal fodder for the more sustainable production of meat. European legislation currently prohibits this, but we are already seeing the appearance on the market of the first foodstuffs for household pets made from insects. QiZen dog food, for example, is marketed as a healthy substitute for meat made from insect meal, a highly nutritious and sustainable superfood. Will an old dog one day eventually be able to teach us new tricks?

Food from a printer

In various sectors 3D printing is seen as the technology of the future. Can this concept also play a role of significance in the food sector? If so, as a consumer you would no longer buy finished products, but would purchase a kind of food-equivalent of a printer cartridge, which would allow you to print off your food or ingredients in your own kitchen.

Different food brands are already testing out this idea, although these early prototypes are aimed in the first instance at the professional market. Chocolate producer Callebaut is working, for example, with the Dutch start-up byFlow on a 3D printer for 'the black gold'. This machine can help chocolatiers to create unique chocolate products. In similar fashion, the Italian pasta manufacturer Barilla demonstrated a printer at the 2015 World Exposition in Milan that is capable of printing 3D pasta shapes that even the most experienced chef could not reproduce. Again, the printer is intended in the first instance for top-end restaurants who wish to give their customers a truly memorable pasta experience.

The summer of 2016 saw the opening of the temporary London Food Ink restaurant, which offered a 3D printed menu for 300 euros. There is no doubt that this was a unique gastronomic experience, but at the moment it still fails to offer any serious challenge to the good old-fashioned food processor!

Supermarkets go into gardening

In August 2016, Metro opened a new supermarket in Antwerp, the highlight of which is a high-tech in-store greenhouse known as InFarm, where fresh herbs are grown under an adjusted form of LED lighting for sale in the store. After a successful pilot project in Berlin, Antwerp was the first Metro store where the concept was rolled out in all its glory over an area of 25 square metre. The technology used ensures that the herbs are not only tastier and more nutritional, but also offer shoppers a range of rarer and more interesting varieties. Just weeks later, Delhaize announced that from 2017 it intended to grow baby tomatoes, lettuce and aubergines in a 320 square metre vegetable garden on the roof of its supermarket in Elsene. Although this is perhaps a copy of a similar Whole Foods initiative in Brooklyn, it is nonetheless a European first. Does this means that supermarkets will soon be competing with market gardeners and fruit auctions?

These two approaches are essentially very different. In theory, the roof of a building is no different from any other plot of 'ground' used for a vegetable garden, except that in this case it simply makes more efficient use of the scarce space in an urban centre. In addition, this 'local' cultivation makes transport unnecessary: the only transport needed is down the stairs and into the store! Of course, the idea of recuperating 'lost' surface area on the roofs of buildings is nothing new: it was one of the basic principles of the world famous architect Le Corbusier.

In contrast, the cultivation of vegetables under LED lighting is very new and very high-tech. The modified light spectrum ensures that the plants enjoy an 'optimal growth process' without the need for any kind of chemical treatment. This method of production is more efficient (it is possible to work at different levels, one on top of the other) and provides superior quality. Moreover, it makes it possible to cultivate in otherwise 'impossible' locations. In London, for example, experiments are already taking place in underground rail tunnels and old bomb shelters.

Metro and Delhaize both received considerable media attention with these initiatives. However, both retailers deny that the projects were little more than marketing stunts. Urban agriculture and market gardening, they say, help to provide an answer to the problems of over-urbanization and population growth. According to both chains, this type of production can also be made financially viable. It also responds to the growing popular demand for greater ethical, local, ecological and qualitative produce from conscious foodies, for whom price is not the decisive factor. Le Corbusier 2.0.

Everyone is a retailer

In place of a customer journey, where the shopper begins with a need and ends with a purchase, in years to come people and (retail) brands will be more or less in constant contact with each other for micro-moments. We are evolving towards a marketing model where brands circle around people instead of consumers, as they used to be defined, circling around brands. In the future of shopping, these clearly defined roles in the current value chain will become blurred. Both the customer journey and the value chain will be much less linear. Everyone will be able to fill the role of retailer, designer, producer and shopper.

> // Consciously or not, people will live more and more inside their own little bubble, created on the basis of big data. //

Consciously or not, people will live more and more inside their own little bubble, created on the basis of big data. Your search results online are already being filtered to show you only what is relevant to you at an individual level. In effect, shoppers are now shown personal collections, which today are still based on categories and (micro-) segments, but in future will be one-on-one offers, so that in a retail context everyone will have their own personal store. And it is already starting: both actively (apps and webshops have options to filter their offers) and passively (large retailers automatically personalize their offers on the basis of customer information). In short, shoppers will increasingly create their own shopping medium, of which they will be both curator and director. We are standing on the brink of a revolution in retail and purchasing behaviour.

People will also be able to sit on the designer's chair in the value chain, at the level of the producer. Via crowdsourcing and co-creation, consumers will collaborate with brands and manufacturers. End users now expect brand manufacturers to understand their needs perfectly and respond to them fully. They think it is normal that they should be heard. If they aren't, they will simply show the brands how it is done (C2B). One size no longer fits all: today's shoppers are highly diverse (with countless different profiles) and they attach great importance to their unique, individual identity (especially the millennials). This need for personalization will become even greater in future. Hyper-personalized products and services will be the norm.

Or why not simply do it all yourself? The short-chain economy is booming. Although the current representatives of the C2C economy in their role as revolutionary disruptors are not always the most sound or sustainable strategic examples to follow - think of Uber or Airbnb - the concept is here to stay. The consumer will become a producer and knock out all the intermediary chains. For people who feel they have something to offer, it has never been easier to enter the market. Platforms provide digital space for almost anyone to sell their own products (self-made or not) and services. And setting up your own business or even opening your own shop has become child's play.

This game of retail musical chairs works in all directions: brands and producers try to get their hands on the entire value chain, hoping to run it in a straight line to their target public, while flagship stores, own brand platforms, pop-ups, shop-in-shops, smart devices that resupply themselves, etc. are all methods that make the traditional retailer surplus to requirements. Even logistical service providers, IT companies and start-ups are trying to take over the retailer's role. In the Netherlands, no less a company than the national postal service PostNL has started its own online supermarket Stockon. The grocery service allows for repeat household purchases delivered every two weeks and keeps a personal shopping list for you via a mobile app. In Germany, DHL has already had its own web supermarket Allyouneedfresh.de for some time.

Power is concentrating in the hands of a few large players (the Big Six), while retailers and brands unintentionally get caught in their web. Google has more than 90% market share as a search engine, a power for which retailers and brands pay a lot in the form of AdWords. However, it means they finance their own competition, because with that revenue Google works on ways to make them superfluous and to serve consumers directly themselves. Amazon is also introducing more and more own brands, competing directly with FMCG manufacturers and traders on its market place.

Does the retailer still have a role to play in the future of shopping? Yes, of course he (or she) does. But it will all be very different from now on... So let's take a brief look at a week in the life of a shopper - and therefore also a retailer - in the years to come.

The new customer journey

Monday, 19.04:

Your smartphone tells you that a courier will be arriving in 26 minutes with your groceries. And yes, the GPS tracking confirms that he is indeed currently in the next-but-one district to yours. So your weekly shopping will be here soon. Because that's the way things will be done in the future: people will have their shopping delivered to their home once a week. There will be no need to order. Your connected household devices (Internet of Things) will have already told your supplier exactly what you need, right down to the fact that your supply of toilet paper has nearly run out.

The box will also contain everything you need for your family meals from Monday to Friday. Recipes, a full list of ingredients, the (fair trade) origins of the products and lots of other relevant information will all be made available to you in augmented reality via an app. The box will have two vegetarian meals for Friday when your two grown-up children - who no longer live at home - will call round. And two less portions for Monday and Tuesday, when your school-going children are sleeping over at your ex-partner's place.

The courier also lets you know that he has just dropped in on your parents, who this week ordered less fresh and more ready-made meals. Are they finding it harder to cook for themselves? It could be a sign. He will keep a check on it in the weeks ahead.

Tuesday, 20.27:

During the streaming of a film, you see the main characters draw the curtain in their bedroom, exactly the kind of curtains you have been looking for. With a click, you find out the name of the manufacturer and the serial number of the pattern. You can order it directly from China, but you first ask your voice assistant if she can't find a place closer to home that sells it more cheaply. Within seconds, she offers you a top three of sales points with the lowest price and the fastest delivery. Even so, that still makes them pretty expensive curtains!

So you decide to do it yourself. You access a design app that works with a fabric supplier. You draw your own design, inspired by the colour and pattern you saw in the film. The dimensions of your windows are not standard, so you use your smartphone to film them and the room in general, allowing the app to calculate exactly how much fabric you need. With augmented reality, you can instantly see how your unique curtains will look when hanging in your room. Perfect! They brighten things up a treat! All arranged while lying in your own bed.

But who will make and deliver the curtains for you? You have ordered the fabric, but what about the finishing? No problem: there are companies enough specialized in personalized textile work. You post your design and your required dimensions on social media and let the bidding begin. Within half an hour, several confectionary retailers have made an offer, but you think the price should still be lower. So you play them out, one against the other. After all, you are in no hurry for your curtains; getting the best price and a good service are more important. Let them stew a bit. 'Okay Alexa, you can turn the film back on now...'

Wednesday, 12.00:

This morning you made a deal with the confectionary company that is going to make your curtains. You picked a company that can print your fabric in their own workshop and will come and hang the finished curtains in your home. That's a lot quicker than letting them come from China and the reviews from your digital assistant suggest their service is reliable. This was confirmed in the short video chat you had with the installer; you are clearly both on the same wavelength. He will come to install the curtains next week, but you won't even need to be at home. Your smart lock will let you know when he arrives via your smartphone, so you can agree to send him the access code and let him deactivatie your door lock during his stay. Okay, his price wasn't the lowest, but what a service!

It's time to pick up the kids from school. The voice assistant in your smart glasses orders you a thirty-minute ride and half an hour later the car is waiting outside your front door. The car tells you that road works on your route will cause a 14 minute delay. Even though the traffic lights have been re-set to take account of the changed traffic situation, the car works out its own new route. You tell the car to stop close to the package collection dispenser next to the school, so you can pick up the new dress you ordered online this morning.

// The voice assistant in your smart glasses orders you a thirty-minute ride and half an hour later the car is waiting outside your front door. //

The smart car could have picked up the children for you and the dress could have been delivered into its boot en route, but today you promised the kids a trip to the park on the edge of town. And they also need some new kit for the school sports day tomorrow. There aren't all that many shops left anymore. Certainly not the big flagship stores, which are only to be found in the large urban centres. But fortunately there are still a number of multi-brand boutiques that have cleverly learnt how to play a key role in local communities. You give the kids a choice: order online for next-day delivery or hunt around in the neighbourhood shops? Hunting it is! The app on which the local retailers have joined forces show that you can find sports shoes in a shop just around the corner from the park. You log on to the shop site and see that it has a wide selection of sizes and styles available. The retailer has noted your interest and sends you a text to say he will have them waiting for you when you arrive.

In the shop, the retailer welcomes you personally and the shoes are indeed waiting, as he promised. The children's feet are measured by a robot assistant, which then fetches the right sizes and models from the storeroom. The children test them on a treadmill and over an obstacle course in a side room, against the backdrop of a giant interactive screen, which takes them on a virtual run through an enchanted forest. The kids are delighted. Not only with their new shoes, but also with the fact that it was such fun and it all went so swiftly!

How was last weekend at their father's place? Fine, but his new partner doesn't make such nice food as at home. He buys all that organic stuff from the local farmer's market. They even had to eat seaweed and insect burgers! And he always uses so much pepper. Dad says his boyfriend learnt that from his grandma, back when they lived in Syria. But it was fun visiting the covered eastern market, with all its colours and smells. You could try everything and there was even a workshop where they taught your how to cook Arabian-style!

Thursday, 19.48:

Oops! Today's recipe needs sambal oelek, but you don't have it in the house. And you also fancy a glass of good wine. Time to pop down to the local supermarket. Lucky that it's now open until midnight! You are recognized via your smartphone as you drive onto the car park and are instantly informed of special offers and the number of points in your loyalty account. Just fifteen more and you can get that smart coffee-maker you have been saving for. And your favourite chocolate is 30 cents a block cheaper this week. They sure know what you like, but that's hardly surprising: they have your complete shopping history for the past five years. But you don't want any distractions today, so you ask your GPS to lead you immediately to the right rows.

Finding a good bottle of wine will be no problem. The supermarket manager knows that a lot of connoisseurs live near his store and he has a fine selection. The touch-screen will tell you which ones best match your meal this evening. A light appears next to each of the candidate wines and you pick one you have never tried before. And the sambal oelek is just as easy to find! You set off for home and as you leave the store the contents of your shopping bag are automatically scanned and paid. How different from when you were a child! No more tills, no more cash, no more waiting in lines...

You wave to the always friendly manager, who is helping an older couple to load their shopping into their car. Now that robots are doing a lot of the work in his store and there is no more check-out, it is useful that he has a bit of extra time for his senior customers. It gives you a feeling of confidence that your ageing parents can also shop here in comfort and safety.

Friday, 21.07:

After the family meal, discussion turns to the annual family holiday. Where will we go this year? You first check with your friends on social media. What would they recommend? You get some tips and some great photos of people's past hols, but these make the choice harder instead of easier. The chatbot of a large travel agency offers to help. Just tell it your desired criteria - budget and child-friendly (although a little bit of glamping would be fine), not too hot and no flights longer than four hours - and it will give you a number of suggestions. It will also offer a number of out-of-the-box ideas of its own, based on its big data.

One location in particular catches your eye, but what's the accommodation like? The chatbot immediately sends you 3D recordings of the camp sites. With your VR headsets, you can imagine that you are already in Morocco! The children love it, but you are still not sure and have a number of practical questions. The chatbot proposes you discuss these with a human travel assistant and makes an appointment for you. What about Sunday evening at five o'clock? Travel agents now understand that not everyone can organize their holidays during what used to be called 'normal office hours' and so they now nearly always work on this appointment basis. This gives you a better made-to-measure service, not only during your holiday, but before it even begins. She can either visit you at home, or you can come into the showroom, where you can see even more VR montages and view all the agency's travel guides (through smart glasses).

Saturday, 11.00:

Today, you finally have some time for yourself. A day in town with your friends: 'shop till you drop!' You arranged things last Thursday with a conference call. Control-freak Elma has booked a group fitting room in one of your favourite shops and online you have already chosen lots of blouses and skirts to try on. They will be waiting for you on arrival (*convenience*). That's great! Of course, a bottle of prosecco to get you in the right mood is even better! (*experience*). Elma looked fantastic in the photo she sent you of the dress she tried on in the shop's virtual AR fitting room. Will it look as good in real life? Or will some things, even in the future, still be just too good to be true?

You are given a warm welcome by name as you enter the store, even though the shop assistant has never met you before. The facial recognition cameras above the door sent her a message the moment you came into view. And all the things they promised would be waiting for you are neatly sorted, person by person, in the fitting room. The assistant is on hand to help, because she is also a stylist who works as a personal shopper. She finds trousers that perfectly match the blouses you chose earlier and it is no coincidence that they are all in your favourite models. And she has shoes to suggest as well. Tempting! Very tempting! Result? You order two blouses in different colours from the ones they have in the shop and a pair of trousers you saw on their internet terminal. You also take with you three of the dresses you just tried on. Now it's time for a girl's lunch. And all those bags? No need to worry about them: they will be delivered to the boot of the car you have booked to take you home later on. All in all, a very successful day!

The new service package of retail

Retail will become a new type of business, which will no longer be based on product rotation and sales, but on service provision. People no longer search for products; they search for solutions, also in retail. If, as a brand, you want to continue playing a role of importance in people's lives, you will need to carefully identify and map out their needs and then respond to those needs as accurately as possible by offering them a personalized package of services.

// People no longer search for products; they search for solutions. //

The products you sell in this new context are almost incidental, since the margins on product retail will be so fine in the future as to be almost negligible. You will create added value both for the shopper and for your own company by providing solutions that make people's lives easier and more comfortable. Shops will be transformed into service points. Shop staff will become service providers. 'In retail there is a formula for customer expectation: time plus experience plus value proposition,' says Jodie Fox, co-founder and CEO of Shoes of Prey.[24]

In the future, (retail) brands need to take accent of four key elements in their strategy:

- Supplementary services;
- Logistics;
- Big Data;
- Media.

A friendly welcome is no longer enough to differentiate yourself as a retailer. **Supplementary services**, from subscription formulas to personal styling, will make it possible to create new relationships between shoppers and (retail) brands, making it possible to rise above the murderous competition of price wars. As a brand, ask yourself what today's shoppers really need and with what network of services you can satisfy those needs. Be ready to go the extra mile!

And also be ready to fight the **logistics** war for the 'last mile', a war that can only get fiercer in future. If time is the decisive factor, automated, technological solutions will be almost unbeatable. Around 40% of domestic purchases will be machine-to-machine. 'Why are you never afraid?' asks one robot. 'Because I have nerves of steel,' replies the other.

Digital disruptors will not rest until they become the fastest to deliver to the shopper. They will break down the entire foundations of the sales process to achieve this goal: they literally want to be able to read their customers' minds and deliver what they need before the customer journey has even begun.

To be able to serve people as they expect - and they will expect an awful lot - **big data** is crucial. A handful of today's global technology players are already raking in data streams from across the entire world, but local omnichannel players can also acquire valuable data if they listen to their community at every possible micro-moment of contact in the customer journey. It is only by correctly analyzing this data and identifying the right emphases you need to set that you will be able to provide the kind of personalized service provision that can bring success.

The physical store will become a **medium** in that process, in a very literal sense. It will be a channel of communication between all the other channels, a radar in the wider brand network. Viewed from this perspective, it is possible to link the store to a new kind of business model, which is no longer exclusively based on product sales, but on its return as a means of communication. From now on, the ROI of a shop will be calculated in the same way as an advert: what is its value in the overall 'big picture' of your brand strategy?

On the reverse side of the coin, media companies will also become retailers, with sales points as an extra channel of communication in their ecosystem. American lifestyle magazine *PopSugar* lets shoppers buy via SMS. Simple yet effective, the women's magazine offers the shopping channel Must Have It, where members are offered a product twice a week - usually with a discount or a temporary offer - that they can easily order by answering 'yes' to the message. The offer comes from commercial partners and advertisers (over 90%), although the editorial teams sometimes select products themselves. Before this service, the Must Have It subscription packages *PopSugar* has been delivering to subscribers on a monthly basis, already accounted for about 20% of the publishers' income.

Likewise, in the future every brand will become media as well, providing exclusive content, blogs, documentaries and so on. When people go shopping, 51% of them have already made up their mind what they want to buy, because they have found all the information they need through the channels available to them. No salesperson can rival the mass of data that can now be found online. What counts is the relevance of your brand and the integration of your online and offline channels. Shoppers expect that retail brands will look further than simple transactions and will provide them with an enriching experience. Is the bike ridden by Tour de France winner Chris Froome better than all the others? Or does it just allow cycling fans to feel like a top rider?

Trust is precious

The internet is an endless shelf, where you will always find the best product at the best price. Especially now that millions of small players are competing with each other in the huge worldwide marketplaces on the platforms of the media giants. There is just one problem with anything endless: you can't see the wood for the trees. People therefore need a guide through those woods.

You must be able to trust a guide. To be certain that a retailer or producer is competent and capable of standing by them every step of the way, shoppers now demand openness and transparency. This is the only way to guarantee that they share the same vision and values. For this reason, all successful companies will become brands - and this includes the retailers. They must have a story, a persona that people can identify with. The shop then becomes a medium to project these values, a service centre and meeting place for the community around the brand.

If a brand stands for an identity, there must be as many brands as there are identities. Despite the bumpy road it faces during the transition, multinational mass retailer H&M has understood that anonymous uniformity is a thing of the past and that today's world is a world of niches: the H&M umbrella now covers a multiplicity of retail brands, ranging from premium (COS and Other Stories) to avant-garde streetwear (Monki and Weekday). This makes H&M a smart Me-tailer: something for everyone.

To keep trust once you have got it requires close collaboration with the shopper. If people are no longer passive consumers but instead are a huge community around the brand, they expect to play an active role. Co-creation and co-innovation will become commonplace. Trust between brands is also crucial for survival. Information transparency will put an end to business secrecy, while the enormous speed of future change will make it impossible to innovate successfully from within your own ivory tower. Innovating together, with your community and other companies, will be a condition for remaining competitive.

This is very different from the past. In recent decades, retailers and FMCG brands were inclined to think top-down, both internally and towards their customers. They were used to doing everything for themselves in an increasingly competitive market. And customers were expected simply to accept what they did. In contrast, many of today's disruptors are open innovators. While classic companies grow everything in neat plantations, the disruptors, according to Peter Hinssen (2017), develop rainforests of organic growth, where cross-pollination and cross-fertilization are the rule rather than the exception. The rapid pace of modern change means that communal thinking and a creative, open mentality are the only way to tackle common challenges with success.

Even at shop level, collaboration offers some enriching possibilities. The offer will go far beyond what existing ranges and stocks can provide, while, paradoxically enough, fewer square metres of shop floor space will be necessary. This freed space can be given a new designation. For example, it can be leased to suppliers or brands that wish to activate shoppers 'in the flesh', live in your store. Or perhaps to create a collection of brands with clear added value.

New business models for the future

To keep retail viable, it will be necessary to find new business models. The idea of the shop as a sales point, which must be capable of standing alone and making a profit, is dead and buried. The old calculation for success - turnover per square metre - no longer holds water. Even when online sales are added, store profitability often remains elusive. In fact, no single channel or touchpoint with the consumer is capable of 'going it alone' in the modern marketplace. The only thing that works is the total package - omnichannel. This is where new ways must be found to make money. And several successful shop formulas show that this is still possible.

> // The idea of a shop as a sales point, which must be capable of standing alone and making a profit, is dead and buried. //

Hyper-personalization and co-creation are the order of the day in the 'creative store' of Stanley/Stella in Antwerp. It is really a wholesale store where the printers of clothes buy their garments, but is now also used by fashionistas who want to print their own unique models. Visitors can see all the styles, feel all the fabrics and compare all the colours, while the real shopping is then done on digital terminals: with just a few clicks, you order what you want and it is printed on the spot. None of the collections are pre-made in advance, so there is hardly any stock and the combinations of each customer are one-of-a-kind. The store also has a catering section and a co-working space, where it possible for people to meet, exchange, share, co-create or just relax together in pleasant surroundings. Workshops, DJ sets and musical performances are also organized: 'A place that stimulates all the senses, and especially the sixth one: the creative sense.' Each month the collection is supplemented with new designs created with the help of external designers and artists. In the meantime, the B2B activities continue to be an important part of their business model. Stanley/Stella is an open platform that works bottom-up. It is not they who create the clothes; it is their customers. Just like the Danish company Mikkeler - 'brewers without a brewery' — which also makes no beer of its own, but serves as a 'beer ambassador' that has all its beers developed and brewed by micro-brewers all across Europe.

It is also possible to apply the successful formula of the online platform in a physical environment, simply by allowing other partners to share floor space in your premises. SCOOP does exactly that (and nothing else) in its stores in the Benelux. It profiles itself as a sales platform for new and unknown labels. Designers rent a piece of their shop for a monthly fee and a commission on any sales. Participating designers receive data, marketing insights and marketing support in return as well. Thanks to this method, SCOOP is already collaborating with more than 75 labels, which also get to sell via the SCOOP webshop and are promoted via its social media sites. On the other side of the Atlantic, Bulletin does the same precise thing in its New York stores, only with an added agenda of female empowerment: they only sell stuff from female-led brands. Moreover, 10% of revenue goes to a planned parenthood organsation.

Thanks to the endless online shelf, shops no longer need to be filled to the rafters with stock. As a result, today's shops have more room at their disposal. By hiring this space to suppliers, other brands or even other retailers, small players and starters can once again be given the opportunity to get a foot in the door of city centre shopping streets, while also adding surprise and inspiration (serendipity) for your existing customers. What's more, this kind of 'blurring' works for both food and non-food. In other words, there are still possibilities enough for physical retail.

We cannot emphasize it enough: it is not about channels, it is about being where the customer wants you to be. This explains why you can find discount supermarket Lidl trying out every possible shopping format these days. The German giant is trying to break through with strategies like premiumization, sustainability and differentiation. At the famous Tomorrowland dance festival, the discounter raised plenty of eyebrows with its pop-up store where party people could stock up on affordable snacks and groceries, although pop-ups have already been part of its game plan for some time: a 'beach club' on the coast, a fashion shop and even a temporary ski shop have all made their appearance in recent times. More permanent are the Lidl webshop, its solid chain of outlet stores and its urban Express concept, which has a smaller range and collection points. The Germans are resolutely playing the omnichannel card. Lidl even shows up at Fashion Weeks, hosting runway shows for its very own fashion collections that it creates in a long-running collaboration with former top model Heidi Klum. It looks like even discount supermarkets are destined to become platforms.

Even if you are an online retailer, a hybrid inline model still seems the way to go, certainly now the e-commerce market is monopolized by only a couple of massive giants. While Amazon and Alibaba are fighting for the major share of the run-shopper cake, there are still plenty of crumbs for the omnichannel retailer to pick up.

When former online pure player Warby Parker reveals plans to reach 100 brick and mortar stores in the US by the end of 2018, it means the retailer of prescription eyeglasses and sunglasses sees added-value in its high street presence. Despite everything virtual technology can do, people still just want to see and feel a pair of glasses on their noses. Likewise, fashion brand ModCloth opened a limited number of physical touch points as service centers, centered around the fitting experience.

Interestingly, even Google prefers omnichannel retailers: retailers and brands with a physical presence will rank higher in product searches than those without.

Making the shopping experience truly relevant

The question that every company needs to ask itself is whether it can add a truly relevant experience to its offer, which it can connect to the consumer at a personal level. Does the brand contribute to the fulfilment of a life style or a life philosophy? Gut feeling and conviction are no longer enough to answer this question. Only a through, data-based knowledge of your target group can confirm that you are on the right track. Better still: open a dialogue with the consumer. Just ask the shoppers what can make your brand more relevant for them. What solutions are they looking for? Find which of these solutions your company can provide and use them as a basis for creating a totality of services and experiences in all contact moments (omnichannel) with potential customers.

To make this experience as consistent and as certain as possible, it is important for brands to control the entire value chain, from production through distribution to marketing. This control is especially critical at all points where the brand comes into direct contact with the shopper. This does not mean that every brand needs to be integrated: collaborations and partnerships (joint purchasing, shop-in-shops, franchises, shared premises, etc.) can also achieve the same results, as long as the brand itself keeps control of direct customer access.

Pick your battles and choose wisely. Whoever makes toilet brushes is probably wasting his time trying to create a unique experience for the end user, although a little creativity can sometimes go a long way: if you see what Oreo can do with a simple biscuit and M&M with a chocolate drop, the sky is potentially the limit!

A brand that has no direct impact on shoppers can make use of new, worldwide technological possibilities instead: marketplaces and machine-to-machine sales are opening up new fields of competition daily. For the producers of commodities, the key is to get as close to the customer as possible and to get there as quickly and efficiently as possible.

Smaller players will have unique opportunities in the new global market to establish niches for themselves. Nowadays, there is a demand for everything, as long as you can find it and can differentiate yourself sufficiently from the crowd. Smart use of all available channels of communication is crucial. From social media through marketplaces to pop-ups, you need to employ everything to win people's trust as a reference in your field. There is also a key role for local players in this scenario, acting as local guides in a worldwide wilderness. 'Think global, act local' is more appropriate than ever.

Today, we are in a transition period, during which retail will be redrawn from top to bottom. At times, it will be a bumpy ride, but from enthusiastic 'adolescence' at the beginning of the new millennium we are now moving towards a degree of maturity. There are still teething troubles, but we are gradually outgrowing them. We are learning by experience and the technological aids to help us are improving all the time. But never assume the process is complete. In new retail, learning is a lifelong task.

// Today we are in a transition period, during which retail will be redrawn from top to bottom. //

We are all witnessing the emergence of new ways of doing business that will allow us to respond to the needs of our changing world. Taking the most important mega-trends as a starting point, the crucial question then becomes: what are the best models for the future? The key is in the hands of each retailer and each brand. The ball is in their court. New best practices are emerging every day. The secret to success is to identify them and apply them in your niche. The future of retail is taking shape as you read these words. The time has come to put all our heads together and share our knowledge.

Everyone is a retailer... and so are we!

Authors usually watch things from the sidelines. But not us. Jorg can be found at least one day a week in the Staopstoelshop pop-up, where he sells relaxation chairs for the elderly that have been refurbished after short-term use. These almost new chairs are hard to distinguish from the real thing, but are much cheaper and also a good example of ecological upcycling: they are reconditioned with specific customers in mind (personalization) and have as their clear value-driven purpose the desire to help older people live longer at home in comfort.

The partnership between the Staopstoelshop pop-up and Kabinet Unique in Antwerp is a good example of local, out-of-the-box retail thinking. Chairs for seniors are hardly likely to create a stampede of visitors, so that the need for collaboration with someone else was clear. In contrast, Kabinet Unique does have a high floor rotation, so the match seemed like an obvious one. A marriage made in heaven, you might say. Kabinet Unique is an association of seven young designers who decided to hire a store that would be manned each day by one of them in turn. As the name implies, theirs are unique products that simply ooze experience: the designers tell their own story and put a smile on shoppers' lips. In the meantime, they have managed to reduce their staff costs to almost zero.

Every object in the store is for sale. And everyone is welcome to display their own products within the pop-up area, in return for a monthly rent or a commission fee. As a result, every square metre of the store is a source of unique experience, but also a source of income for all involved. The collaboration also creates a new kind of brand experience: what used to be seen as 'old-fashioned' - and it doesn't come much more old-fashioned than 'granny chairs' - has been given a new look and a new angle of approach that is now capable of activating children and grandchildren to provide their elderly relatives with more comfortable support for their ageing posteriors.

In addition, a pop-up strategy helps to generate customer awareness. This results in excellent brand value and positioning, so that customers will then have the confidence to place orders online as well.

As you can see, it was the perfect laboratory for writing this book.

A final word

Why this book? And why with two authors? And why 'The Future of Shopping', which brings together experts and retailers to think about the years ahead? And why Home of Retail, our experience centre for FMCG and retail professionals in Antwerp?

These are questions I am often asked and the answer to all of them is simple: because it is our passion! There is no other way to describe it. Or perhaps there is: it is our purpose, our mission to increase the power of the collective brain in the fascinating sector of retail and FMCG. So that fewer stores need to close; so that fewer jobs are lost; so that fewer people see their life's work go up in smoke; so that more people can discover a love for entrepreneurship in the profession.

This is the passion that I share with Pauline, the remarkable lady with the wheelchair who came into my life while I was writing a text one evening in front of the television. My son Jente was watching as well and he said he thought it was tremendous that the disabled ex-triathlete Marc Herremans was now giving training to cross-country runners. Almost without thinking, I replied from behind my PC that there are probably a lot of people with a physical limitation who are able to do a lot, but don't always get the chance to show it.

I couldn't sleep that night for thinking about what Jente had said, so I decided to see if I could turn my own words into practice. A week later, I heard from a recruitment office that they had some interesting CVs for me to see. In my mind, I had the idea of taking on a blogger for a few hours a week - after all, I only had a small start-up - but in the end I chose a young woman who was on the point of graduating from the Vlerick Business School. Everyone said I was mad - including Pauline! When I asked her why I should take her on, she replied: 'Simply because I can write better than you, and in three languages.' 'That's fighting talk, missy,' I thought to myself. 'Let's see if you can prove it.' But prove it she did - and with verve.

People who know RetailDetail well call her my secret weapon. In these times of change, I can recommend everyone to find themselves this kind of weapon. I wouldn't be without her for all the tea in China. And I never want to hear anyone talk to me again about 'the disabled'. Pauline and everyone else is definitely able.

This book was derived from a unique interplay of people. For the initial development, we could rely on the co-operation of some of the best journalists and retail savants in the country, a synergy that resulted in the fulfilment of a dream. Every day we are active in retail, every day we write about retail, every day we talk about retail. We love retail and that is what we want to share with you today in this book.

With our common brain we wish to enhance the common brain of the sector. Thank you for joining us on the journey towards the future of shopping. We hope that you will find this journey an inspiring one and will enjoy it as much as we have enjoyed writing about it. May it give you plenty of new insights, 'aha' moments and creative ideas.

Have a great read!
Jorg (and Pauline, of course)

// Roland Palmer / Managing Director Alibaba Group Benelux, Head of Alipay in Europe, Middle East and Africa //

"Snoeck and Neerman invite us to step into the new retail world where shopping is intuitive, constant and everywhere. A world that has changed from push to pull, where data is key and where service is taken to the next level by chatbots and robots. A world which is about to accelerate thanks to the internet of things. A must-read for those seeking an insightful guidebook for tomorrow's change."

// Cor Molenaar / Professor eMarketing and Distance Selling RSM Erasmus University Rotterdam //

"What this well-written book above all makes clear is that there is now a fragmentation of demand and a corresponding fragmentation of supply, with technology as the matching partner. This makes necessary both concentration (platforms) and a careful curation of the offer. These problems are discussed in a broad framework to underline that what we are now experiencing is just the start of 'the future of retail'. This is an essential insight if you want to survive in this new world."

// Bob Phibbs / CEO The Retail Doctor //

"A chilling reminder of where we are in retail with hope for a different future that changes more in the next ten years than it has in the past 100. Using their keen observations, Snoeck and Neerman point the way to retailers who are already defining the trends and will be table stakes for anyone in retail in the near future."

// Frank De Moor / CEO Q-Park //

"Retail is still the mirror of society. As society is changing faster than ever before, everyone who deals with customers also needs to adjust at the same lightning speed. To be among the winners, you don't need to listen to the prophets of doom or take part in expensive seminars on 'disruption'. All you need are a few concrete guidelines to start your journey. In short, a combination of true passion for your work and the useful practical tips that are the trademark of this book."

// **Dirk Van den Berghe** / Executive Vice President Walmart Inc, Regional CEO Asia and Canada //

"As Snoeck and Neerman put it very aptly, the retail industry is about to change more in the next 10 years than over the past 100 years. These monumental changes are already manifesting in countries like China, Japan, the US and Japan, where a lot of traditional retailers threaten to miss their window. Healthy paranoia, curiosity and common sense to follow up on new, disruptive trends in retail and technology are absolutely necessities to remain successful — or even just relevant — in the future. This innovative book is a very good place to start."

// **Frans Colruyt** / COO Colruyt Group //

"Even though I already know quite a bit about (online) retail, this book was still able to surprise me. The way it is littered with practical examples is fantastic. This is a book that triggers every reflex: it encourages reflection and every few pages gives you serious pause for thought."

// **Erik Van Heuven** / International retail consultant, former Manager INNO, KARSTADT, RENO//

"This book is one of the most interesting and practice-relevant books on the retail industry. As a former CEO and Advisory Board member of the holding of a major German retailer, I recommend this book to all employees as a must-read to understand and tackle today's retail challenges - a valuable gift for your employees, excellent!"

// **Erik Saelens** / Executive strategic director Brandhome //

"Retail is at the heart of a perfect storm and will undergo more changes in the next five years than it did in the past 500 years. This book provides an accessible insight into the challenges, risks and opportunities the entire retail world faces. Everyone who is connected to retail (and wants to remain connected), in every shape or form, needs to read this book."

// **Wouter Kolk** / CEO Ahold Delhaize Europe & Indonesia, CEO Albert Heijn //

"As the Western European population ages and diversifies, the global population is rapidly growing. We face worldwide challenges, like resource scarcity, which have an enormous impact, even close to home. We cannot find the solutions alone. Technology will bring everyone together and provide never-before-seen opportunities. We cannot escape the future, but whoever reads this book, is ahead of the pack!"

// **Sander Van Der Laan** / International CEO Action //

"We are in a rapidly changing world that stimulates customers from all angles. There is no industry as dynamic as the retail industry. What is new, attractive and distinguishable today, could be outdated tomorrow. The authors offer a fascinating window into the development that our customers and industry face. This book quickly offers an insight into the wondrous world of retail. Highly recommended."

// **Billie Whitehouse** / CEO Wearable X //

"What I love about Snoeck and Neerman is their look at the experience from a 360 perspective: everything from the data to the human centric design. As they show, the future of retail isn't just about a shift from physical to digital and back again, its about the spaces in between. The future of shopping isn't just about the environments but also what is being sold, and both these experiences being designed for a future that we want to live and participate in. The future is about enchanted shopping experiences through technology."

// **Wijnand Jongen** / CEO Thuiswinkel.org, Chair Executive Committee Ecommerce Europe //

"A great readable and engaging book on the future of retail. I love the fascinating insights and practical cases: a must read for all who are looking to understand the challenges our industry is facing and who want to take action to thrive in the new state of retail."

// **Howard Saunders** / Retail Futurist and Speaker Twenty Second & Fifth Ltd //

"There cannot be a more pressing issue, at such a significant time, than the future of retail. After all, the way we shop defines our towns, cities and critically, our communities. Jorg's book is a prescient summary from a man who instinctively understands retail and has a clear vision on where it is heading."

// **Piers Fawkes** / Founder and President PSFK //

"I've been an admirer of the work of Jorg Snoeck and Pauline Neerman for a long time and I am excited to see that their extensive knowledge and experience in the field of retail and FMCG now manifests in this engaging and educational first book. Loaded with international examples, the book offers the best insight into the European retail landscape today (and tomorrow)."

// **Mattia Crespi** / IFTF Research Affiliate and Founder Qbit Technologies //

"A great reference for anyone looking to understand the forces that are reshaping the future of retail and the consumer experience with brands. A must read for anyone working in retail."

// **Gino Van Ossel** / Professor Retail Management at Vlerick Business School //

"At last a book that offers a holistic and comprehensive overview of all the trends that are shaping the future of shopping. A must read for retailers and brand manufacturers who want to address the tremendous challenges they are facing."

// **Mike Dawson** / International Desk Editor Lebensmittel Zeitung //

"This book is a must read for every professional within the retail space."

// **Frank Quix** / Managing Director Q&A Insights & Consultancy, Assistent Professor University of Groningen //

"The future of retail is a book that provides great insight into how retail has developed the past decades and gives good guidance for the future. To me, it shows that there is a need for speed: not technology is disruptive but speed is."

 // **Jonathan Reynolds** / Academic Director Oxford Institute of Retail Management University of Oxford //

"Full of practical examples and grounded in a profound understanding of retailing and of the consumer, Snoeck and Neerman have provided a remarkable guide to the transformational changes affecting the sector."

// ENDNOTES //

1   **S. Maybin**, *Busting the attention span myth*, BBC World Service [Online]. 10 Mar. 2017 [Accessed on 15 Aug. 2017] http://www.bbc.com/news/health-38896790.

2   **A. Van De Peer**, *Jongeren dragen steeds vaker reclamekleding: gratis is het nieuwe cool* [Online]. 29 Jun. 2017 [Accessed on 15 Aug. 2017] https://charliemag.be/lijf/reclamekleding/.

3   **R. Thompson**, *Wearable for your dick wants to measure thrusts, girth and warn you about STIs* [Online]. 2 Mar. 2017 [Accessed on 15 Aug. 2017] http://mashable. com/2017/03/02/penis-wearable-thrustsgirth/# 1_oYgkIPPSqs.

4   **M. Stifter**, *Migranten wohl bald in Mehrheit - Ängste sind unbegründet* [Online]. 19 Apr. 2016 [Accessed on 15 Aug. 2017] http://www.augsburger-allgemeine.de/politik/Migranten-wohl-bald-in-Mehrheit-Aengstesind-unbegruendet-id37523542.html.

5   **D. Ballegeer**, *Antwerpen en Brussel kunnen bevolkingsgroei fiscaal niet aan*, De Standaard [Online]. 13 Jul. 2017 [Accessed on 15 Aug. 2017] http://www.standaard. be/cnt/dmf20170713_02970947.

6   **T. Drissen**, *Positieve reviews kosten webwinkels klauwen met geld* [Online]. 11 Aug. 2016 [Accessed on 15 Aug. 2017] https://www.rtlz.nl/business/bedrijven/positieve-reviews-kostenwebwinkels-klauwen-met-geld.

7   **E.K.**, *Europese winkels onthullen werkelijke kost van groenten en fruit*, Knack Weekend [Online]. 24 Jun. 2016 [Accessed on 15 Aug. 2017] http://weekend.knack.be/lifestyle/culinair/europese-winkels-onthullenwerkelijke-kost-van-groenten-en-fruit/articlenormal-720723.html.

8   **N. Morrison**, *Products in 'eco-look' packaging seen as better quality* [Online]. 11 Jul. 2016 [Accessed on 15 Aug. 2017] http://www.foodnavigator.com/Market-Trends/Products-in-eco-look-packaging-seenas-better-quality.

9   **Vandenberghe, P.**, *Voedseloverschotten: supermarkten zijn niet de grote boosdoeners* [Online]. 29 Oct. 2014 [Accessed on 15 Aug. 2017] http://www.mo.be/opinie/voedseloverschotten-supermarktenzijn-niet-de-grote boosdoeners.

10 **CIPS**, *The Pro's and Con's of Local Sourcing* [Online]. [Accessed on 15 Aug. 2017] https://www.cips.org/en/knowledge/procurement-topics-and-skills/srm-and-sc-management/global-supplychains/the-pros-and-cons-of-local-sourcing/.

11 **R. Spoler**, *Predictive e-mailmarketing: zo zet je 7 stappen naar maximale relevantie* [Online]. 19 Apr. 2017 [Accessed on 15 Aug. 2017] https://www.frankwatching.com/archive/2017/04/19/predictive-emailmarketing-zo-zet-je-7-stappen-naarmaximale-relevantie/.

12 **K. Morley**, *Exclusive: End of fixed prices within five years as supermarkets adopt electronic price tags* [Online]. 24 Jun. 2017 [Accessed on 15 Aug. 2017] http://www.telegraph.co.uk/news/2017/06/24/exclusive-end-fixed-priceswithin-five-years-supermarkets-adopt/.

13 **L. Ulanoff**, *iRobot CEO: "We will always ask your permission to even store map data"* [Online]. 25 Jul. 2017 [Accessed on 15 Aug. 2017] http://mashable.com/2017/07/25/irobot-wants-to-sell-homemapping-data/.

14 **A. Gabbatt**, *Married to money: 'smart' wedding ring doubles as payment method* [Online]. 6 Jan. 2017 [Accessed on 15 Aug. 2017] https://www.theguardian.com/technology/2017/jan/06/tappy-smartwedding-ring-ces-2017.

15 **P. Olson**, *Report: Facebook Is Turning Messenger Into A Mobile Wallet*, Forbes [Online]. 29 Mar. 2016 [Accessed on 15 Aug. 2017] https://www.forbes.com/sites/parmyolson/2016/03/29/facebookmessenger-businesses-payments/.

16   **Torfs**, *Werken met hart en ziel [Online].*
[Accessed on 15 Aug. 2017] http:/ /www.
werkenbijtorfs.be/werken-methart-en-ziel.
html.

17   **Redactie**, *Waarom ook Elvea een pop-up
opent, RetailDetail* [Online]. 12 Dec. 2015
[Accessed on 15 Aug. 2017] https://www.
retaildetail.be/nl/news/food/ waarom-ook-
elvea-een-pop-opent.

18   *Verkeer in Nederland daalt terwijl economie
en arbeidsmarkt langzaam aantrekken; Blijft
tweede land van Europa met hoogste filedruk*
[Online]. 16 Mar. 2016 [Accessed on 15
Aug. 2017] http://inrix.com/pressreleases/
scorecard-nl/.

19   **Doro**, *Deze tien slimme oplossingen moeten
de Antwerpse mobiliteit verbeteren, Gazet
van Antwerpen* [Online]. 13 Jan. 2017
[Accessed on 15 Aug. 2017] http://www.gva.
be/cnt/dmf20170113_02672260/deze-tien-
slimmeoplossingen-moeten-de-antwerpse-
mobiliteitverbeteren.

20   **K. Koelemeijer**, *De digitalisering van
winkelgebieden moet sneller, RTL Z* [Online]. 9
Apr. 2017 [Accessed on 15 Aug. 2017] https://
www.rtlz.nl/opinie/column/kitty-koelemeijer/
de-digitalisering-vanwinkelgebieden-moet-
sneller.

21   **C. Stern**, *Forget something? H&M under fire
for casting Ashley Graham in new H&M Studio
campaign - but NOT selling plus sizes in stores,
Daily Mail* [Online]. 12 Aug. 2016 [Accessed
on 15 Aug. 2017] http://www.dailymail.
co.uk/femail/article-3736306/Forget-H-M-
fire-casting-Ashley-Graham-new-H-M-Studio-
campaign-NOT-selling-plus-sizes-stores.html.

22   **Filippa K Lease**: *A way to sustainable
consumption* [Online]. [Accessed on 15 Aug.
2017] https://www.filippa-k.com/be/filippak-
world/lease.

23   **Postnord**, *Swedish innovation takes grocery
shopping into the future– Swedish companies
first to test in-fridge delivery of groceries*
[Online]. 20 Apr. 2016 [Accessed on 15 Aug.
2017] http://www.postnord.com/en/media/
press-releases/postnord-sverige/2016/
swedish-innovationtakes-grocery-shopping-
into-the-futureswedish-companies-first-to-
test-in-fridgedelivery-of-groceries/.

24   *'There's an equation in retail around customer
expectations: time plus experience, plus
value proposition.' In: H Milnes, How custom
footwear retailer Shoes of Prey cut its delivery
time to two weeks, Digiday* [Online]. 8 May
2017 [Accessed on 15 Aug. 2017] https://
digiday.com/marketing/ custom-footwear-
retailer-shoes-prey-cutdelivery-time-two-
weeks/.

// BIBLIOGRAPHY //

Akkanto, *RepTrak Belgium 2016 Once again, Colruyt is Belgium's most reputable business* [Online]. 28 Apr. 2016 [Accessed on 15 Aug. 2017] http://www.akkanto.com/network/reputation-institute/667-reputationmanagement/259-once-again-colruyt-is-belgiums-most-reputable-business.

Alizila News, *Alibaba is Building an 'E-Commerce Media Ecosystem'* [Online]. 2 Mar. 2016 [Accessed on 15 Aug. 2017] http://www.alibabagroup.com/en/ir/article?news=p160302.

Anderson, C. (2006), *The Long Tail: Why the Future of Business is Selling Less of More*, New York: Hyperion Books.

[Anoniem], *Ikea lanza un nuevo concepto de tienda*, Revista Info Retail [Online]. 5 Feb. 2015 [Accessed on 15 Aug. 2017] http://www.revistainforetail.com/noticiadet/ikea-lanza-un-nuevo-concepto-de-tienda/c081822c0f13acf7d-95c2112a502f180.

[Anoniem], *Moet de bezoeker (van de binnenstad) gratis parkeren, Parkeer 24* [Online]. May 2016 [Accessed on 15 Aug. 2017] http://cormolenaar.nl/wp-content/uploads/2016/06/PDFartikel-molenaar-mingardo-gratis-parkeren.pdf.

[Anoniem], *Slechts 0,27% betalingen gebeurt contactloos*, Het Belang van Limburg (21 Apr. 2017), 6.

Arline, K., *What is C2B?*, BusinessNewsDaily [Online]. 2 Jan. 2015 [Accessed on 15 Aug. 2017] http://www.businessnewsdaily.com/5001-what-is-c2b.html.

Aussems, M., *Waarom bitcoin geen toekomst heeft maar de blockchain wel* [Online]. 9 Feb. 2017 [Accessed on 15 Aug. 2017] http://www.techpulse.be/achtergrond/211916/waarombitcoin-geen-toekomst-heeft-maar-de-blockchain-wel/.

Ballegeer, D., *Antwerpen en Brussel kunnen bevolkingsgroei fiscaal niet aan*, De Standaard [Online]. 13 Jul. 2017 [Accessed on 15 Aug. 2017] http://www.standaard.be/cnt dmf20170713_02970947.

Ballon P. (2016), *Smart Cities*, Leuven: Lannoo-Campus.

Beltman, A., *Gaastra, Hugo Boss en H&M: zo duurzaam is uw favoriete kleding*, HP De Tijd [Online]. 29 Apr. 2014 [Accessed on 15 Aug. 2017] http://www.hpdetijd.nl/2014-04-29/gaastra-hugo-boss-en-hm-zo-duurzaam-isuw-kleding/.

Bernaerts, N., *15 miljoen euro = 10.000 auto's uit file*, Het Laatste Nieuws [Online]. 27 Aug. 2016 [Accessed on 15 Aug. 2017] http://www.hln.be/regio/nieuws-uit-schoten/15-miljoeneuro-10-000-auto-s-uit-file-a2841213/.

Biggs, C. e.a., *What China Reveals About the Future of Shopping* [Online]. 4 May 2017 [Accessed on 15 Aug. 2017] https://www.bcg.com/en-be/publications/2017/retailglobalization-china-reveals-future-shopping.aspx.

Bosteels, K., *Antwerpse Wilde Zee stilaan te duur voor zelfstandigen?*, RetailDetail [Online]. 4 Aug. 2016 [Accessed on 15 Aug. 2017] https://www.retaildetail.be/nl/news/vastgoed/antwerpse-wilde-zee-stilaan-te-duur-voorzelfstandigen.

Bosteels, K., *Plan tegen winkelleegstand in Roeselare werkt*, RetailDetail [Online]. 17 Mar. 2016 [Accessed on 15 Aug. 2017] https://www.retaildetail.be/nl/news/algemeen/ plan-tegen-winkelleegstand-roeselare-werkt.

Boston Retail Partners (2017), *POS/Customer Engagement Survey. 18th Annual Survey*, Boston: BRP.

Castillo, M., *Adidas Is Letting Fans Design Jerseys For Their Favorite Football Team*, PSFK [Online]. 11 Aug. 2016 [Accessed on 15 Aug. 2017] https://www.psfk.com/2016/08/adidas-lets-fansdesign-jerseys-for-favorite-football-team.html.

CEV-SCvV (2016), *Jaarlijks verslag 2016: Studiecommissie voor de Vergrijzing*, Brussels: SCvV.

Clark, D. (2016), *Alibaba: The House That Jack Ma Built*, New York: HarperCollins.

Compendium voor de Leefomgeving, *Indicator Leegstand van winkels, 2004-2016* [Online]. 8 Sep. 2016 [Accessed on 15 Aug. 2017] http://www.clo.nl/indicatoren/nl215104-leegstand-winkels.

Corbin, D., *Jack Ma: The C2B business model is an "undeniable trend"*, Tech in Asia [Online]. 15 Jul. 2014 [Accessed on 15 Aug. 2017] https://www.techinasia.com/jack-ma-softbank-world-alibaba-business-model.

Corstjens, M. & Corstjens, J. (1995), *Store Wars: The Battle for Mindspace and Shelfspace*, New Jersey: Wiley.

Corstjens, M. (2015), *Penetration. The New Battle for Mind Space and Shelf Space*, Norwich: Bertrams.

Crain's New York, *Free parking isn't worth the stress, the hazards and the wasted time* [Online]. 18 May 2016 [Accessed on 15 Aug. 2017] http://www.crainsnewyork.com/article/20160518/OPINION/160519889/free-parking-isnt-worth-the-stress-the-hazards-and-the-wasted-time.

Crul, M. & Schneider J. (2013), *Superdiversiteit*, Amsterdam: Vu University Press.

Dawson, M., *Marcel Corstjens debunks marketing myths* [Online]. 26 Feb. 2016 [Accessed on 15 Aug. 2017] http://www.german-retail-blog.com/topic/past-blogs/Professor-Marcel-Corstjens-demolishes-another-round-of-marketing-myths-365.

Deckmyn, D., *TV boeit vooral nog ouderen* [Online]. De Standaard, 26 Feb. 2016 [Accessed on 15 Aug. 2017] http://www.standaard.be/cnt/dmf20160225_02150510.

Deloitte, Food Marketing Institute & Grocery Manufacturers Association (2016), *Capitalizing on the shifting consumer food value equation*, New York: Deloitte Development LLC.

Deloitte (2016), *Retail Volatility Index*, New York: Deloitte Development LLC.

Del Rey, J., *55 percent of online shoppers start their product searches on Amazon* [Online]. 27 Sep. 2016 [Accessed on 15 Aug. 2017] https://www.recode.net/2016/9/27/13078526/amazon-online-shopping-product-search-engine.

De Panafieu, O. e.a. (2016), *Robots and retail: What does the future hold for people and robots in the stores of tomorrow?*, Parijs: Roland Berger.

De Morgen, *Straks meer luiers voor senioren dan voor baby's* [Online]. 28 Nov. 2015 [Accessed on 15 Aug. 2017] https://www.demorgen.be/plus/straks-meer-luiers-voor-senioren-dan-voor-baby-s-b-1448671203444/.

DNB/Betaalvereniging Nederland (2016), *Betalen aan de kassa 2015*, Amsterdam: DNB & Betaalvereniging Nederland.

De Reu, M., *In beeld: De route van een online pakketje*, Data News, [Online]. 22 Dec. 2016 [Accessed on 15 Aug. 2017] http://datanews.knack.be/ict/nieuws/in-beeld-de-route-van-een-online-pakketje/article-normal-793517.html.

De Waele, S. (2014), *Retail 4.0 – the Fun(doo) case. Omnichannel and multichannel are dead* [Presentation]. 19 Mar. 2014 [Accessed on 15 Aug. 2017] https://www.slideshare.net/webwinkelvakdag/presentatie-eshop-expo-2014-fundoo-presentatie-retail-detail-v01.

Doro, *Deze tien slimme oplossingen moeten de Antwerpse mobiliteit verbeteren*, Gazet van Antwerpen [Online]. 13 Jan. 2017 [Accessed on 15 Aug. 2017] http://www.gva.be/cnt/dmf20170113_02672260/deze-tien-slimme-oplossingen-moeten-de-antwerpse-mobiliteit-verbeteren.

Duhigg, C., *How Companies Learn Your Secrets* [Online]. 16 Feb. 2012 [Accessed on 15 Aug. 2017] http http://www.nytimes.com/2012/02/19/magazine/shopping-habits.html.

E.K., *Europese winkels onthullen werkelijke kost van groenten en fruit*, Knack Weekend [Online]. 24 Jun. 2016 [Accessed on 15 Aug. 2017] http://weekend.knack.be/lifestyle/culinair/europese-winkels-onthullen-werkelijke-kost-van-groenten-en-fruit/article-normal-720723.html.

Engelen, G. e.a. (2015), *Duurzaam inkopen doe je zo*, Brussel: FEVIA, Boerenbond, The Shift, Fairtrade Belgium en Vredeseilanden.

Drissen, T., *Positieve reviews kosten webwinkels klauwen met geld* [Online]. 11 Aug. 2016 [Accessed on 15 Aug. 2017]; https://www.rtlz. nl/business/bedrijven/positieve-reviews-kosten-webwinkels-klauwen-met-geld.

El País, *Alicia Borrás, Miss España 1965, baila para Desigual en su último videoclip* [Online]. 10 Mar. 2016 [Accessed on 15 Aug. 2017]; https://smoda. elpais.com/imperdibles/2016/03/alicia-borras-miss-espana-1965-baila-para-desigual-en-su-ultimo-videoclip/

Eurostat, Wronsk, A. red. (2015), *European Commission Demography Report. Short Analytical Web Note 3/2015*, Luxembourg: Publications Office of the European Union.

European Commission (2015), *Growing the European silver economy*, Luxemburg: European Commission.

Fawkes, P. red. (2016), *PSFK Future of Retail 2016 Report*, New York: PSFK Labs.

Fawkes, P. red. (2017), *PSFK Future of Retail 2017 Report*, New York: PSFK Labs.

Fawkes, P. red. (2016), *The Future of Advertising: The New Rules Of Consumer Engagement*, New York: PSFK Labs.

Galloway, S. (2017), *The Four: The Hidden DNA of Amazon, Apple, Facebook, and Google*, Londen: Penguin.

Göbbel, T., Goeken, C. & Onnen (2017), A., *Catch the waves in consumer goods: Mastering disruption in dynamic markets*, München: Roland Berger.

Google, *Your Guide to Winning the Shift to Mobile*, Think with Google [Online]. Sep. 2015 [Accessed on 15 Aug. 2017] https://www.thinkwithgoogle. com/marketing-resources/micro-moments/micromoments-guide-pdf-download/.

Google/Shopper Sciences, *The Zero Moment of Truth Macro Study* [Presentatie], Apr. 2011.

Gozin, L., *Micro Moments: Begrijp, pas toe en win*, Invisible Puppy [Online]. 18 Jul. 2017 [Accessed on 15 Aug. 2017] https://www.invisiblepuppy.com/ blog/micro-moments-begrijp-pas-toe-en-win.

Gratton, L. & Scott, A. (2016), *The 100-Year Life: Living and Working in an Age of Longevity*, Londen: Bloomsbury.

Grieder, P. e.a., *The future of retail: How to make your bricks click* [Online]. Sep. 2014 [Accessed on 15 Aug. 2017]; via http://www.mckinsey.com/ business-functions/marketing-and-sales/our-insights/the-future-of-retail-how-to-make-your-bricks-click.

Guérin, S. (2015), *Silver Génération - 10 idées reçues à combattre à propos des seniors*, Paris : Michalon.

Hermanides, E., *'Veel vrijheid, het kan niet gek genoeg in de stad'*, Trouw [Online]. 26 Mar. 2016 [Accessed on 15 Aug. 2017] https://www.trouw. nl/home/-veel-vrijheid-het-kan-niet-gek-genoeg-in-de-stad-~a21dcaaf/.

Hinssen, P., *Het jaar van het 'bakske'. De Glazen Bol 2017*, De Tijd [Online]. 31 Dec. 2016 [Accessed on 15 Aug. 2017] http://www.tijd.be/opinie/ algemeen/Het-jaar-van-het-bakske/9847309.

Hinssen, P. (2017), *The Day After Tomorrow: Hoe overleven in tijden van radicale innovatie?*, Leuven: LannooCampus.

Hinssen, P. (2010), *The New Normal: Explore The Limits Of The Digital World*, Gent: Mach Media.

Hochman, D., *Shoes Of Prey Delivers Women's Custom Footwear In Two Weeks At Retail Prices*, Forbes [Online]. 31 May 2017 [Accessed on 15 Aug. 2017] https://www.forbes.com/sites/ davidhochman/2017/05/31/shoes-of-prey-delivers-womens-custom-footwear-in-two-weeks-at-retail-prices/.

IDC, *IDC Worldwide Quarterly Wearable Device Tracker* [Online]. 2 Mar. 2017 [Accessed on 15 Aug. 2017] http://www.idc.com/getdoc.jsp?containerId=prUS42342317.

Inci, E., Who pays for free parking?, *The Milken Institute Review* (2016), First Quarter, 66-74.

Inge, S., *Fake Italian restaurant tops TripAdvisor ranking* [Online]. 23 Jun. 2016 [Accessed on 15 Aug. 2017] https://www.thelocal.it/20150623/fake-italian-restaurant-gets-top-spot-on-tripadvisor.

Iskyan, K., *China's middle class is exploding*, Business Insider [Online]. 25 Jul. 2017 [Accessed on 15 Aug. 2017] http://uk.businessinsider.com/chinas-middle-class-is-exploding-2016-8.

Julius, How the "Oreo Dunk Challenge" was catalyzed by influencer marketing [Online]. 19 Apr. 2017 [Accessed on 15 Aug. 2017] https://medium.com/juliusworks/how-the-oreo-dunk-challenge-was-catalyzed-by-influencer-marketing-e9f15c846017.

Kaptein, M. (2015), *Persuasion Profiling: How the Internet Knows What Makes You Tick*, Amsterdam: Atlas Contact.

Kjeldsen, C., *The future of SME and the evolution of business clusters* [Presentation]. 14 Oct. 2013, Copenhagen: Instituttet for Fremtidsforskning.

Kenney R. & Fleming, N. (2016), *Mobile Shopping Focus Report: Actionable Insights from 400 Million Shoppers*, Burlington: Demandware.

Koelemeijer, K., *Opinie: Retail blijft mensenwerk*, RTL Z [Online]. 12 Feb. 2017 [Accessed on 15 Aug. 2017] https://www.rtlz.nl/opinie/column/kitty-koelemeijer/retail-blijft-mensenwerk.

Koelemeijer, K., *De digitalisering van winkelgebieden moet sneller*, RTL Z [Online]. 9 Apr. 2017 [Accessed on 15 Aug. 2017] https://www.rtlz.nl/opinie/column/kitty-koelemeijer/de-digitalisering-van-winkelgebieden-moet-sneller.

Kopinga, W., *Digimeter: 'Slechts 6 procent van de Vlamingen heeft geen enkel slim digitaal toestel in huis'* [Online]. 25 Jan. 2017 [Accessed on 15 Aug. 2017] http://datanews.knack.be/ict/nieuws/digimeter-slechts-6-procent-van-de-vlamingen-heeft-geen-enkel-slim-digitaal-toestel-in-huis/article-normal-805965.html.

Lamarque, C. (2017), *Influencers*, Leuven: LannooCampus

Lamrabat, R. (2017), *Etnomarketing: Het vertrouwen van de nieuwe consument*, Antwerp: Pelckmans Pro.

Lanzieri, G. (2011), *The greying of the baby boomers. A century-long view of ageing in European populations*, Luxemburg: Eurostat.

Latten, J., *Levensverwachting 65-jarige 5 jaar hoger sinds AOW-wet* [Online]. 30 Jul. 2016 [Accessed on 15 Aug. 2017] https://www.cbs.nl/nl-nl/nieuws/2016/22/levensverwachting-65-jarige-5-jaar-hoger-sinds-aow-wet

Lemaitre, F. & Rombauts, A. (2016), *Framily: Hoe millennialouders het gezin hertekenen*, Tielt: Lannoo.

Lemmens, R., Donaldson, B. & Marcos, J. (2014), *From Selling to Co-creating*, Amsterdam: BIS Publishers.

Leung, G. & Lesko, Z. (2014), *The Collaborative Economy: Empowering Freelancers, Gig-Workers and Sharers*, Boston: AGC Partners.

Lewis, L. & Dart, M. (2014), *The New Rules of Retail: Competing in the World's Toughest Marketplace*, New York: St. Martin's Press.

Lodewijckx, E., *Aantal alleenwonenden in Vlaanderen sinds 1990 toegenomen met 50%* [Online]. Jan. 2016 [Accessed on 15 Aug. 2017]; https://www.vlaanderen.be/nl/publicaties/detail/aantal-alleenwonenden-in-vlaanderen-sinds-1990-toegenomen-met-50-1

Maheshwarijuly, S., *As Amazon's Influence Grows, Marketers Scramble to Tailor Strategies* [Online]. 31 Jul. 2017 [Accessed on 15 Aug. 2017] https://www.nytimes.com/2017/07/31/business/media/amazon-advertising.html.

Maier, A. (2017), *Eeuwig houdbaar : de ongekende toekomst van ons lichaam*, Amsterdam: Prometheus.

Manyika, J. e.a., *Independent work: Choice, necessity, and the gig economy*, Report McKinsey Global Institute [Online]. Oct. 2016 [Accessed on 15 Aug. 2017] http://www.mckinsey.com/global-themes/employment-and-growth/independent-work-choice-necessity-and-the-gig-economy.

Marine Stewardship Council, *Gecertificeerde visconsumptie in opmars* [Online]. 15 Aug. 2016 [Accessed on 15 Aug. 2017] https://www.msc.org/nieuws/nieuws/gecertificeerde-visconsumptie-in-opmars.

Maybin, S., *Busting the attention span myth*, BBC World Service [Online]. 10 Mar. 2017 [Accessed on 15 Aug. 2017] http://www.bbc.com/news/health-38896790.

Meeker, M., *2015 Internet Trends*, Kleiner Perkins Caufield Byers [Presentation]. 25 May 2015 [Accessed on 15 Aug. 2017] http://www.kpcb.com/blog/2015-internet-trends.

Meijers, C. e.a. (2014), *Cross channel retail update 2014: De invloed van online winkelen*, Amsterdam: ABN Amro.

Molenaar, C. (2017), *De kracht van platformstrategie: het is buigen of barsten*, Amsterdam: Uitgeverij Boom.

Molenaar, C. (2011), *Het einde van winkels? De strijd om de klant*, Amsterdam: Uitgeverij Boom.

Molenaar, C. (2012), *Red de winkel: zo kan het niet langer*, Amsterdam: Academic Service.

Molenaar, C. (2014), *Kijken, kijken ... anders kopen*, Amsterdam: Academic Service.

Montague, T. (2013), *True Story: How to Combine Story and Action to Transform Your Business*, Brighton: Harvard Business Review Press.

Montini, L., *Marketing Trend: Shift to Native Advertising Explained (Infographic)*, Inc. [Online]. 23 Apr. 2014 [Accessed on 15 Aug. 2017] https://www.inc.com/laura-montini/infographic/the-shift-to-native-advertising-in-marketing.html.

Morley, K., *Exclusive: End of fixed prices within five years as supermarkets adopt electronic price tags* [Online]. 24 Jun. 2017 [Accessed on 15 Aug. 20177] http://www.telegraph.co.uk/news/2017/06/24/exclusive-end-fixed-prices-within-five-years-supermarkets-adopt/.

Morris, H., *A weird and wonderful journey to M&M's World, London's most peculiar tourist attraction*, Telegraph [Online]. 27 Jan. 2017 [Accessed on 15 Aug. 2017] http://www.telegraph.co.uk/travel/destinations/europe/united-kingdom/england/london/articles/m-and-ms-world-london-weirdest-tourist-attraction/.

Morrison, N., *Products in 'eco-look' packaging seen as better quality* [Online]. 11 Jul. 2016 [Accessed on 15 Aug. 2017] http://www.foodnavigator.com/Market-Trends/Products-in-eco-look-packaging-seen-as-better-quality.

Murray, K. (2013), *The Retail Value Proposition: Crafting Unique Experiences at Compelling Prices*, Toronto: University of Toronto Press.

Najberg, A., *Hema supermarket offers shoppers a 'new retail' experience*, Alizila News [Online]. 17 Jul. 2017 [Accessed on 15 Aug. 2017] http://www.alizila.com/hema-supermarket-offers-shoppers-new-retail-experience/.

Neerman, P., *Er kan maar één de goedkoopste zijn, de rest moet iets anders verzinnen*, RetailDetail [Online]. 3 May 2011 [Accessed on 15 Aug. 2017] https://www.retaildetail.be/nl/news/retaildossier/%E2%80%9Cer-kan-maar-%C3%A9%C3%A9n-de-goedkoopste-zijn-de-rest-moet-iets-anders-verzinnen%E2%80%9D.

Neerman, P., Saskia Van Uffelen (Ericsson): *"Waarom laten we de consument niet zelf zijn product maken?"*, RetailDetail [Online]. 16 Jan. 2017 [Accessed on 15 Aug. 2017] https://www.retaildetail.be/nl/news/algemeen/saskia-van-uffelen-ericsson-%E2%80%9Cwaarom-laten-we-de-consument-niet-zelf-zijn-product-maken.

Neerman, P., *"Shopping should be stripped of its worthless moments"*, RetailDetail [Online]. 20 Mar. 2017 [Accessed on 15 Aug. 2017] https://www.retaildetail.eu/en/news/general/%E2%80%9Cshopping-should-be-stripped-its-worthless-moments%E2%80%9D.

Neerman, P., *Thomas Vaarten (A.S.Adventure, JUTTU): "Omnichannel betekent doen hoe de klant het wil"*, RetailDetail [Online]. 26 Jan. 2017 [Accessed on 15 Aug. 2017] https://www.retaildetail.be/nl/news/algemeen/thomas-vaarten-asadventure-juttu-%E2%80%9Comnichannel-betekent-doen-hoe-de-klant-het-wil%E2%80%9D.

Neuvy, F. (2016), *Is the silver economy entering its golden age* [Presentation]. Paris: L'Observatoire Cetelem.

OECD (2006), *Live longer, work longer*, Paris: OECD Publishing.

Olson, P., *Report: Facebook Is Turning Messenger Into A Mobile Wallet*, Forbes [Online]. 29 Mar. 2016 [Accessed on 15 Aug. 2017] https://www.forbes.com/sites/parmyolson/2016/03/29/facebook-messenger-businesses-payments/.

Open Companies, *Infographic | Hoe belangrijk zijn online reviews nou echt?* [Online]. [Accessed on 15 Aug. 2017] https://www.opencompanies.nl/blog/infographic-online-reviews/.

Panetta, K., Gartner, *Top Trends in the Gartner Hype Cycle for Emerging Technologies, 2017* [Online]. 15 Aug. 2017 [Accessed on 15 Aug. 2017] http://www.gartner.com/smarterwithgartner/top-trends-in-the-gartner-hype-cycle-for-emerging-technologies-2017.

Parker, G., Van Alstyne M. & Choudary S. (2016), *Platform Revolution: How Networked Markets Are Transforming the Economy And How to Make Them Work for You*, New York: W. W. Norton & Company.

Pratz, A. e.a. (2016), *Cashing In on Cashless Commerce*, New York: A.T. Kearney.

PSFK (2017), *PSFK New York City Retail guide*, New York: PSFK.

Qadar, S., *Shoes of Prey: flying high, but at a price*, SBS Small Business Secrets [Online]. 12 Feb. 2017 [Accessed on 15 Aug. 2017] http://www.sbs.com.au/news/article/2017/01/30/shoes-prey-flying-high-price.

Quartier, K., *The sense and nonsense of technology* [Online]. 5 May 2017 [Accessed on 15 Aug. 2017] https://www.linkedin.com/pulse/sense-nonsense-technology-katelijn-quartier?articleId=6266154151684771840.

Quix, F. (2016), *Retailmarketing*, Groningen: Noordhoff Uitgevers.

Ramli, D., *Jack Ma Sees Decades of Pain as Internet Upends Old Economy*, Bloomberg News [Online]. 23 Apr. 2017 [Accessed on 15 Aug. 2017] https://www.bloomberg.com/news/articles/2017-04-23/jack-ma-sees-decades-of-pain-as-internet-upends-older-economy.

Redactie, *Rachel Shechtman (STORY): "Maximaliseer je beleving, want dat is de sleutel"*, RetailDetail [Online]. 26 Mar. 2015 [Accessed on 15 Aug. 2017] https://www.retaildetail.be/nl/news/algemeen/rachel-shechtman-story-maximaliseer-je-beleving-want-dat-de-sleutel.

Redactie, *Waarom ook Elvea een pop-up opent*, RetailDetail [Online]. 12 Dec. 2015 [Accessed on 15 Aug. 2017] https://www.retaildetail.be/nl/news/food/waarom-ook-elvea-een-pop-opent.

Rowinski, D., *Here Are Two Companies That Set An Example For The Future Of Retail*, ARC [Online]. 17 Feb. 2017 [Accessed on 15 Aug. 2017] https://arc.applause.com/2017/02/17/future-of-retail-shoes-of-prey-indochino/.

Saelens, E. (2017), *Marketing of Meaning: Why purpose markets itself*, Antwerp: Brandhome publishing.

Schwab, K. (2016), *The Fourth Industrial Revolution*, Genève: World Economic Forum.

Shoup, D. (2011), *The High Cost of Free Parking*, Los Angeles: Planners Press & American Planning Association.

Silverman D. red. (2016), *IAB internet advertising revenue report*, New York: PricewaterhouseCoopers.

Snoeck, J., *Metro Group schakelt versnelling hoger in groeiplannen*, RetailDetail [Online]. 7 May 2015 [Accessed on 15 Aug. 2017] https://www.retaildetail.be/nl/news/algemeen/metro-group-schakelt-versnelling-hoger-groeiplannen.

Snyders, H., *Mastercard laat je betalen met een selfie*, Financieel Dagblad [Online]. 4 Oct. 2016 [Accessed on 15 Aug. 2017] https://fd.nl/economie-politiek/1170025/mastercard-laat-je-betalen-met-een-selfie.

Soenens, D., *Betalen met een selfie*, De Morgen [Online]. 19 Aug. 2015 [Accessed on 15 Aug. 2017] https://www.demorgen.be/economie/betalen-met-een-selfie-b0045564/.

Spoler, R., *Predictive e-mailmarketing: zo zet je 7 stappen naar maximale relevantie* [Online]. 19 Apr. 2017 [Accessed on 15 Aug. 20177] https://www.frankwatching.com/archive/2017/04/19/predictive-e-mailmarketing-zo-zet-je-7-stappen-naar-maximale-relevantie/.

Steenbergen H. red. (2015), *Food inspiration trend report 2015*, Wageningen: Shoot my food.

Stephens, D. (2017), *Reengineering Retail: The Future of Selling in a Post-Digital World*, Vancouver: Figure 1 Publishing.

Stephens, D. (2013), *The Retail Revival: Reimagining Business for the New Age of Consumerism*, New Jersey: John Wiley & Sons.

Stern, C., *Forget something? H&M under fire for casting Ashley Graham in new H&M Studio campaign - but NOT selling plus sizes in stores*, Daily Mail [Online]. 12 Aug. 2016 [Accessed on 15 Aug. 20177] http://www.dailymail.co.uk/femail/article-3736306/Forget-H-M-fire-casting-Ashley-Graham-new-H-M-Studio-campaign-NOT-selling-plus-sizes-stores.html.

Stifter, M., *Migranten wohl bald in Mehrheit - Ängste sind unbegründet* [Online]. 19 Apr. 2016 [Accessed on 15 Aug. 2017] http://www.augsburger-allgemeine.de/politik/Migranten-wohl-bald-in-Mehrheit-Aengste-sind-unbegruendet-id37523542.html.

Stone, B. (2013), *The Everything Store: Jeff Bezos and the Age of Amazon*, Londen: Bantam Press.

Sundararajan, A. (2016), *The Sharing Economy: The End of Employment and the Rise of Crowd-Based Capitalism*, Massachusetts: MIT Press.

Tanghe, N., *Cash geld nog lang niet uitgeteld*, De Standaard [Online]. 6 Apr. 2017 [Accessed on 15 Aug. 2017] http://www.standaard.be/cnt/dmf20170405_02819988.

Taryn, L., *Gillette to introduce new razor for women* [Online]. 9 Jan. 2015 [Accessed on 15 Aug. 2017] https://www.bostonglobe.com/business/2015/01/09/gillette-introduce-new-razor-for-women/y1tcVwXvir6qi58MrRTmWO/story.html.

The Economist, *The grey market. Older consumers will reshape the business landscape* [Online]. 7 Apr. 2016 [Accessed on 15 Aug. 2017] https://www.economist.com/news/business/21696539-older-consumers-will-reshape-business-landscape-grey-market.

Thompson, R., *Wearable for your dick wants to measure thrusts, girth and warn you about STIs* [Online]. 2 Mar. 2017 [Accessed on 15 Aug. 2017] http://mashable.com/2017/03/02/penis-wearable-thrusts-girth/#1_oYgkIPPSqs.

Thomson Reuters (2017), *State of the global Islamic economy report 2016/17*, Dubai: Dubai Islamic Economy Development Centre.

Toch, H. (2014), *Happy Profit: Ga voor winst en wees er trots op*, Leuven: LannooCampus.

Toch, H. (2013), *Transformeren om te overleven: Marketing in het nieuwe tijdperk*, Leuven: LannooCampus.

Tokmetzis, D. & Martijn, M. (2016), *Je hebt wél iets te verbergen*, Amsterdam: De Correspondent.

Torfs, *Werken met hart en ziel* [Online]. [Accessed on 15 Aug. 2017] http://www.werkenbijtorfs.be/werken-met-hart-en-ziel.html.

Trefis, *How Important Is Germany For Amazon?* [Online]. 18 Jan. 2017 [Accessed on 15 Aug. 2017] http://www.nasdaq.com/article/how-important-is-germany-for-amazon-cm735034.

Trotter, C., *High Street of the Future: How is Tech is Changing Retail Spaces?* [Online]. 20 May 2016 [Accessed on 15 Aug. 2017] https://www.speakerscorner.co.uk/blog/the-future-of-retail.

Trotter, C., *Is Micro Retail the Future of the High Street?* [Online]. 8 Jun. 2016 [Accessed on 15 Aug. 2017] https://www.linkedin.com/pulse/micro-retail-future-high-street-cate-trotter.

Tsjeng, Z., *Teens These Days Are Queer AF, New Study Says* [Online]. 10 Mar. 2016 [Accessed on 15 Aug. 2017] via https://broadly.vice.com/en_us/article/kb4dvz/teens-these-days-are-queer-af-new-study-says.

Ulanoff, L., *iRobot CEO: "We will always ask your permission to even store map data"* [Online]. 25 Jul. 2017 [Accessed on 15 Aug. 2017] http://mashable.com/2017/07/25/irobot-wants-to-sell-home-mapping-data/.

Van Belleghem, S. (2012), *De Conversation Company: gebruik de feedback van je klanten nu ook echt*, Leuven: LannooCampus.

Van Belleghem, S. (2013), *De Conversation Manager*, Leuven: LannooCampus.

Van Belleghem, S. (2014), *When digital becomes human: Klantenrelaties in transformative*, Leuven: LannooCampus.

Van Craeynest, B. (2016), *Superstaat: Wat België moet doen om geen failed state te zijn*, Gent: Borgerhoff&Lamberigts.

Vancoppenolle, D. red. (2017), *Het kind in Vlaanderen 2016*, Brussel: Kind en Gezin.

Van De Peer, A., *Jongeren dragen steeds vaker reclamekleding: gratis is het nieuwe cool* [Online]. 29 Jun. 2017 [Accessed on 15 Aug. 2017] https://charliemag.be/lijf/reclamekleding/.

Vandenberghe, P., *Voedseloverschotten: supermarkten zijn niet de grote boosdoeners* [Online]. 29 Oct. 2014 [Accessed on 15 Aug. 20177] http://www.mo.be/opinie/voedseloverschotten-supermarkten-zijn-niet-de-grote-boosdoeners.

Van der Hamsvoort, C. e.a. (2011), *Rethinking the F&A Supply Chain: Impact of Agricultural Price Volatility on Sourcing Strategies*, Utrecht: Rabobank International.

Vandist, S. (2017), *Eneco Trendrapport. Duurzame innovatie in retail: 7 inspirerende trends*, Brussels: Eneco.

Vandresse, M. red. (2017), *Demografische vooruitzichten 2016-2060: Bevolking en huishoudens*, Brussels: Federaal Planbureau.

Van Haver, K., *Klimaat kruipt in DNA van bedrijven*, De Tijd [Online]. 11 Dec. 2015 [Accessed on 15 Aug. 2017] http://www.tijd.be/dossier/klimaattop/Klimaat-kruipt-in-DNA-van-bedrijven/9709386.

Van Ossel, G. (2014), *Omnichannel in retail: het antwoord op e-commerce*, Leuven: LannooCampus.

Van Looveren, Y., *Amazon lanceert fysieke betaaloplossing Amazon Pay Places* [Online]. 25 Jul. 2017 [Accessed on 15 Aug. 2017] https://www.retaildetail.be/nl/news/m-tail/amazon-lanceert-fysieke-betaaloplossing-amazon-pay-places.

Van Looveren, Y., *Moeder Kruidvat zet zwaar in op fysieke winkels*, RetailDetail [Online]. 28 Jun. 2017 [Accessed on 15 Aug. 2017] via https://www.retaildetail.be/nl/news/drogmetica/moeder-kruidvat-zet-zwaar-op-fysieke-winkels.

Van Rompaey, S., *Elektrohandel wordt hippe belevingswinkel* [Online]. 30 May 2017 [Accessed on 15 Aug. 2017] https://www.retaildetail.be/nl/news/elektronica/elektrohandel-wordt-hippe-belevingswinkel.

Van Rompaey, S., *"Fairtradekopers zijn waardevolle shoppers"*, RetailDetail [Online]. 26 Apr. 2016 [Accessed on 15 Aug. 2017] http://www.retaildetail.be/nl/news/'fairtradekopers-zijn-waardevolle-shoppers'.

Van Rompaey, S., *Lidl zet in op zonne-energie*, RetailDetail [Online]. 15 Jun. 2016 [Accessed on 15 Aug. 2017] https://www.retail-detail.be/nl/news/food/lidl-zet-op-zonne-energie.

Van Rompaey, S., *Visconsument vindt duurzaamheid belangrijker dan prijs*, RetailDetail [Online]. 15 Jul. 2016 [Accessed on 15 Aug. 2017] https://www.retaildetail.be/nl/news/food/visconsument-vindt-duurzaamheid-belangrijker-dan-prijs.

Van Rompaey, S., *Zo gaan robots de retail redden*, RetailDetail [Online]. 29 Jun. 2017 [Accessed on 15 Aug. 2017] https://www.retaildetail.be/nl/news/algemeen/zo-gaan-robots-de-retail-redden.

Verbuiksonderzoek i.o. VLAM, *Rechtstreeks kopen bij de boer, makkelijker dan ooit* [Online]. 25 Aug. 2016 [Accessed on 15 Aug. 2017] via https://pers.vlam.be/nl/pers/detail/5177/rechtstreeks-kopen-bij-de-boer-gemakkelijker-dan-ooit.

Verkeer in Nederland daalt terwijl economie en arbeidsmarkt langzaam aantrekken; Blijft tweede land van Europa met hoogste filedruk [Online]. 16 Mar. 2016 [Accessed on 15 Aug. 2017] via http://inrix.com/press-releases/scorecard-nl/.

Vredeseilanden (2014), *Achtergronddossier campagne 2015: Hoe redden we de toekomst van ons voedsel?*, Leuven: Vredeseilanden.

Wang, S., *Jack Ma Is Ahead of Jeff Bezos in Grocery Store Ambitions*, Bloomberg [Online]. 17 Aug. 2017 [Accessed on 15 Aug. 2017] https://www.bloomberg.com/news/articles/2017-08-17/jack-ma-is-ahead-of-jeff-bezos-in-grocery-store-ambitions.

Wolfe, J., *Roomba vacuum maker iRobot betting big on the 'smart' home* [Online]. 24 Jul. 2017 [Accessed on 15 Aug. 2017] via http://www.reuters.com/article/us-irobot-strategy-idUSKBN1A91A5.

World Bank, International Monetary Fund (2016), *Global Monitoring Report 2015/2016 : Development Goals in an Era of Demographic Change*, Washington: World Bank; via https://openknowledge.worldbank.org/handle/10986/22547.

World Economic Forum, *The Future of Jobs: Industry Profile The Consumer* [Online]. 2016 [Accessed on 15 Aug. 2017] http://reports.weforum.org/future-of-jobs-2016/consumer-2/.

Zuboff, S., Big Other: Surveillance Capitalism and the Prospects of an Information Civilization, *Journal of Information Technology* (2015), 30, 75–89.